THUCYDIDES AND THE PELOPONNESIAN WAR

'Cawkwell is an important historian . . . [this book] is typical of his style, his scholarship and his humanity, and ought to be read.'
Hugh Bowden, *King's College, University of London*

Understanding the history of Athens in the all important years of the second half of the fifth century BC is largely dependent on the legacy of the historian Thucydides. Previous scholarship has tended to view Thucydides' account as infallible. This book challenges that received wisdom, advancing original and controversial views of Thucydides' account of the Peloponnesian war; his misrepresentation of Alcibiades and Demosthenes; his relationship with Pericles; and his views on the Athenian Empire. Cawkwell's comprehensive analysis of Thucydides and his historical writings is persuasive, erudite and is an immensely valuable addition to the scholarship and criticism of a rich and popular period of Greek history.

George Cawkwell arrived in Oxford in 1946 as a New Zealand Rhodes Scholar and, like the lotus-eaters, 'forgot the way home'. In 1949 he became a Fellow of University College, Oxford where he tutored in Ancient History until 1995. He is the author of *Philip of Macedon* (1978) and many articles in learned journals on the history of Greece from the eighth to the fourth century BC.

THUCYDIDES AND THE PELOPONNESIAN WAR

George Cawkwell

London and New York

First published 1997
by Routledge
11 New Fetter Lane, London EC4P 4EE

Simultaneously published in the USA and Canada
by Routledge
29 West 35th Street, New York, NY 10001

Typeset in Garamond by Routledge
Printed and bound in Great Britain by Creative Print
and Design (Wales), Ebbw Vale

British Library Cataloguing in Publication Data
A catalogue record for this book is available from the British Library

Library of Congress Cataloguing in Publication Data
Cawkwell, George.
Thucydides and the Peloponnesian War / George Cawkwell.
Includes bibliographical references and index.
1. Thucydides–Political and social views. 2. Greece–History–
Peloponnesian War, 431–404 BC–Historiography. 3. Thucydides.
History of the Peloponnesian War. I. Title.
DF229.T6C37   1997
938'.05'072–dc21   96–37755
CIP

ISBN 0–415–16430–3 (hbk)
ISBN 0–415–16552–0 (pbk)

CONTENTS

PREFACE

For about fifteen years, off and on, I lectured on 'Thucydides and the War' in the School of Literae Humaniores in Oxford, but when in 1992 I was invited to fill a temporary gap in the Lecture List and return to the fray, I declined. Lecturing was for me a fray indeed. I used to take enormous pains over it and at the end of an hour felt physically exhausted. It seemed unwise to engage again. So I resolved instead to seek to publish what I would have delivered; foolishly perhaps, for lectures are essentially an *agōnisma es to parachrēma* and such is this book.

I resolved to refer in the notes only to works accessible to the majority of those likely to use the book. Thus the list of works referred to is confined mainly to works in English. A few articles in French have crept in, but almost no works of German scholarship are listed (though in one or two places in the notes I have weakened). So such a masterpiece as Beloch's *Griechische Geschichte*, a work for which I take this opportunity to profess supreme admiration, is not mentioned. In short, the list is not a bibliography, which would be immense.

Especial thanks are due to Rachel Chapman, Madeline Littlewood and Susan McCann at the Classics Faculty Office, without whose kindness this work would not have gone beyond manuscript.

Perhaps I should dedicate it to the many Greats, men and women, who have patiently and politely persisted with me, at least longer than a beautiful and intelligent young lady I once met at a party, who told me that she had been to my lectures 'or, rather, to one of them', but actually I prefer to dedicate it *honoris causa* to Simon Hornblower.

George Cawkwell
University College, Oxford, March 1996

vii

ABBREVIATIONS

ATL   *The Athenian Tribute Lists*, B. D. Meritt, H. T. Wade-Gery and M. F. McGregor (eds). Volume I, Cambridge, MA: Harvard University Press (1939); Volumes II and III, Princeton, NJ: The American School of Classical Studies at Athens, Princeton (1949).

CAH   *Cambridge Ancient History*, 2nd edn. (1961–), Cambridge: Cambridge University Press.

FGH   *Fragmente der griechischen Historiker*, F. Jacoby (ed.), Leiden: Brill (1923–).

GHI   *A Selection of Greek Historical Inscriptions* II, M. N. Tod (ed.), Oxford: Clarendon Press (1948).

HCT   *Historical Commentary on Thucydides*, A. W. Gomme, A. Andrewes and K. J. Dover (eds), 5 volumes, Oxford: Clarendon Press (1945–81).

IG   *Inscriptiones Graecae*, Berlin: de Gruyter (1873–).

Meiggs and Andrewes, *Sources for Greek History between the Persian and Peloponnesian Wars*, R. Meiggs and A. Andrewes (eds), Oxford: Clarendon Press (1951).

ML   *Greek Historical Inscriptions I^2*, R. Meiggs and D. M. Lewis (eds), Oxford: Clarendon Press (1969).

SEG   *Supplementum Epigraphicum Graecum*, Amsterdam: Gieben (1923–)

VS   *Fragmente der Vorsokratiker*, H. Diels and W. Kranz (eds), 7th edn., Berlin: Weidmann (1954).

1

THUCYDIDES

For good or ill, we students of Greek History are utterly beholden to the *Histories* of Thucydides, and inevitably one begins with a profession of belief about that great man. Gone are the days when he was accorded the sacrosanctity once accorded to Holy Writ, as it may be fairly supposed he was accorded by his great commentator, A. W. Gomme. A more tempered regard is now inevitable. Indeed, his reputation is under assault and some prefatory statement is necessary from anyone about to engage in discussion of the history of the Peloponnesian War.

What little is known about the life of Thucydides is to be gleaned almost entirely from his book.[1] Unfortunately, we cannot be very precise about the date of his birth. It is commonly supposed that he was born not long before 454, for he returned to Athens in 404 (5.26.5) and probably passed some time making revisions, and in the *Life* of Marcellinus (§34) it is stated that he was over 50 at his death. The source of this statement is, however, very uncertain. It is more suggestive that Thucydides has Nicias speak of Alcibiades as young for the generalship in 415 (6.12.2) and under 420, the year of Alcibiades' first recorded generalship (Plut. *Alc.* 15.1), Thucydides himself declared (5.43.2) that any other city would have regarded him as 'young' (*neos*). The age at which a man could be elected general is not known, but since thirty was the required age for entry to the council, the 'young' man is likely to have been at least 30. Alcibiades had assets both material and moral that Thucydides lacked and it would be no surprise if the latter's less brilliant career began at a considerably later age.[2] So he may have been at least 40 when he entered in 424 on his only recorded generalship and have been born as early as the mid-460s. Consistent with this would be Thucydides' claim to have begun at the outset of the war the work

1

of recording what happened (1.1.1 and 5.26.5); young men of 23 are more minded to fight than to record wars; by the age of 34 a more reflective habit of mind would have come upon him. Let Thucydides then be born by the mid-460s.

But, it may be asked, 465 or 454, does it matter? It does indeed. If he was 15 or so when the remains of his great kinsman Cimon were laid to rest in the so-called 'Cimonia' (Plut. *Cim.* 19.5), the occasion must have left its mark. And if he had heard, or heard of, the high praise of Cimon uttered in Cratinus' *Archilochi* (ibid. 10.4) shortly after his death, family pride would have been much touched, and Thucydides' conversion to admiration of Cimon's great rival, Pericles, would have been a most striking independence of mind. Not able to attend the Ecclesia until he was 18, he may have missed the excitements of Callias' return from negotiating the Peace that bears his name,[3] but growing up in such circles the boy must have heard the great issue of peace or war with Persia seriously discussed, and as he rose to manhood, the Parthenon began to rise on the Acropolis, and his education would have been completed amidst the intellectual and artistic ferment of the 440s. It is, then, no wonder that he should acquire an intense admiration of Athens, her empire and her whole way of life, so lauded in the Funeral Oration he put into the mouth of Pericles, the author of all this power and beauty. Thucydides himself beheld day by day this power of the city and loved it indeed (2.43.1).

His admiration for Pericles is at any rate plain enough (2.65). Yet it was Pericles who above all sought to maintain and foster the Empire and who also prized and developed the democracy, and Thucydides' attitude to the Empire and to democracy must be closely examined. If he shared Pericles' views on those matters, it was a radical change of stance. That is not, however, surprising in a man who, in his attitude to religion, displayed unusual independence of mind.

It has been much debated whether Thucydides was an atheist. If he had been so, he would have been unusual but far from unique. It is difficult to name atheists of the fifth century, though atheism was clearly conceivable as the celebrated fragment of Critias' *Sisyphus* shows[4] (*VS* 88 B25), and we are ill-informed about the trials of which we hear of those accused of it.[5] So it is hard to say how widespread such opinions were. Indeed, where atheism was an offence, prudence dictated reserve. Athens was a remarkably tolerant society. Plato could criticise democracy and propose without fear an idealised Spartan constitution for his ideal city. But religion was different. Unorthodox opinions about the gods could bring down the wrath of the gods not just on the free-thinking individual, but on the whole city.[6] The Mysteries could be profaned by men of advanced opinions, but the price had to be paid, even by the man whose education was thought to have corrupted the young. By the fourth century, however, to judge by Plato's Laws, unbelief was widespread and frank (cf. 885c, 886d, 888b, 908b and c). So it would not be surprising if Thucydides was an atheist, albeit discreetly so.

Unfortunately, the evidence he provides is ambivalent.[7] To all Greeks of earlier ages and to most in the second half of the fifth century, the divine will was manifested to men partly in exceptional natural occurrences like earthquakes, plagues and eclipses, the meaning of which was plain to all, partly in signs and portents which required the specialist interpretation of seers (manteis), and partly by oracular utterances.[8] Herodotus was, on the whole, so minded.[9] For him, man may misinterpret but oracles do not err.[10] The gods constantly intervene to secure the result they want. His whole cast of mind is theological. Thucydides is vastly different.[11] Only one of the oracles given during the war happened to come true (5.26.3). Only those lacking experience of climatic conditions were terrified by thunder and lightning (6.70.1). The gods are, indeed, conspicuous by their absence and wherever he makes his speakers appeal to them, it is sure presage of disaster.[12] Nowhere does Thucydides reveal himself more tellingly than in the chapter (2.54) he wrote immediately after his account of the Plague. To the Greeks generally, plagues came from the gods.[13] For Thucydides, this mighty plague came from Ethiopia and spread widely over Egypt, Libya and the Persian Empire before it came to the Piraeus (2.48), doubtless imported by merchants; he had observed that it was spread by contagion (2.47.4, 50, 51.5). That was his view of its origin unlike those who 'knew the oracle given to the Spartans when they asked the god whether they should make war and the god gave the response that if they fought with all their might victory would be theirs and he said he would lend a hand.' For them, the Plague was divine aid for Sparta. Thucydides gives his answer. First, he manifests his sceptical attitude to portentous utterances: men, he says, take the version that seems to fit in with their present conditions. Then, most revealingly, he declares that men interpreted the Spartan oracle to match what was happening; the Plague began

3

when the Peloponnesians had invaded and it did not go into the Peloponnese to any extent worth mentioning. So the Plague was seen as divine punishment; but not by Thucydides. Of course, it would have been unwise, probably dangerous, for him to say openly that the gods had nothing to do with it.[14] He makes his viewpoint clear by implication. The Plague 'settled on Athens most, and after that on the most populous places (*ta polyanthrōpotata*).' The contagion was worst where people were most crowded together. That was all there was to it. The whole chapter is a notable exercise of scepticism.

Thucydides seems in general rationalist and scientific, both in what he says and in what he does not. The eruption of Etna is remarked (3.116) without suggestion that a god is engaged. The relation of tidal waves and submarine earthquakes is noted (3.89). His comment may be sly: he recounts the coincidence of the second outbreak of the Plague and widespread earthquakes in Athens, Euboea, Boeotia, and especially in Orchomenus (3.87), and so rebuffs the idea that the Plague expresses the displeasure of heaven with Athens by remarking that what is popularly supposed to be divinely engineered, the earthquake, was so widespread, with its epicentre in Boeotia, that it had no relevance to the Plague – which, in any case, as already remarked, came from Ethiopia.[15]

There is one passage, however, that has seemed to many to mean that Thucydides did hold to the traditional view. In 1.23 in pursuit of his thesis that the Peloponnesian War was the greatest war, he remarks that not only did it go on for a very long time, but also in the course of it an unparalleled number of what he terms *pathēmata* occurred. These included events involving human suffering, such as droughts, famines and the Plague. So, by *pathēmata* he can mean 'sufferings' and 'afflictions', but he also includes 'eclipses of the sun' which, as far as we know, the Greeks did not suppose entailed suffering. Their inclusion suggests that these *pathēmata* are not chance concomitants of the war, but are due to powers more than human. If this interpretation of the word 'eclipses' is correct, Thucydides was not wholly rationalist, or not rationalist all of the time.[16] The chapter is an uncomfortable fact. It does not destroy the general impression that Thucydides was one of the free-thinkers of the age, but it shows he was not always so.

At least one may beware the easy labelling of his views. Thucydides was a most elusive person who says almost nothing directly of his opinions which, in consequence, have to be teased out of his text. A common starting-point is his remark about the rule of the Five Thousand in 411 (8.97.2) from which it has been presumed that Thucydides was a moderate oligarch. In so far as such a judgement is dependent on taking the phrase *eu politeusantes* to mean 'having a good constitution', it can be brusquely repudiated.[17] In talking of the Athenians' disregard of Pericles' policy (2.65.7) when the constitution remained unchanged, he uses the converse phrase (*kakōs es te sphās autous kai tous xymmachous epoliteusan*) which must mean 'They conducted policy badly.' So in itself the phrase used of 411 does not argue that Thucydides approved of the constitution of the Five Thousand. What he says is to be judged in the light of a passage of Xenophon's *Memorabilia* (4.4.16), where the essence of good government is declared to be concord (*homonoia*). But Thucydides does go on to explain why the Athenians had good government at that time. 'The mixture with regard to the few and the many was moderate.' So he *does* seem to be commending the moderateness of the oligarchy of 411. However, it is also clear that this had not always been his view.

The surest thing one can say of his political sympathies is that he greatly admired Pericles (2.65). Pericles was the man principally responsible for the development of the Athenian Empire as well as being a notable fosterer of the democracy. Was Thucydides then an imperialist and a believer in democracy? The reason for Pericles' powerful position was in part his judgement (*gnōmē*), but Thucydides does not speak of his particular judgements, and one might wonder whether it was Pericles' skill in judging what best served his purposes that Thucydides admired, not those purposes themselves. However, if one looks at the obituary he wrote for Themistocles (1.138.3), the position is plainer. He too played a notable part in the development of the Empire and of the democracy.[18] Thucydides did not allude specifically to that. Rather, he commended Themistocles' judgement, his very great ability quickly to decide what had to be done (*ta deonta*). That is the tell-tale phrase; there is nothing about his purposes and his choice of ends, but simply his ability to decide on the necessary steps. That is, for Thucydides, there is only one course open and the best statesman is the man who best discerns it. Consistently with this, in the speeches in the *Histories*, it is never the balancing of justice and advantage, always purely the calculation of advantage. That is how he thinks statesmen really think. A man who thinks like this is inevitably imperialist, for no sane man would not prefer his city to have power over another rather than to be in some other city's power. In some sense, therefore, Thucydides was imperialist. Why, after all, did he choose to include that laudation of imperial Athens, the Funeral Oration? It is Pericles' profession of faith, but it was included, one presumes, because the man to whom Thucydides accorded admiration and allegiance spoke for him too.

The Funeral Oration expounds at length the sentiment expressed in Pericles' last speech.

> Realise that the city has a very great reputation with all mankind for not giving in to disasters and for having expended a great many lives and made great efforts in war, and that it possesses power previously unmatched, the memory of which, should we go down somewhat (for in the nature of things everything diminishes), will remain with posterity for ever, that as Hellenes we had empire over a very great number of Hellenes, that we held out in very great wars against our foes both separately and in concert, and that we dwelt in a city admirably provided with everything and very great.
>
> (2.64.3)

Here is the boast of imperial power and of the imperial city. One suspects that in these two speeches Pericles speaks for his great admirer too.

We can, generally speaking, have no great confidence in drawing on the speeches to elucidate Thucydides' opinions. It is clear that they are not like any of the samples of oratory that have survived. They tend to the general and the intellectual too much to be seriously regarded as the record of the uttered words. In some way, they have been sublimated, but one can never be sure whether they express what Thucydides thought or what he thought the speakers thought. If it is the latter, it is possible that he made them think in his own way, the speaker's presumed thoughts being run, as it were, into the mould of Thucydides' own ways of thought. In that case, discerning the genuinely Thucydidean from, for example, the Cleonic or the Nician should be suspected of being largely subjective. The speeches of Pericles, however, are different. He was the man 'who led the city with moderation (*metriōs*) and kept it safe, and in his time it became very great' (2.65.5), and it seems not unreasonable to treat his speeches on the greatness of Athens as speaking for Thucydides too.[19]

Imperialist, then, let him be; but was he also, like Pericles, a believer in democracy? He seems at moments somewhat dismissive

6

of popular assemblies and their inconstancy. The words he uses (*ochlos, homilos*) seem more appropriate to a fickle mob than to the sovereign People.[20] When, however, one considers the manner in which the sovereign People behaved on the two successive days of the Mytilene debate (cf. 3.36.4), the charge of fickleness is not to be denied and certainly would not have been denied by Pericles himself (cf. 2.59). Such behaviour was, and indeed is, only to be expected. But for Pericles the important point about democracy was not that everyone participated so much as that anyone who had the ability to serve the city was not prevented by poverty (2.37) and that there was a career open to talent. Could Thucydides have thought differently? In his famous chapter on the decline of Athens after Pericles (2.65) the emphasis is on the quality of leadership, and since it is a fact of life that statesmen of high quality are rare, he must have favoured that system which gave the highest hopes of their appearing.[21] The disadvantages of the system had to be borne, and in any case, if Athens was to have the great advantages of having empire, it had to be a naval empire, which meant a 'naval multitude' (*nautikos ochlos*) which would require and maintain democracy (8.72.2; cf. Arist. *Pol.* 1304a22f.). Shocking as it will be to some latter-day sages, it may well be that Thucydides gladly accepted both empire and democracy. The Spartan alternative could no more appeal to him, than it did to Pericles (2.39). Quite apart from their national character (1.70) and their rumoured dark deeds at home (4.80), Spartans could not behave themselves when they got abroad (4.81), and their claim to accord their allies independence was a sham (1.19). The Funeral Oration makes it all clear.

Thucydides began work for his book, if we may believe him (1.1), in 431, and it looks as if there was an original version of the events of the Archidamian War – or 'the ten-year war', 'the first war', as he variously termed it (5.25.1, 24.2, 26.3) – for he chose to reintroduce himself when he set out to describe the breakdown of the Peace (5.26.1). But his account of that first war bears evidence of rewriting after his return to Athens from exile in 404 (e.g. 2.65), while there are several passages which must have been written well on in the course of the war (e.g. 2.100.2, 4.81). Likewise, for the period after 421, whatever the order in which he wrote up the confusions in the Peloponnese, the Melian campaign, and the Sicilian Expedition, it is clear that important revisions were made (e.g. 6.15.3 and 4, perhaps 6.91.6, 7.27.5). Book 8, which has been termed 'the workshop of Thucydides', is far from complete and therefore gives us some idea of how Thucydides set about his task. However, for the rest of the *History*, the more the matter of the composition of the work is debated, the less clear it becomes that any part would not have been further revised in the course of time.[22]

This is of some importance when one considers various charges that have been made against him. Few errors have been detected,[23] but this is not saying very much, for generally Thucydides provides the only evidence there is. However, the zeal for acquiring information was presumably very great. In a world without photographs, proper maps, written records of detailed military history, memoirs of generals and politicians, the manifold sources, in short, now available to those attempting to record a war through which they have themselves lived, it must indeed have been hard work discovering what happened (1.22.3 *epiponōs de hēurisketo*) with a very great deal of questioning of participants. Whether what Thucydides tells us is true or false or a blend of truth and error, he must have been a quite exceptional man – a monster in his inquiries. As far as we know, no one had previously done anything similar. Herodotus had collated accounts, no doubt with considerable shrewdness, but had not shrunk from including a merry mix of nonsense in his account of the Persian Wars. In eschewing that, Thucydides manifested a new concern with the truth, a veritable passion.

How he went about gathering his information one can only guess. He knew Athens and Athenians and after his exile in 424 he probably had the epistles of various well-informed persons to guide him, and documents may have been relayed to him. For instance, in Book 8 he gives the two preliminary drafts of the Spartan-Persian treaty of 411, the final version declaring itself by having, unlike the earlier versions, a proper prescript and dating.[24] The two preliminary versions would never have been published and Thucydides must have obtained them from either someone in Sparta (which seems unlikely) or someone in the know in Persia. Alcibiades is the obvious guess, but there were, no doubt, Greek secretaries at Sardis. If Thucydides got hold of that sort of document, it is easy to imagine him receiving a good deal from friends within Athens. In a sense, Athens was easy.

Sparta was not, 'because of the secretiveness of the state' (5.68.2), and the search required a rare determination to discover the truth. In nothing was Sparta more secretive than about keeping Helots in their place. In Book 4, Thucydides recounted a dark deed (80.3–4).

He did not date it and, as to the precise manner of death for these uppish Helots, he had to declare that 'no one knew'. Like the Polish officers in the Katyn Forest, they ceased to exist. But to have got even this far was remarkable penetration of the darkness, a sign of persistence and diligence. It is notable too how many names of Spartans, and with patronymics, appear in the work, notable also how often he gives their social status and how often he does not (or presumably cannot).[25] He had been to Sparta and other places in the Peloponnese (5.26.5) and had used his opportunities well. The national festivals, especially the quadrennial gathering at Olympia,[26] would have afforded him occasions where he could meet a wide variety of Greeks and gather the names of the commanders of sometimes quite small detachments of troops (cf., for example, Sargeus of Sicyon at 7.19.4). So he could have got, for instance, the names of the three Corcyran commanders at Sybota (1.47.1) without ever going to Corcyra. However, given that he was working without the sort of written and graphic evidence that we would have at our disposal, it is hard to conceive of his writing as he did without a great deal of travel and autopsy,[27] and the abundance of detail in his work argues a monstrous passion for seeking out the truth.

Detail makes for credibility as accomplished liars know, but Thucydides was never accused of untruthfulness or deliberate misrepresentation in the ancient world, as far as we know. Indeed, to judge by what Dionysius of Halicarnassus says in his essay *On Thucydides*, 'the most celebrated philosophers and orators supposed him to be the model historian' (ch. 2), and he declares that Thucydides was very greatly concerned with the truth (ch. 8).[28] It has been left to modern times for Thucydides to be accused of something akin to deliberate misrepresentation, a charge which will hardly succeed. Yet he has also been charged with over-confidence which leads him to present his account as clear and certain when common experience suggests that no single account ever can be wholly correct or wholly beyond question.[29] Unlike Herodotus, he does not give himself away by indicating which of the variant accounts he prefers; he draws his own conclusions and presents them to his readers. In this way, his version is beyond question. But how credible is he?

Much of his narrative is of a sort that, given persistence and thorough method, we could all discover what had actually happened, and the very full detail of Thucydides' account suggests that he did have the necessary persistence and thoroughness.

Military engagements are much more questionable, but modern examples of confusion of memory may not be properly used to discredit Thucydides. For one thing, the element of high explosive makes the greatest possible difference to one's power to comprehend what is happening. For another, modern battles are extended over a wide area. One may (or may not) with radio communication have a mental picture of what is happening; no one can literally see the whole. But this was not the case with the engagements of the Peloponnesian War. Before the advance to battle, participants could well see where the battle was to be fought, and although once the dust-clouds, which must almost always have arisen on Greek battlefields, obscured the overall view,[30] hoplite battles of the fifth century were of a fairly standard pattern and the range of variations was small. So there was much less for accounts to differ on, and the uncertainties of the night battle on the Epipolae, on which Thucydides commented (7.44.1), were very much the exception. Of course, fear is a great distorter of memory and the well-directed spear was probably more formidable than the random bullet, but to accuse Thucydides of describing battles as if he had, and as if there could be, no doubt about the accuracy of his account seems misdirected. A multitude of notes to the effect of saying 'I am not at all sure about this, but on the whole this seems to me the likeliest account' would certainly have comforted us in our confidence that we could do better, but it would certainly have clogged the flow of the narrative. Ancient authors did not have the luxury of footnotes and appendices and Thucydides just had to do his best without them, a best that seems not to have discontented the ancient world.[31] It may be added that it hardly seems proper to extend 'the fog of war' to cover his whole narrative.

There are disqualifications, however, which are not to be denied. The first is his curious addiction to superlatives.[32] It is not that he can be proved to be exaggerating in any particular case: the 120 Athenians killed in Demosthenes' Aetolian campaign, for instance, may indeed have been 'the best men lost in this war' (3.98.4); he certainly maintained this view in retrospect (4.73.4). Again, First Mantinea he declared (5.74.1) to be 'the greatest of Greek battles for a very long time engaging most important cities'; the battle of Tanagra forty years earlier had probably involved larger numbers (cf. 1.107.2 and 5), but 'a very long time' may have been intended to allow for the 'greatness' of that battle, or Mantinea may have been thought by him to be 'greatest' in the sense of 'most important'. So he cannot be convicted of exaggeration. Nonetheless, frequent recourse to the superlative is not reassuring. More seriously there are moments when one is very uneasy about his critical judgement. For instance, in Book 6 he asserted (55.1) that Hippias was the oldest son of Pisistratus, declaring that he had special and reliable information,[33] but went on to say that one could work it out for oneself by noting that the inscription on the altar of the Twelve Gods described the younger Pisistratus as 'son of Hippias', and the inscription on the pillar recording 'the wrongdoing of the tyrants' ascribed five sons to Hippias and none to his two brothers. Since both these brothers may have had infertile marriages, the argument is of little worth. His following argument (§2) that Hippias was listed immediately after his father Pisistratus is more respectable, but the whole discussion is hardly encouraging.[34] Another instance is provided by his excursus on Pausanias the Regent (1.128–134), the unsatisfactoriness of which has been often remarked. The account can hardly stand as it is, and one would have expected Thucydides, with his knowledge of Sparta, to be more critical. One may seek to excuse it as early work that he never got around to revising, but excuses are certainly due.[35] A less frequently remarked case is provided by his account of the rebuff of the Spartan embassy at Athens in 420 (5.44.3–46.1). Thucydides has Alcibiades persuading the Spartans to deny in the assembly what they had asserted before the Council, and then rounding on them for perfidy. The story would be acceptable were it not that the assembly was interrupted by an earthquake and adjourned to the next day. Overnight, Nicias could and surely would have found out why the Spartans had gone back on their word to the Council and the next day he could, and surely would, have exposed Alcibiades' deception.[36] There is a more humdrum explanation of why the Spartans behaved as they did: namely, that they had their terms of reference as to how far and no further they were free to negotiate and they had been called on in the assembly to exceed them.[37] Thucydides' colourful version is perhaps to be explained by his relation to Alcibiades, but hardly increases our respect for his historical judgement. Likewise, with his references to the Persian Wars. He showed his independence and his acuteness in twice having speakers declare that the Persians' failures were largely of their own making (1.69.5, 6.33.5), including on the second occasion the opinion that the Persians in 480 did not outnumber the Greeks – in all this he was, I believe, quite right as well as wholly out of tune

11

with the views of other Greeks.[38] However, in another speech he has the Athenians declare that the Athenian victory at Salamis checked the Persian advance to the Peloponnese – a conventional enough opinion. He then goes on to give as the most important evidence of this that after losing the sea-battle, Xerxes quickly 'retired with the major part of his army' (1.73.5). This is, indeed, the view of Herodotus (8.115), but since the force under Artabazus that escorted the king promptly returned to the army under Mardonius (Hdt. 8.126), it is a very dubitable view and Thucydides should have doubted it. Of course, it might be said in his favour that what he made the Athenians say was not necessarily what he himself thought. So perhaps he should have the benefit of such a doubt, but in general it may be affirmed that his historical judgement appears not to be flawless.

Blackest of all is the mighty cloud that now hangs over him, which if it bursts will deluge his reputation. For long scholars have haggled over the date of the alliance between Athens and Segesta, for which the only evidence we have is provided by a fragmentary inscription (*IG* 1³11 = ML no. 37). The last two letters of the Archon's name are sure, namely 86; the rest are not. The name long preferred for the most part, Habron of 458/7, has been objected to on far from convincing grounds (*v.i.*) and the suggestion that various marks on the stone are consistent with the name Antiphon, archon for 418/17, was little heeded for two, as it seemed, over-whelming objections. First, Thucydides, in recording the appeal of the Segestans to Athens in 416/15, has them appeal not to a recently made alliance, but to one made in the Archidamian War (6.6.2), and made probably with Leontini. But even if that alliance had been between Athens and Segesta, it is inconceivable that the Segestans would have appealed to that rather than to an alliance so recently made in 418/17, if such there had been. Secondly, if there had been an alliance made in 418/17, Thucydides' whole account would be vitiated. Once Athens had sworn 'to think the same friends and enemies', the only possible response to the appeal of winter 416/15 would have been to send military aid at the first possible moment. In Thucydides' account, however, the Athenian response was to send envoys to discover whether the Segestans had the money which they claimed they had (6.6.3); when the envoys returned with a favourable report, the Athenians voted to send a fleet of sixty ships (6.8.2). It is true that Thucydides does not mention that a treaty of alliance was made after the envoys returned,[39] but the point made by Alcibiades in the speech Thucydides gives him (6.18.1) is decisive, namely, 'we must defend them since we exchanged oaths with them.' That was not how Thucydides made the Athenians respond to the appeal of 416/15. So Thucydides' account is not reconcilable with a Segestan alliance in 418/17. In support of Thucydides, one may cite Diodorus' account of the beginning and course of the war between Segesta and Selinus (12.82f.). It is evidently not derived from Thucydides and so provides independent testimony that Segesta did not appeal to Athens until she did so jointly with the exiled Leontinans whom we meet in Thucydides (6.19.1, 12.1). But now the debate is transformed. It is claimed[40] that by passing a laser beam through the stone, a stark, precise iota is revealed in the place where the name Antiphon would have it, and that Thucydides' account is wrong, a result greeted with shocked horror by his faithful and with exultation by his denigrators – an iota of difference indeed.

If the Segestan alliance was indeed made in the archonship of Antiphon, 418/17, it will be necessary to revise our estimate of Thucydides radically. Mere historians can only look on, as the epigraphists engage, with emotions of the sort attributed by Thucydides to the Athenians watching the last sea-fight in the Great Harbour at Syracuse. *Ne sutor supra crepidam*, but it is to be remarked that directly above the claimed iota is to be seen an extended mark which cannot be a letter but which may be part of a long scratch and the claimed iota may belong to it.[41] Until the opponents of the iota have surrendered to its champions, I (and I expect many others) will continue to believe that the Segestan alliance was not made in 418/17, and Thucydides' reputation has not been severely deflated.[42]

Nonetheless, enough has been said to show that idolatry is out of place, and consideration of Thucydides' omissions supports such tempered judgement. Omissions are of several kinds. First, there are matters which Thucydides regarded as beneath his history, such as the financial history of Athens[43] or the various imperial arrangements, cleruchies, the *Hellespontophylakes*, *episkopoi* and so on. These were too lowly for his lofty-toned 'possession for ever'. Similarly, he was not interested to record the small change of Athenian politics. Hyperbolus makes only one fleeting appearance (8.73.3), though the Comic poets were constantly concerned with him. Likewise, Cleophon, of whom Thucydides might well have had much to say concerning the events of 410 and 406, gets no mention, though he was coming into prominence before the *Histories* came to a stop, just as Cleon's hostility to Pericles (Plut. *Per.* 33.8) goes unmentioned.[44] Indeed, his treatment of Cleon is illuminating: only when there are great issues to be recorded or when Cleon has a military role does he make much of him. He mentions that Cleon proposed the decree putting all the adult males of Scione to death (4.122.6), but, the issue having been fully treated in the case of Mytilene, in 423 Thucydides gives Cleon the merest mention (though one would like to know whether and how strongly he was opposed). In themselves, party politics (though our phrase is misleading for Athens) did not interest Thucydides.

Then there were the matters he ruthlessly excluded. Religion was not for him an important consideration. Since plagues were, for the Greeks, divine visitations, the incidence of the Plague must have, in view of the Delphic oracle given to the Spartans (1.118.3, 2.54.4), greatly encouraged the Spartans and discouraged the Athenians, and the decision to seek peace in 430 (2.59.2) was, one presumes, a measure of that discouragement. Not a murmur of such thoughts is uttered in his account. It may be that, quite apart from superstitious fancies, Thucydides vastly disapproved of the decision in 430 to seek peace; it certainly gave the Spartans to think that Pericles had been wrong to claim that Spartan power would not move Athens, and it thus frustrated the Periclean plan for the war, explicitly commended by Thucydides (2.65.5). So this dismissal of the Athenian appeal for peace is as much a reflection of his admiration for Pericles as due to his contempt for religion. But this latter even affects his military narrative. The decree of Charinus (Plut. *Per.* 30.3) added to the oath sworn by generals a clause that they would twice yearly invade the Megarid. The first invasion was in autumn 431 (2.31.3), fully enough recounted, but he concluded by remarking that these invasions happened every year until Nisaea was captured (which happened in 424). Later, we learn that they happened twice a year (4.66.1) and, in view of the justification for passing the original decree advanced by Pericles (1.139.2, Plut. *Per.* 30.2), it seems likely that instead of offering the Megarians the Sacred Truce for the Mysteries, since they had murdered the herald Anthemocritus in spring 431, these invasions were made shortly after the Mysteries.[45] However, to Thucydides these invasions were mere religion, irrelevant to the war, even though they finally moved some Megarians to take political action (4.66.1). Other omissions may be of no great significance. Philochorus (*FGH* 328 F130) recorded under the year 424/3 an Athenian campaign against Euboea. No such campaign appears in Thucydides. Its purpose is only to be guessed, and there is no reason to suppose that Thucydides has omitted a matter of considerable importance. Again, the omissions of his account of the Pentekontaetea are, generally speaking, due to the incompleteness of that part of his history.[46]

There is one topic, however, consistently and constantly underplayed by Thucydides, which raises the question whether his failure fully to treat of it does not seriously distort his work. I refer, of course, to the matter of Athenian relations with Persia. There is not a word about the peace negotiations in the Pentekontaetea; the abortive embassy of 425/4 is mentioned (4.50.3), but there is no word of a peace treaty being subsequently made with King Darius. Negotiations with Tissaphernes are described (8.56), but there is no account of how Athens came to support the rebel satrap, Amorges, who features somewhat mysteriously in Book 8; alliance with Amorges is to be presumed (28.2 and 54.3) and that is all. According to Andocides (3.29), the Athenians were persuaded by the exile Amorges, which sounds as if Amorges presented himself in person at Athens, but the date is uncertain, though possibly 415/14.[47] Thucydides denies us all this, but whether Amorges appeared in person or not, there must have been a debate in the Assembly, and one would have thought it would have been of interest and importance to Thucydides. For whatever reason, there had been no hostilities between Athens and Persia for nearly 40 years; shortly, Sparta and Persia were in alliance, and the alliance gave Sparta the confidence (and support) to see her through to victory. Some explanation of all this was, one would think, essential. It should also have been very appealing to Thucydides. Did the growth of Athenian power make the Persians 'afraid and force them to war', another 'truest cause' for another clash of giants? Was there to be sooner or later a Panhellenist crusade, and the sooner the better – the view of Cimon, Gorgias, Lysistrata and all that ilk? Or was some pact between powers that could not for the present come to grips with each other inevitable – the view of Pericles? It must have been for Thucydides a fascinating debate and should have engaged his pen whenever it happened, whether in Book 6, 7 or 8. It is no mere omission. It is a scandal. No matter whether supporting Amorges broke the Peace with Persia or merely roused the dormant beast, the matter should have been described.

15

If one asks why Thucydides has so underplayed Persia, there is no obvious reply. There are powerful reasons for holding that Athens made a formal peace with Persia in the middle of the century, which was probably renewed after the accession of Darius II in 423. In his summary of Athens after Pericles (2.65.10–12), he did acknowledge the important part played by Cyrus the Younger, and perhaps revision would have done something to make amends. Down to the coming of Cyrus in 407 (Xen. *Hell.* 1.4.3), regardless of whether there was formal peace or not, the Persians must have seemed to Thucydides of no great importance since they did not decisively interfere, and in the period described in Book 8 they purposely kept out and pursued the policy which Alcibiades advocated (8.46), probably needlessly, for Tissaphernes was the arch bystander (§5) and needed no such advice. For the brief period when Artaxerxes bestirred himself and began actively to court Sparta, Thucydides did not omit record (4.50), but, Artaxerxes dead, Athenian–Persian relations reverted to normal and Thucydides did not feel moved to record them. So much might be said by way of *apologia*.

Such *apologia* is limp. We, of course, know what Thucydides could not, i.e. that in the longer term, Persian policy was successful in utterly excluding the Greeks of the mainland from Asia. Indeed, all too successful: in the fourth century the Great King – as Isocrates (4.121) complained and Xenophon, when it suited him, depicted (*Hell.* 7.1.33–8) – was much involved in the politics of Greece and provoked the Panhellenist sentiment which Philip of Macedon was able to exploit. So our interest in the development of Persian policy towards Greece is inevitably more lively than Thucydides' could, or should, have been. Nonetheless, he saw the end of the war and knew that Persian money gave Sparta the aid and the will to see it through, and if he could add the version of 2.65 that we have, comment on the successors of Brasidas (4.81.2), reflect on the loss of Alcibiades for the closing years (6.15.3 and 4) and so on, he could, and should, have added the Persian dimension. A record of Athenian contacts and an analysis of Persian policy would have greatly enriched the *Histories* and our understanding.

There are, thus, serious qualifications to be made about the truthfulness of Thucydides. Whether or in what sense he was unfair in his treatment of individuals has to be discussed. He certainly did not think well of Cleon, but if Cleon did not deserve to be well thought of, that cannot stand to Thucydides' discredit. His attitude towards Alcibiades is more questionable, and will be questioned. Likewise, his view of Demosthenes – who was, it will be argued, the greatest general of the fifth century and whose greatness is not immediately evident from the pages of Thucydides.[48]

Why he so treated Demosthenes is for conjecture, but it must be questioned how good a judge of war Thucydides was. There is no way of knowing how much military experience he had before his unlucky generalship in Thrace in 424, which resulted in his exile, but since the Old Oligarch remarked that the People elected as generals 'those most able' to exercise the office (Xen. *Ath. Pol.* 1.3), his experience of war will not have been confined to the year 424. It is not to be excluded that he served in Samos in 440 and that was why he was able to furnish a comparatively full account of the campaign when all else between 446 and 433 required research for which he lacked the time, but whatever his earlier military experience, he obviously had enough to be the historian of a war. However, for the judgement of strategy, experience, though essential, is not necessarily sufficient. Experienced generals can differ greatly, as one sees in the debate of the generals about the campaign in Sicily (6.47–49). Nicias' contribution is to be discounted; his heart was not in the enterprise. Lamachus was, indeed, experienced. His first known *stratēgia* was in 425/4, but when Aristophanes in the *Acharnians* picked on him as the typical man of war, not only was the name suitable, but also it is to be presumed that Lamachus had already a considerable military reputation. He was probably not general in 429/8 when another member of his tribe is known to have held office, but he could have been general in 428/7, 427/6, and 426/5. He was general in 425/4 and in 424/3 and the only year between then and the Sicilian Expedition in which he is not known to have been so is 418/17. So Lamachus was indeed experienced.[49] By contrast, Alcibiades was much less so. His first three generalships (420/19, 419/18, ?418/17) were much concerned with politics and diplomacy and he did not take part in the battle of Mantinea; active command of an army before the Sicilian Expedition occurred only in 417/16. Plato (*Symp.* 219e–221b) shows him on active service in 432 and 424 and, no doubt, that was not all his military experience, but as general he was greatly Lamachus' junior. Later, Thucydides (6.15.4) was to concede that Alcibiades 'most effectively conducted the business of the war'. Lamachus' greater experience in 415 was matched by Alcibiades' potential. The judgement of each of them about how to conduct the campaign was seriously to be considered, but they differed somewhat. Lamachus advocated sailing straight to Syracuse, landing and engaging the Syracusans in battle and so persuading other states that Athens was the better bet (6.49). Alcibiades advocated not beginning the attack on Syracuse until they had assembled a force large enough to fight the war and secured the food supply for the army (6.48). Bowing perhaps to Alcibiades' known diplomatic gifts, Lamachus went over to support Alcibiades (6.50.1), but there may have been more to it.

Implicit in Alcibiades' plan was the intention to carry through the attack on Syracuse without pause. If Syracuse did not prudently come to terms, there would have to be a siege, for which speed in circumvallation would be essential. Alcibiades was no doubt well aware that, as Nicias had pointed out (6.20.4) and as the Athenians would have to acknowledge (6.71.2), the force was seriously lacking. There was no point in going against Syracuse until the necessary forces had been assembled.[50] So Lamachus' whole strategy was misconceived and it is no surprise that he accepted the superior good sense of Alcibiades.

What is surprising is that Thucydides, in his famous parenthetical remark in his own person (7.42.3), takes the view that Nicias could have and should have gone directly against the Syracusans, who would not even have sent for forces from the Peloponnese, but would have been walled off before help could reach them.[51] The Athenians simply did not have the necessary hands and resources to begin a siege when Nicias arrived, and Thucydides seems here to make a serious military misjudgement.

At one other point, Thucydides surprises us by his silence. In recounting the Boeotian order of battle at Delium in 424, he remarks that the Thebans were 25 deep (4.93.4), but he utters not a word about the oddity of such depth nor about its purpose. It is, however, a challenging fact. At the battle of Leuctra, the Thebans were 50 deep (Xen. Hell. 6.4.12). At Nemea in 394, having agreed that the confederate army should be drawn up 16 deep, the Thebans, when their turn came to command, made the phalanx 'really deep' (ibid. 4.2.18; cf. 13). Both Leuctra and Nemea were battles quite unlike First Mantinea in 418, and one suspects that the process which culminated in Theban predominance in Greece had begun. If it had, Thucydides cared for none of these things enough to enquire the reason why. So one wonders about him as a military historian. He may have faithfully recorded, as his experience qualified him to do, but his understanding of a Demosthenes may well be less reliable.[52]

'A possession for ever' (1.22.4) assuredly, but in what sense? From one point of view, the *Histories* might seem a somewhat jejune military narrative. The Sicilian Expedition is engaging and moving. Much else is not, and one might wonder what, when he began, Thucydides thought he was about. Perhaps he had no more in mind at the very beginning than to record a war that seemed likely to last more than the mere year or two taken by the Persian invasion of Greece (1.23.1), a clash of Titans. He could not know in 431 that he would be writing an account of the fall of the great Imperial power, and his work must have developed significance as the war developed. In its latest form, it was the obituary of imperial Athens.

Essentially, Thucydides was concerned with power. The moral was to use it wisely or lose it woefully. The military narrative is to demonstrate how Athens used and lost her power, but the heart of the matter is in the speeches which show how wisely and unwisely statesmen might be supposed really to think about the maintaining and extending of power. For behind all the rhetoric and fine pretensions, states 'have no friends, only interests' and statesmen are good and bad in so far as they reckon those interests well or badly. The speeches in Thucydides present such reckoning. That is why his *Histories* are an education for ever.

2

'THE TRUEST EXPLANATION'

There are three accounts of the causes of the Peloponnesian War to be considered seriously.[1] First, there is the view that Sparta resolved to destroy Athenian power, the view argued for by de Ste Croix.[2] Secondly, there is the view that Athens under Pericles' guidance sought to bring on the war, the view which de Ste Croix laboured to discredit and which Badian[3] seeks to re-establish. Thirdly, there is Thucydides' view that 'the truest explanation' was that 'the growth of Athenian power made the Spartans afraid and forced them to go to war' (1.23.6), which is plainly different from each of the other views. Which is to be preferred?

There is, however, a preliminary question. Did Thucydides change his mind? Were there, at different times, two Thucydidean views? It has been argued[4] that §6 of 1.23 was written at a considerably later date than §5 and, if this is correct, it is necessary to explain why the addition was made. In §5 Thucydides explained why he had first recorded the matters of dispute leading to the war and in the following chapter he proceeds to set down that record. If §6 is a later addition, it is an intrusion and some account of why it was made is due. Does it represent a change of mind, or 'a shift of emphasis', or a development of some sort? Did Thucydides come to think differently about the cause of the war?

If §6 was a 'late' addition, it must have satisfied Thucydides that it fitted in well enough for him not to have rewritten the whole chapter, and if it satisfied him, it will hardly be obvious to us. Nonetheless, §6 does seem to be an addition. In §5 he appears to think that whoever inquires as 'to the origins of so great a war coming on the Greeks' will be satisfied by reading the Corcyra and Potidaea affairs, but in §6 he thinks that anyone who really wishes to know what is most truthfully to be given in explanation must read

20

the Excursus on the Pentekontaetea, a change of some sort. Now the Excursus bears the marks of being written after 404[5] and so with the 'late' Excursus goes the 'late' addition of §6. Did Thucydides then change his mind about the cause of the War? There certainly seems to be some tension in Book 1. Consistently with 'the truest explanation', the Corcyrans are made (1.33.3) to speak as follows:

> As to the war for which we could be useful, if anyone of you thinks it will not happen, he is mistaken and does not see that Spartans out of fear of you desire war . . . [6]

In explaining why the Athenians voted as they did at the end of the Corcyra Debate, Thucydides asserted that the Athenians thought the Peloponnesian War was inevitable (1.44.2) and the Spartan ephor Sthenelaïdas called on the Spartan assembly 'not to allow the Athenians to become greater' (1.86.5). The introductory account of the Corcyra and Potidaea affairs is rounded off with a reassertion of 'the truest explanation' (1.88) before the Excursus on the Pentekontaetea begins. On the other hand, in Book 1, far from Sparta seeming to be forced to war out of fear at the growth of Athenian power, it would appear that a reluctant Sparta was being pushed and pulled by an insistent, urgent Corinth, for the Corinthians are made to conclude their speech at Sparta by threatening (1.71.4–6) that if the Spartans do not help the Potidaeans by promptly invading Attica, Corinth will be forced to look elsewhere for military support, clearly enough Argos.[7]

This tension has prompted theories of a change of mind in Thucydides about the cause of the war[8] – namely that originally he saw the war as primarily Corinth's war and only later did he come to 'the truest explanation'. Such theories require that the passages mentioned above were added to an original version or, rather, that they were part of subsequent rewriting of that version. This may indeed be the correct way of resolving the tension, though with regard to one of the passages it is hardly comfortable. Thucydides must have given some explanation in his original version of why the Athenians voted as they did at the end of the Corcyra Debate, and whatever explanation he gave was a matter of report, not of interpretation. After all, Thucydides was either present or well able to inquire what had moved his countrymen. When he says 'for it seemed that the war against the Peloponnesians was coming anyway' (1.44.2), that is very likely to record the mood of the time

21

and to have moved Thucydides at that time to his 'truest explanation'. That is, he may well have had the 'truest explanation' in mind before ever he put pen to paper.

In any case, this tension may be more apparent than real. In Book 7 (18.2), speaking of the Spartans' preparations for the fortifications of Decelea in 414/13, Thucydides declared that they considered that 'in the former war they themselves had transgressed the peace',[9] that although there was a clause in the former treaty forbidding hostilities if the other side was willing to submit to arbitration, they had taken no notice of the Athenians proffering just that. What was generally admitted in Sparta in 414 could well have been strongly held by a considerable number of Spartiates in 432, who had to be persuaded against their better judgement that Sparta must go to war without delay. All may have accepted that the only way to check the alarming growth of Athenian power was war, but some were demanding strict adherence to the Thirty Years Peace.[10] It was they who had to be over-persuaded by the Corinthians, Sthenelaïdas and his kind. If that was the case, there was no inconsistency in Thucydides' account that is to be explained away.

Thucydides may have changed his mind for all we know, but we have no reason for thinking that he did and his account of the events leading up to the outbreak of the war may be accepted as expounding a single and consistent view. But why then, it must be asked, did he add §6 to the twenty-third chapter and illuminate it by inserting the Excursus on the Pentekontaetea?

The answer may be proposed that, although Thucydides did not, as far as we can see, change his mind about the cause of the war, he did make a historiographical change. When he began, he thought that if he wrote up the *aitiai* and the *diaphorai*, that would suffice for those who wished to know 'the origins of so great a war coming on the Greeks' (1.23.5), just as Herodotus had prefaced his history with an account of the *aitiai* and *diaphorai* between Greece and the powers of the Orient (1.1–5). So the first version of Thucydides' *History* contained no more than the Corcyran and Potidaean affairs; 'the truest explanation' was not spelled out. In time, he came to see that this first version was inadequate for so great a conflict and that it was necessary to make the implicit explicit. So he added §6 to chapter 23 and wrote up the history of the Pentekontaetea, or rather, as much as he had time for.

22

There is no good case to be made for the view that there were two Thucydidean versions of the cause of the war. So the question may be put whether Thucydides was correct in his 'truest explanation'.

First, some elucidation is called for. When Thucydides spoke of the Spartans being afraid because of the growth of Athenian power, he was presumably thinking of the period between 446 and 432. In 446 they had contentedly settled for the Thirty Years Peace when they cannot have thought that they had to. Bribery of Plistoanax, the king in command of the Peloponnesian army in the invasion of Attica (1.114.2), had been alleged (2.21.1, 5.16.3), but since Athens was in a difficult position and felt obliged to make concessions (4.21.3), it is likely enough that Plistoanax led his army home because Athens had indicated that it was ready to return Nisaea, Pegae, Troezen and Achaea (ibid.), and that Sparta considered that the Peace was a good deal. After all, they appear to have gained a statement from Athens that the autonomy of the subject allies would be respected.[11] So Spartan fear of the growth of Athenian power had either been allayed or was not strong once the Peace had been made, and it seems likely that it was between 446 and 432 that the alarming growth occurred which Thucydides alluded to in his 'truest explanation'.

This period is the very part of the Pentekontaetea that Thucydides did not describe apart from his comparatively full account of the Samian Revolt, and one can only surmise what he had in mind, but one can surmise with some confidence. The most decisive event of those years was probably the successful settlement of the Samian Revolt. It was a tense time. The Samians came near, according to Thucydides (8.76.4), to wresting control of the sea from Athens, and if Lesbos and Chios had sided with Samos instead of with Athens (1.116.2), the combined naval power of the allies would have been at the least a very serious challenge indeed. Once Samos had been dealt with, the balance of power between Athens and her allies swung decisively in Athens' favour, and even major allies could think of revolt only if Spartan aid was secured (cf. 3.2.1). So from 439 onwards Athens was very much more powerful.

Secondly, there was the foundation of Amphipolis in 437. Not only did it secure for Athens an abundant supply of timber for shipbuilding as well as control of the rich mining area of Mount Pangaeus, but also the strategic importance of the site was enormous (4.108.1; Livy 45.30.3). Whoever controlled it controlled the crossing of the lower Strymon. In the fourth century, Philip had

23

to have it if he was to expand eastwards; in the fifth the loss of it occasioned the Athenians 'great fear' (4.108.1). Its foundation was a great increase in strength.

Again, although the development of Athenian naval skill can hardly be traced in any detailed way, their crews were continually practising (1.142.5 and 6) when their future opponents were not, and there is a lively demonstration of this in the contrast between the battle of Sybota in 433 (1.48f.) and the operations of Phormio at the mouth of the Corinthian Gulf in 429 (2.83ff.). In the latter engagement, the Athenians with 20 ships faced ultimately 77[12] (2.86.4), and although the Peloponnesians had some success, the Athenians plainly out-sailed them and out-manoeuvred them as the Peloponnesian commanders seem to have expected. At Sybota, before the Athenians began in a limited way to be involved, the fighting was conducted in a very old-fashioned way, 'being more like a land battle' (1.49.2f.). 'There were no *diekploi*, but they fought the sea-battle more with dash and strength than with skill' (*epistēmē*). When one considers that Corinth and Corcyra were, after Athens, the two leading naval powers of the Greek world, it is clear that Athens was, navally speaking, far ahead of everyone else and formidable indeed. Of course, Sparta may not have exactly appreciated how far ahead Athens was, but they must have heard enough to be afraid.

In general, Athens must have appeared dauntingly strong. She had built up a reserve fund of 6000 talents (2.13.3), by Greek notions quite enormous, and her control of the Empire must have been tightening every year. We do not know when the tithe on cargoes coming through the Hellespont began to be imposed, but it would seem to have been in place at the time when the first Callias Decree was passed and was probably enough pre-war.[13] The more regular ordering of the annual gifts to Athena on the (so-called) Tribute Lists[14] is perhaps symbolic. The real index is the appearance on the Tribute Lists in the 430s of rubrics[15] showing that cities were taking on themselves the payment of tribute, that even individuals were doing so, presumably to be able to enjoy 'the benefits of empire', i.e. not to be excluded from trading (cf. [Xen.] *Ath. Pol.* 2.12).[16] The empire was becoming from one point of view an ever more successful protection racket, and Sparta must have known it and been pressed by *émigrés*[17] to act to stop the consolidation of imperial power.

Most seriously, Sparta had lost the hegemony of the Greek world. In the sixth century, after Croesus had opted for Sparta (Hdt. 1.69.1) and Sparta had accepted her role as champion of Greek independence (cf. Hdt. 1.152.3), it was natural for others to look to her, and her leadership during Xerxes' invasion was inevitable (Hdt. 8.2.2). But after the decisive debate of 478 (Diod. 11.50), Athens came ever more to supplant her. It was not just the great increase of Athens' political power whereby she was on the lowest assessment by the late 460s a partner of Sparta in the hegemony of Greece and by 446 secure in her control of the Greek cities in and around the Aegean, but also, as the Funeral Oration declares (2.37), her democratic way of life was a model for others and the whole city was an 'example to Greece' (2.41.1). Whatever precisely Thucydides meant by this phrase,[18] Athens was, indeed, the centre of Greece for drama, for philosophy, and for the writing of history. Other states gave employment to architects and artists, but none on the scale of Athens which seemed twice as large as life (1.10). At the Panathenaea and the Dionysia, the city, so wonderfully provided (2.36.3, 64.3), would have been thronged with visitors and the impression it made on them must have been very great indeed; democracy worked and wealth and power came with it – for Sparta a fearsome spectacle.

Certainly Athenian power had grown. But what exactly had Sparta to fear? Athens had been forced in 446 to abandon what she had got hold of during the First Peloponnesian War (1.115.1), and it was unlikely that Pericles, bent on developing sea-power, would want to become involved again in war or politics in the Peloponnese. So Sparta had nothing exactly to fear, but fears do not have to be exact to be compelling.[19] The Spartans controlled the Peloponnese by maintaining oligarchy (1.19). Argos, their faded rival, was democratic (5.29.1), but if democratic ideas should spread to the populous states of the northern Peloponnese, Spartan control would weaken with imaginable consequences.

The 'truest explanation' is intelligible, but is it right? The principal alternative theory is that Athens provoked the war,[20] that in furtherance of imperial policy Pericles not only was responsible for measures that alarmed and provoked the Peloponnesians, but also was so intransigent and unwilling to give an inch in discussion with Spartan ambassadors that war became inevitable.

The responsibility of Pericles for Athenian policy is plain, both in general (2.65.9) and in relation to Sparta. Indeed, Thucydides not only recorded that in 430 the People held Pericles to blame for their misfortunes 'considering that he had persuaded them to go to war' (2.59.1), but also when he introduced Pericles (1.127.3), he pronounced him 'the most powerful man of his time and leader of the state' who 'opposed the Spartans in everything and would not allow the Athenians to give way but urged them to go to war', and he made Pericles begin his speech in answer to the final Spartan embassy: 'my judgement is constant and unchanging, namely that we should not give way to the Peloponnesians' (1.140.1). Even if Plutarch (*Per.* 29.1) had not explicitly stated that it was Pericles who persuaded the Athenians to make a defensive alliance with the Corcyrans, it could have been presumed that when on the second day of the Corcyra Debate the People changed round (1.44.1), it was Pericles who made the decisive speech.

In Thucydides' account, however, that debate would appear to be the first occasion when the Athenians took a decision seriously affecting relations with the Peloponnesian League, for neither does the Corcyran speaker argue that Athens would be inconsistent if she rejected the Corcyran appeal, nor does the Corinthian call on Athens to renounce hostile policy already begun. The impression one gets is that the Corcyran affair is a cloud in a previously clear sky, and that that was indeed the case seems to be suggested by what we know of the building of the Propylaea. It was begun in 437/6 and, according to Heliodorus, was 'utterly finished in five years' (Harpocration *s.v. Propylaia tauta*) – clearly intended gloriously to complete the building-programme for the Acropolis.[21] However, the work was in fact cut short, not completed, and this was, one feels bound to presume, because of the approach of war.[22] If the approach of war caused a cessation, it seems unlikely that the grandiose plans would have been started in 437 if Periclean policy was, for years before the Corcyra Debate of 433, pursuing aims that could lead to war. Perhaps the impression we derive from Thucydides' account of that debate is not false, and before 433 Athens under Pericles was not pursuing policies that could provoke war.

Apart from the possibility, and it is only a possibility, that Athens increased the tribute of Potidaea from 6 to 15 talents in some year before 433/2, possibly as early as 438/7,[23] there is no clear sign of Athens flexing her imperial muscles in any way that directly affected any member of the Peloponnesian League. In any case, a mere raising of the tribute, by no means unparalleled, would hardly be felt even in the metropolis of Potidaea, Corinth, which continued to send out annual magistrates until 432 (1.56.2).[24] It would, however, greatly affect our judgement of Athens' conduct in the years immediately before 433 if the passing of the Megara Decree and the Athenian interference in Aegina – the two specific complaints made to Sparta in 432 (1.67) – could be shown to precede the Corcyra Debate. That, however, cannot be shown, and the probability is that both belong to 433/2.

First, the dating of the Megara Decree. When Thucydides made the Corinthians argue in the Corcyra Debate that instead of taking on Corinth's enmity by helping Corcyra, 'it would be wise for Athens rather to detract from the suspicion incurred through the Megarians' (1.42), he did so in such general terms as to make it unlikely that he was referring to anything as specific as the Megara Decree which, for the Megarians (1.67.4) as for the Spartans (1.139.1), was a plain breach of the Thirty Years Peace, a source of 'resentment', not merely 'suspicion'. The alternative explanation which makes the Corinthians allude to the Megarians joining Athens in the First Peloponnesian War (1.103.4) – the source of the 'special hatred' of Corinth for Athens – is much preferable.[25] Other arguments, however, suggest that the Decree was passed at no great interval before the Megarians went to Sparta with their complaint in 432 (1.67). In commenting on the claim in Aristophanes' *Peace* (605f.) that Pericles got the Megara Decree passed to distract attention from the corrupt dealing of Phidias, the Scholiast remarked, by way of showing that the two matters were quite unconnected, that Philochorus dated the prosecution of Phidias in 438/7 but recorded the Megarian protest to Sparta about the Megara Decree under 432/1. He did not explicitly say that Philochorus dated the Decree to that year (though Philochorus may well have done so),[26] but the manner of his argument suggests that the decree did not greatly precede the protest. One cannot affirm with any certainty that the passing of the decree was recorded by Philochorus, but it seems very likely that this famous event was not omitted by him, and the Scholiast would have had to be a dolt or a rogue to argue as he did if the decree was recorded by Philochorus well before the protest of 432. To this one may add the general consideration that since the Megarians believed the Decree constituted a breach of the Thirty Years Peace (1.67) – in which it will be argued they were probably justified – they would surely have made their complaint to Sparta without delay.[27] So it is no surprise that Thucydides makes the speakers in the Corcyra Debate speak as if no exceptionable act of Athens had yet taken place.

It has been argued[28] that Thucydides did not describe the origins of the dispute with Megara as he did in the cases of Corcyra and Potidaea because the Decree had been passed long before the Corcyra Debate and only assumed importance in the final negotiations. But Thucydides also did not describe the Athenian intervention in Aegina (1.67.2). Is that event likewise to be thought to have occurred long ago and to have been of no importance in itself? It would seem, at any rate, proper to pose the same sort of explanation for Thucydides' brevity in both matters. Since both the Aeginetans and the Megarians considered that Athens was in breach of the Thirty Years Peace, there may well be another explanation why Thucydides did not fully describe, and it may be proposed that the reason he fully described the Corcyran and Potidaean affairs but not the Megarian and Aeginetan was that he was concerned fully to describe those affairs that involved actual hostilities and those affairs only. So the argument for an early date for the Decree based on Thucydides' failure fully to describe it is not compelling.[29]

The date (and precise nature) of the Athenian intervention in Aegina is even more problematic. In March 432, the Aeginetans paid either 9 or 14 talents tribute, much less than the 30 talents they seem regularly to have paid since 454/3,[30] and one inevitably connects this with their protest to Sparta in 432. Some have suggested that Aegina made a short payment in 432[31] and was punished for it, perhaps by installation of a garrison, but it is very unlikely that if they were defaulting they would not have defaulted entirely. The reduced amount is far more satisfactorily explained by supposing that the interference in Aegina's autonomy, presumably by installation of a garrison, had already taken place and her tribute reduced in compensation.[32] Unhappily, no entry for Aegina on the Tribute Lists survives in the preceding years as far back as 440 and it is open to believe that the intervention Aegina complained of in 432 had occurred well before the Corcyra Debate. But, again, one would expect them not to delay in their complaint. Thucydides (at 1.67) gives no hint that 432 was not the first occasion that Aeginetans had complained and so, in view of the tone of the Corcyra Debate in Thucydides' account, it seems likely enough that before that debate Athens had put the screw on neither Megara nor Aegina.

In all this, it must be remembered that, at the first assembly concerning Corcyra, the Athenians had been in half a mind to accept Corinthian arguments (1.44.1). So if Athens had been pursuing policies or approving measures that directly affected Sparta or her allies, there should have been no havering about whether or not to deny Corinth the chance to win over the third largest naval force in the Greek world (1.36.1); therefore, no Athenian should have failed to realise that war was coming (1.34.3, 36.1). Given the nature of the evidence, one cannot be sure, but it very much seems that if Pericles brought on the war, it is on the period following the making of the defensive alliance with Corcyra that one must concentrate the inquiry.

But what, it will be objected, of the Callias Decrees (ML 58) which have been generally regarded as amounting to a war budget? In the first decree, the treasures of gods other than Athena are to be assembled on the Acropolis and put in the care of a specially created board of Treasurers of the Other Gods,[33] and the money which is left over after payments due to the Gods have been made is to be used 'for the dockyard and the walls'. In the second decree, which is on the back of the first but is in a much poorer state of preservation, it would appear that the decision to curtail work on the Propylaea is presumed and that arrangements for repair and maintenance are being made. For over 60 years it has been widely accepted that both decrees were passed on the same day, and for many scholars that day has been supposed to belong to 434/3. To quote the commentary of Meiggs and Lewis (1969):

> There is little doubt that Callias moved his decrees in 434/3. We may perhaps be a little more precise and suggest that it was after the Great Panathenaia of 434 and shortly before the elections [in the spring?] of 433. If this date is approximately right these decrees precede Athens' acceptance of Corcyra's appeal for help against Corinth in the summer of 433.

If that were right, not only would the Athenian readiness to accept the arguments of the Corinthians in the first assembly of the Corcyra Debate (1.44.1) be utterly paradoxical, but Thucydides' whole account of the debate would also have to be pronounced quite misleading.[34]

It is not necessarily so. Over 20 years ago it was pointed out[35] that the claim that the second Callias Decree had exactly the same prescript as the first and, therefore, was passed by the assembly on the very same day, went far beyond what the marks on the stone strictly justified. This criticism has recently been restated by Kallet-Marx[36] in a radical reconsideration of the dating and the relation of the two decrees, which, if it were correct, would take both decrees out of 434/3. It certainly would be very odd if two decrees proposed on the same day by one and the same person manifested different spellings and different terms. The fact that the two decrees are inscribed on the two faces of a single stone by the same mason[37] does not prove they were passed on the same day. They deal with related matters and the second decree, which evidently comes after the first, could have been inscribed by the same mason, though perhaps at no very great interval.

If the arguments of Kallet-Marx are accepted and the first decree is assigned to 430/29, the Callias Decrees become irrelevant to the question of Athenian policy in the period before the Corcyra Debate. But even if she is not correct, even if both decrees belong to 434/3 and were proposed in the Council at no great interval apart, the decrees may well belong to the period between the debate and the end of the Panathenaic year 434/3 (as is argued elsewhere in this book).[38] If they can be placed in that period, in view of the tone of the Corcyra Debate, let them be so placed. Certainly they do not necessarily prove that Athens was pursuing a policy likely to lead to war before the crisis of the Corcyran appeal.

All in all, those who argue that Athens deliberately brought on the war must seek their ammunition in the period after the Corcyra Debate.

As already argued, at some time between the Corcyra Debate and March 432 when the tribute was paid, Athens had interfered in Aeginetan affairs and prompted the complaint made later at Sparta (1.67.2). The settlement of a cleruchy on the island came in the first year of the war (2.27.1) and the reasonable guess is that what happened in 433/2 was that Athens installed a garrison. The only conceivable purpose of that must be that it was to ensure that the island was not used as a base for hostile operations of the sort that occurred in the fourth century. In the later years of the Corinthian War, the Spartans made piratical raids on Attica from there (Xen. *Hell.* 5.1.1 and 29), and Teleutias in 387 made a successful attempt on shipping in the harbour of the Peiraeus (ibid. 18–24). Similarly, Spartan piracy from Aegina played its part in the war of 378–5 (ibid. 6.2.1) and in 376 the corn ships were checked from sailing to Athens (ibid. 5.4.61). So in 433/2, Athens had good reason to be afraid. If Pericles in 433 saw 'war bearing down on Athens from the Peloponnese', a celebrated dictum (Plut. *Per.* 8.7), it is likely enough that in declaring, at that time or shortly afterwards, with regard to Aegina that Athens must 'remove the sore in the eye of the Peiraeus' (ibid., and cf. Aristotle *Rhet.* 1411a15), he had in mind the installation of a garrison. Aegina might and did complain, but it was only common precaution, a strategic preliminary to the war.

Megara is more troubling. In view of the prominence of the Megara Decree in the final negotiations (cf. 1.139), it would be helpful to know what its purpose was. According to de Ste. Croix, the Decree had no political purpose at all; the Megarians had offended by encroaching on the land sacred to the Twin Goddesses of Eleusis and piety required that action be taken. The Spartans, in their poverty of proper grounds for complaint against Athens, fixed on the Megara Decree and demanded its repeal.[39] There is much to be said by way of comment on this theory,[40] but the important point is that it does not explain why the Megarians themselves were persuaded that the Decree constituted a breach of the Thirty Years Peace (1.67.4).

An explanation may be suggested. There was a clause of the peace treaty constituting the League of Corinth in 338/7 to the effect that 'those sharing in the peace should sail the sea, and that no one should prevent them or force a ship of any of them to beach' (Dem. 17.19).[41] If there was such a clause in the Thirty Years Peace, the Megarian belief that Athens had acted 'contrary to the treaty' (1.67.4) is understandable. In the Peace of Gela of 424 there was a clause to the effect that if a single Athenian ship sailed in to Gela, it should be welcomed, but not a larger number unless they had been summoned (6.52). This, of course, concerns warships, but presumably a single merchant-ship would not be excluded. A similar decision was taken during the revolution at Corcyra in 427 (3.71.1). In the year's truce between the Athenians and the Spartans in 423, the Spartans and their allies are accorded the right to use the sea off their own shores and that of their allies, not with a warship, but with an oared merchant ship up to a stated tonnage (4.118.5). So it is apposite to ask whether a clause of some sort pertaining to use of the sea was in the Thirty Years Peace. There is a hint that there was. In describing the Spartan preparations in 432/1, Thucydides said that 'for the rest they made no move and received Athenians on a single ship until these preparations were made' (2.7.2). Why did they do so? Why should they? A clause of the Thirty Years Peace is a reasonable guess.[42]

It may be objected that no such clause asserts itself in the Peace of Nicias. But perhaps the contracting parties deliberately eschewed the matters that had caused friction under the Thirty Years Peace. It is notable that there is no trace of the clause which the Aeginetans had claimed in 432 that Athens had transgressed (1.67.2). That clause would, it seems, have been of general bearing. When Pericles responded finally to the Spartan ultimatum in 432/1, after dealing with the complaint about Megara he dealt with that about Aegina by recommending Athens to reply 'that we will let the allied cities be autonomous if we actually had them in an autonomous state when we made the treaty' (1.144.2). But in 421 the only clause which raises the question of autonomy is that confirming a special status on the cities of the Thracian district of the Empire that had revolted in 432 (5.18.5). For the rest, the nebulous topic of autonomy for all is absent. So too, perhaps, the maritime clause, present in the truce of 423, was avoided.

If this hypothesis of a maritime clause is right, Megara had just cause to complain in 432. Since much of the trade that was carried on in the Peiraeus involved metics, de Ste Croix presumes the same was the case with Megara. Athens, however, was exceptional: she was the great entrepôt of the Aegean, and what was true of Athens may well not have been true of Megara.[43] In so far as Megarians traded in the Aegean – and there was some, probably enough, traffic between her and her colonies on the Bosphorus, Byzantium and Chalcedon, even if, as de Ste Croix improbably maintains, Megarians were not excluded from the Peiraeus – Megara must have realised they would feel the pinch and have strongly resented. The Spartans very properly took up the Megarian complaint and made it the crucial issue, not because they lacked a real cause for complaint, for they could have picked on the trouble over Aegina, but because it was to them 'a very clear case' (1.139.1).[44]

But why did Pericles choose to propose and secure the passing of such a decree? To judge by the speech of Dicaeopolis in the *Acharnians* (495–556, esp. 530–8), and there is no other evidence, the effect of the decree was said to be to cause the Megarians to feel hunger. This is no doubt comic exaggeration, for if it is right to place the Decree after the Corcyra Debate, there was hardly time for Megarians to feel greatly deprived, but it is represented as having struck them in their bellies. It was not merely that their noses were put out of joint. They were affected economically. But it was not, generally speaking, characteristic of Greek states to seek to foster their economic well-being. Athens, the state about which we are most fully informed, did pay close attention to the corn supply and had some concern for materials for the navy,[45] and Thasos had a law forbidding a Thasian merchantman importing foreign wine,[46] and no doubt there were other such attempts to control trade, but in general trade was very much a matter for individuals and *laissez-faire*, and it is wholly unlikely that Pericles had any economic objective in the case of the Megara Decree.

The means were economic, but the purpose was, in all likelihood, political – an attempt to draw Megara into seeking its own salvation by leaving the Peloponnesian League and becoming an ally of Athens, just as she had been in the First Peloponnesian War (1.103.4). During that war Attica was kept immune because, by virtue of the Megarian alliance, Athens kept guard in Mt. Geraneia, difficult enough to cross unguarded (1.107.3), until in 446 Megara returned to her former allegiance and Attica was invaded (1.114.1). For the coming war it was highly desired that Megara should be induced by whatever means to do the same again, and the economic exclusion ordered by the Decree was perhaps the chosen means. Experience has shown that such sanctions rarely achieve their purpose, but men nonetheless constantly expect them to do so. If, then, it is right to place the Megara Decree after the Corcyra Debate, the Decree may be regarded as a strategic preliminary to the imminent war.

With the Megara Decree, Pericles essentially breached the Thirty Years Peace but, perhaps, not without the semblance of an excuse. When the Spartans came confidently to demand the repeal of a measure so blatantly in breach of the Peace, they were met with the justification that the Megarians had worked the sacred land as well as 'the undefined land' and had given refuge to runaway slaves (1.139.2). This was a smart card to play which Pericles had kept up his sleeve, and it caused the Spartans to stop talking about Megara and issue a general ultimatum (ibid. §3). But the underlying truth was that, for sound strategic reasons, Megara was to be forced, if possible, to join the Athenian alliance.

Precaution is not aggression. But there is a serious question. Why was Athens so intransigent about the Megara Decree? If it was a strategic precaution for the coming war, why, when Sparta had declared that if Athens repealed the decree there would not be war,

33

did Athens refuse to give an inch? In such confrontations one side or the other or both must make some concession if strife is to be avoided. Is not the Athenian intransigence a sign that Pericles actually wanted the war? He had persuaded the Athenians to break the Peace over Megara and Aegina. Now he was refusing to make any concession. Does not the responsibility for the Peloponnesian War belong fairly and squarely to Athens?

Such is the case presented by Professor Badian,[47] who argued that

> it is Thucydides' main aim, in his account of the origin and outbreak of the war, to show that it was started by Sparta in a spirit of ruthless *Realpolitik* and that this was the culmination of a long series of attempts, unscrupulous and at times treacherous, to repress Athenian power, on several occasions when opportunity seemed to offer, between the withdrawal of the Persians and the final vote for war.
>
> (p. 128)

He speaks of 'Thucydides' disinformation and misleading interpretations' (p. 155).[48] Here, where attention is being concentrated on the period between the Corcyra Debate and the outbreak of war, Badian's discussion of 'the decisive point, the votes for war and the negotiations that preceded its outbreak' (p. 145) will be specially considered.

First, he argues that what Thucydides presents as a vote at Sparta for war was no more than a declaration that 'the treaty seems to have been breached and the Athenians to be in the wrong' (1.87.2) – the quoted words of the motion, but in his account of the preceding debate he pronounced that 'the proposals of the majority agreed in declaring that the Athenians were in the wrong and that war must be quickly begun' (1.79.2). The Spartans are then represented as wishing to summon all the allies and put it to the vote 'in order that they might make war, if they decided to do so, on a common resolution' (1.87.4), i.e. Sparta was said to be bent on nothing short of war. Then, when Thucydides records the meeting of the Peloponnesian League, he makes them vote for war (1.125.1), but Badian asserts

> we can be all but certain ... that the congress of the allies merely confirmed Sparta's own decision and made it binding on the League, that Athens had broken the treaty. ... That would presumably imply negotiations to undo the wrong that

had been done, and ultimately it would empower Sparta, if negotiations failed, to declare and begin war on behalf of the whole League.

(p. 150)

He points to the fact recorded by Thucydides (1.125.2) that the Peloponnesians took the best part of a year in preparation for attacking Attica. So much for war 'quickly' beginning (1.79.2).

Second, Badian argues that Thucydides' account of the negotiations, which followed the vote of the Peloponnesian League, is so sketchy that any serious desire to avoid war which the Spartans manifested is concealed, despite the fact that it would seem that there was quite a lot of coming and going in the process[49] (cf. 1.139.2 *phoitōntes*). Pericles would have nothing of it, for he was bent on war. Thucydides' 'truest cause' will be credited only by those gullible enough to be misled by Thucydides' guile.[50]

By way of answer to Badian's views, the following points can be made. First, to judge by the question posed to the Delphic Oracle and the Oracle's response, the decision of the Spartan assembly would appear to have been a decision for war. There are two accounts of the consultation. At 1.118.3 the Spartans are said to have asked 'whether it would be better for them if they waged war' and 'the god answered them, so the story goes, that if they waged war with all their might victory would be theirs and he said that he himself would lend a hand whether he was called on to do so or not.' At 2.54.4 the Spartans are said to have 'asked the god whether they should wage war'; the response is given in the same words. If the allies in the Peloponnesian League were told this (and not only does the speech put in the mouth of the Corinthian suggest at 1.123.1 that they were, but also the Spartans would have been stupid not to let it be known), they can hardly have been in any doubt about the intention of the vote at Sparta (1.87). Why should Pericles or the Athenians in general have doubted that they were bent on war? Why should we?

Second, one may wonder how seriously Sparta was bent on negotiations. The delay of nearly a year is not surprising. Sparta would invade Attica when the corn was ripe and the only choice would have been in which year to attack.[51] Archidamus had pleaded for a delay of two or three years for preparation and training (1.82.2). Indeed, Sparta called on Sicilian cities which took her side to build ships and contribute money (2.7.2). But Sparta would not

35

wait. Invasion occurred at the first possible moment. That is the point of Thucydides' comment. In no way does it suggest that the Spartans had been seriously seeking to negotiate. But had they? Thucydides claimed that the embassies were only to secure the greatest excuse for waging war, unless the Athenians 'hearkened to them' (1.126.1). They began their negotiations by trying to get Pericles exiled (1.126.2) though Thucydides declared that they were not seriously expecting that to happen (1.127.2). Whether Thucydides was correct about that or not, it was a curious start to 'serious' negotiations. Why did Sparta from then on consistently refuse to submit disputed matters to arbitration? The Thirty Years Peace required it. Badian may not regard such procedure seriously – 'arbitration would turn out to be a farce if tried and direct negotiations obviously seemed the only chance of avoiding war' (p. 151). But the Spartans had committed themselves to arbitration, if arbitration was demanded, just as they were to do in the Peace of Nicias (5.18.4), and they took it sufficiently seriously as very much to blame themselves for not having heeded the Athenian call in 432/1 (7.18.2). Athens would not relent over the Megara Decree, but the Spartans would not have anything to do with arbitration. Why were they so intransigent about that? Even as they were engaging in embassies to Athens, they were preparing for war (2.7.2). How serious was Sparta?

Badian believes that when Sparta declared that if Athens repealed the Megara Decree there would be no war, she was 'undertaking to change to a purely defensive posture toward the Athenian Empire' (p. 156). If that had been so, it would have been grievous folly. Corinth had reviled her for her defensive posture and threatened to seek a more effective leader (1.71.4), and Sparta had to act. Why should she have given Athens the chance to discredit her utterly with her allies? If Sparta had failed to act, the results would have been disastrous for Spartan hegemony in the Peloponnese.

Athens had, probably, breached the terms of The Thirty Years Peace in her precautionary moves over Megara and Aegina and there was a strong reason why she should not respond to Spartan pressure. Pericles' whole strategy of war was to be directed at proving to Greece that she and her sea empire were unassailable, and his whole political strategy in the closing months of the peace must have been directed at proving to her subject allies that there was no outside help that could save them. To concede one inch to Sparta would have been, psychologically speaking, to concede a mile to the subject allies' hopes. Once Athens had passed the Megara Decree, prudence dictated that there should be no turning back. Only if Sparta had not, in fact, been bent on war would the passing of the Decree have brought on a war Athens did not need to fight. So one returns to the crucial question. Was Sparta bent on war by 433?

Thucydides wrote as if Sparta was so intending, but was he right to do so? Sparta had certainly acted as if she was; Plistoanax had been exiled as punishment for not carrying on with the invasion of Attica in 446 (2.21.1). During the Samian Revolt, Sparta had had the Peloponnesian League debate whether Athens should be attacked (1.40.5), which almost certainly implies that Sparta had proposed war. So Thucydides' report of the Corcyran speech in 433 (1.33.3 and 36.1) and of the reason for the Athenian decision (1.44.2) may not be false. The Spartans would have been very silly if they had not been bent on war. They saw Athens' power growing and believed that war could put a stop to it. Until one can accept that Thucydides was no other than an artful apologist for Athens' dark designs, one will continue to hold that Athens did not provoke the Peloponnesian War.

It was the thesis of de Ste. Croix that Spartan 'hawks' brought on the war. By 'hawks', a word much in vogue in the early 1970s, he meant

those who were unwilling to accept the 'dual hegemony' of Sparta and Athens, with Sparta as the acknowledged leader in at least the Peloponnese, Megara and Boeotia, and Athens dominant in the naval Confederacy of Delos which by the mid-fifth century had become the Athenian empire.[52]

First, it is to be noted that there is nothing in Thucydides' account of 433 to 431 to suggest that there was such a division at Sparta into 'hawks' and 'doves'. Archidamus is represented as opposing precipitate action, but it is clear that he wanted time to prepare for a war that would be no simple walk-over (1.81.4–82.1) and the conclusion of his speech is that Sparta should, at the same time as she protested to Athens, prepare for war (1.85.2). No other opponent of war appears.[53] However, just as at Athens Cimon had in 465 called on the Athenians 'not to see Greece lame or Athens deprived of her yoke-fellow' (Plut. *Cim.* 16.10), thus showing himself the advocate of dual hegemony, so too at Sparta there had been those who had advocated the sharing of power with Athens and there would be such in later times. Plistoanax had been the latest example before the debates of 432 just as the Spartan ambassadors in 425 were to conclude their appeal for peace with a cynical call for shared hegemony (4.20.4). So it is worth considering whether there was not a sharp difference of opinion at Sparta between those who wanted to confront the rising power of Athens and those who were content to let it be.

The coming of the Persians in 480 had raised the question of which state was to lead the Greeks in naval operations. On land there was no dispute. Sparta was the unquestioned *hēgemōn*.[54] On sea, Sparta had so few ships (cf. Hdt. 8.1.2 and 43) and so little naval experience that Herodotus is probably reliable in attributing to Athens aspirations to leadership of the Greek navy (8.3.1; cf. 7.161). The rest of the Greeks would not at that time stand for it, but the idea of shared hegemony had taken root; the dual aspect of war against Persia required dual leadership. In Sparta it was accepted in late 478, in the decision not to contest with Athens her taking over the leadership (1.95.7, of which Diod. 11.50 is the Ephoran version),[55] that Athens should be in command of the Greek naval operations, and perhaps they, no more than Themistocles (1.93.7), had no great expectations of having to fight again against the Persians in Greece. However, at the same time as the war of revenge got going, the Panhellenist idea of a national crusade began to grow. The full flowering of this poisonous theory was to come in the fourth century with Isocrates and his followers, but Gorgias was an early bloom[56] and clearly, to judge by the wild anachronisms Herodotus could foist on to various characters in his *Histories*,[57] the theory was by mid-century thriving. The celebrated dictum of Cimon already quoted (Plut. *Cim.* 16.10) reflects it. In what cause were Athens and Sparta to be 'yoke-partners', and along which course might Greece become 'lame'? It is reasonable to suppose that Cimon, 'in every way the best of Hellenic men' as the poet called him after his death (Plut. *Cim.* 10.4), was thinking of a great joint assault on Persia under the joint hegemony of Athens and Sparta.

The Peace of Callias must, however, have given such musings a severe jolt.[58] While Athens collaborated with Persia, ideas of national crusade were unthinkable. Indeed, there is in Herodotus an indication of this. When the Spartans heard in the winter of 480/79 that Alexander of Macedon had come to Athens to bring the Athenians into agreement with the Barbarian, they promptly sent a counter-embassy, 'remembering the oracles that they, along with the other Dorians, would have to be expelled from the Peloponnese by the Medes and the Athenians' (8.141.1). When precisely such oracles were delivered, one can only guess. Perhaps the period after Athenian envoys gave 'earth and water' in the late sixth century (Hdt. 5.73.2) is credible enough, though it could well have been after Callias had been at Susa (Hdt. 7.151) in the late 460s when Athens' allies 'were observing them giving up the enmity with the Mede' (3.10.4), and then retrojected to 480/79. Whenever it was, once Athens had made peace with Persia these oracles must have been much in Spartan minds and any thoughts of shared hegemony laid aside. Prudence might dictate tolerance of the other side, as in 425 when Sparta had come to terms to recover the men trapped on Sphacteria, but it required the unholy alliance of Lysander and Cyrus and the abandonment of the Greeks of Asia for Panhellenism truly to revive; witness the celebrated dictum of Callicratidas (Xen. *Hell.* 1.1.7).

In 446, the Spartans were perhaps evenly divided, Plistoanax and his supporters gaining acceptance of a treaty of peace which, by requiring Athenian withdrawal from the cities on the mainland (1.115.1) and assurances of autonomy for the cities of the Empire, seemed to clip Athenian wings. Athens was in a tight spot (4.21.3), and coexistence seemed possible. Repentance swiftly followed. The following year Plistoanax had to flee into exile (2.21.1) and in the succeeding years the power of Athens grew to 'a glorious and enviable height'. There was no longer room for thoughts of tolerance or coexistence. By 433 there must have been near unanimity in Sparta that the growth of Athenian power must be stopped. Allied to that opinion was the conviction that Athens could quickly be dealt with militarily (4.85.2, 5.14.3). To resolve on war was not 'hawkishness'. It was plain prudence. The Peloponnesian War began not because some Spartans were wicked. It began because a substantial majority (1.87.3) saw that it was the only way to remove the threat presented by the growth of Athenian power.

'The truest explanation' was correct. 'The growth of Athenian power made the Spartans afraid and forced them to go to war.'

3

THUCYDIDES AND THE STRATEGY OF THE PELOPONNESIAN WAR

Thucydides considered that Pericles judged well the power of Athens compared to that of the Peloponnesians and that if the Athenians had followed his advice, the city could easily have survived the war (2.65.6f. and 13). Was this judgement sound?

The Spartans began the war with great confidence that the Athenians would shortly submit. They had, they thought, only to ravage Athenian territory and Athens would come to terms and relinquish her empire (5.14.3, 4.85.2, 7.28.3). In 446, the Spartan king Plistoanax had been duped (or bribed)[1] into giving up the invasion of Attica (2.21.1); this time there would be no mistake. No matter how much of her food Athens imported in the late 430s, she would not be able to survive with her own wheat and barley destroyed by fire, her olive-trees damaged with ring-barking,[2] and her vines cut; she would have either to concede defeat or to come out and fight. If she did come out and fight, defeat – and disastrous defeat at that – was certain. In 431, Sparta was still by far the most formidable military power in the Greek world. Her ruling class, the Spartiates, devoted the whole of life to training for war both as individual fighters and as an army. On the battlefield of First Mantinea in 418, King Agis attempted a complicated manoeuvre which involved the rearrangement of the battle order of his army while the whole army was already advancing against the enemy (5.71); it did not succeed, but it was only conceivable in an army which was highly trained and, indeed, trained for that very movement. Their tactical skills and changes of formation were the wonder of the Greek world ([Xen.] *Lac. Pol.* 11). Although hardly surprising to us, Thucydides felt it necessary to explain to his readers (5.66.3) their practised system of transmitting orders, presumably because such discipline was lacking elsewhere in the

40

Greek world. They were trained to load the transport wagons ([Xen.] *Lac. Pol.* 11.2) – not the sort of thing other Greeks bothered themselves with – and at that battle of Mantinea while their opponents were being roused to valour by stirring appeals by their commanders, the Spartans in their separate units sang the martial songs of Tyrtaeus which they had had dinned into them from boyhood (5.69.2).[3] When their opponents began their eager, angry advance, the Spartans moved slowly to the sound of the flute, keeping their distances and their formation (5.70.1). Above all, these men, expertly trained in the use of spear and sword, were also trained never to yield ground or turn tail (Hdt. 9.53.2, 55.2). 'Come back with your shield or be carried back on it' was the women's parting cry (Plut. *Mor.* 241F), and with iron resolve they advanced with purple cloaks and polished shields, the crest waving on their helmets above their long locks, the boast in ancient Greece of unchallengeable might and valour ([Xen.] *Lac. Pol.* 11.3).[4] For many of their opponents, the mere sight of the Spartans was enough and they would turn rather than face them (5.72.4). In a world of amateurs, the Spartans were in 431 the professionals. There was no hope that Athenians could match them.

Indeed, as a land power the Athenians were of little account. Apart from their victory in 490 against the Persians, they had remarkably little to boast about, and even that victory was not what they boasted it to be. Much paper has been spent on the question of what part the Persian cavalry had in that battle, but it is notable that there is no mention of cavalry in the fighting on the beach when the Persian army was re-embarking, and since it must have taken quite a long time to get horses aboard horse-transports, it is evident that that had already been done when the Athenians attacked. In short, the victory was won only when the Persian command had decided that the Athenians were not going to fight and had gone quite a long way in re-embarking their army.[5] The glorious victory was less glorious than national pride let on, and after 490 there was nothing to boast. The all-decisive battle of Plataea, which forced the Persians out of Greece in 479, was won essentially by Spartan valour (Hdt. 9.71.2). In 457 at Tanagra, the full Athenian army supported by 1,000 Argives and a good number of their other allies (the whole force totalling 14,000) was defeated by a smaller Spartan army, the core of which consisted of a mere 1,500 Spartans. It is not to be denied that, shortly afterwards, the Athenians were successful against the Boeotians (1.108.2) and, no doubt, they had their successes at the head of the Delian League against sundry barbarians (cf. ML 33 and 48), but there was no reason whatsoever for the Spartans in 431 to fear a reverse on land. So within the limited Spartan premises they had every confidence. Athens would be defeated within a few years.

It was not the case that this was the sole strategic notion that occurred to Spartan minds. If we may trust Thucydides, the Corinthians before the war spoke of 'different ways of fighting the war' (1.122.1), including 'causing their allies to revolt, which most of all would deprive them of the revenues on which they flourish'. Even if Thucydides was writing anachronistically, it is evident that, from the start of the war, there were those who chafed at the strategy of merely ravaging Attica and sought more dramatic methods of attacking Athens' imperial power. Their leader would appear to have been Brasidas, the hero of the later years of the Archidamian War who, with limited forces but with great dash, sought to liberate the northern cities of the Athenian Empire. This was after the Athenians had the good fortune to capture on Sphacteria a number of Spartiates and so were able to threaten that, if Attica was invaded, the prisoners would be put to death (4.41.1). Sparta was therefore forced to follow the strategy advocated by Brasidas and his ilk. Even earlier they took what opportunities they could, making efforts to assemble a fleet (cf. Gomme *ad* 2.72), fostering revolt in Lesbos (3.16.3), attempting a raid on the Piraeus (2.93f.), and founding the city of Heraclea that would reveal its purpose when Brasidas made his hurried march to Thrace (3.92). Sparta was not without strategic imagination.[6]

Sparta persisted with the strategy of ravaging Attica for a very good reason: it was working or appeared to be working. After two years of Spartan invasion, and despite the fierce opposition of Pericles, the Athenians sought to make peace (2.59.2). The offer was rejected. Presumably, they were not yet ready to concede as much as Sparta required. But they continued to want peace and, it would seem from a remark Thucydides made about the Spartan appeal for peace in 425, they continued to seek it (4.21.1).[7] Thus Sparta saw no need to change her strategy. The Delphic oracle had given the assurance of Apollo that Sparta would win, and had promised divine assistance (2.54.4). The devastating plague of 430 which lasted for two years – and its recurrence in winter 427 which lasted for over a year (3.87) – was plainly heaven-sent to the Greeks.

Sparta was confident that she would win and that her strategy was the right one.

With matching confidence, Pericles persuaded the Athenians to follow the strategy he proposed – a purely defensive strategy. He said that if they remained on the defensive and carefully maintained the navy, abstained from increasing their empire while the war was on and took no risks with the city, they would survive (2.65.7; cf. 1.144.1, 2.13.2). The key word was 'survive'. He was not looking for the defeat of Sparta, merely for a confession that Athens and her imperial power were untouchable. Militarily, this would be a negative result. Politically, it would bring immense gains. Not only would the subject states of the Empire have to resign themselves to the fact that the state they had looked to to liberate them could not do so, and so have to make the best of their ill condition, but also the prospects for the extension of Athenian Empire were boundless. In the speech which Thucydides has Pericles deliver to the Athenians, shortly before his death and at a time when Athens was suffering most dreadfully from the Plague, he declared:

> And I'll tell you this too which you don't seem ever to have realised is open to you as regards imperial greatness, nor have I spoken of it in my earlier speeches, and I wouldn't say it now since it makes a somewhat boastful claim if I didn't see you unreasonably dispirited. You think you have empire over just the allies, but I declare that of the two zones available for exploitation, I mean land and sea, you are in complete control of the latter both to the extent that you now occupy it and still further if you are willing. There is no one of the present powers, be it the King of Persia or any other people, who will, given your existing naval armament, stop you sailing the seas.
>
> (2.62.2)

Thus, he promised the Athenians the hope of, in Virgil's phrase, 'boundless empire', if only they would follow his defensive strategy.

The navy and naval power were, for Pericles, all-important, and it is important to realise how far ahead, navally speaking, the Athenians were in 431. It was not just that they possessed a very large number of ships,[8] that they had in the Piraeus by far the greatest maritime centre of the Aegean, stocked, as no purely naval base would have been, with all the materials shipping of all sorts required, that all the mercenary rowers of the Aegean went there where they were most likely to be sure of employment,[9] but also

Athens was far ahead of other Greek naval powers in seamanship and naval tactics. The battle of Sybota in 433 is the revealing occasion (1.49). Thucydides shows that the Greeks in general were 50 years behind Athens. For, in that battle, the two other major naval powers fought 'in an old-fashioned way'. It was more like a land-battle than a sea-fight, with ships stationary, side by side, with their marines slugging it out just as the Phoenicians in Xerxes' navy had wanted to do. 'Determination and strength', Thucydides says, 'not science', whereas in 429 we see the Athenian general, Phormio, with an inferior number of ships circling round a Peloponnesian force, like a stoat round a rabbit, terrified of Athenian tactical skill (2.85–90). Sparta talked of assembling an enormous fleet (2.7.2). Even if they had assembled a matching number, to catch the Athenians up in seamanship would not be easily done. As Pericles had said (1.142.6),

> they won't readily develop naval skill. You Athenians practised from the Persian invasion onwards and were never prevented. How are farmers and land-lubbers to develop it, when we will not allow them to practise?

He was right. Athens was supreme and almost as untouchable by sea as the Spartans were on land. The irresistible force could not meet the immovable object.

In the sense already noted, the Periclean strategy did not fail. By seeking peace within eighteen months of the start of the war, the Athenians not only encouraged Sparta to persist in its strategy, but also thereby nullified Pericles' claim that Athens would prove that she could not be affected by Spartan hostility. His strategy did not fail. It was not properly tried. It may also be noted that it should not be thought properly to have succeeded. When the Spartans appealed for peace in 425, it might seem that Pericles was proved right in arguing that the city would survive. Clearly, the Athenians did have the chance in 425 to make what one might term a Periclean peace, and indeed they did make one of a sort in 421, unstable though it proved. But not even Pericles, supremely provident as he was in Thucydides' judgement (2.65.6), could have foreseen that the Spartan commander of the forces sent to deal with the Athenian occupation of Pylos would commit the appalling strategic blunder of putting part of his army on to the island of Sphacteria, whereby at a stroke the besiegers became the besieged, nor is it likely that Pericles was all that clearly aware of Sparta's peculiar problem of the decline in the numbers of Spartiates, whereby the besieged on Sphacteria were, demographically, too precious to lose.[10] Athens' biggest bit of luck was Sparta's folly. It made a Periclean 'survival' possible, but only by the strangest of chances.

Pericles' strategy was not properly tried, but in so far as it was tried, it succeeded only by accident. In itself and by its nature it was likely to fail. Sparta went to war in 431 because her whole position as leader of the Peloponnese was at stake. She had too much to lose for her to give in without trying everything possible.[11] What was possible and what was ultimately tried and succeeded[12] was the strategy advocated by King Archidamus, or at any rate the strategy attributed to him by Thucydides.

Scholars have always wondered, and always will wonder, whether the speech attributed to Archidamus (1.80–85) in the fateful debate at Sparta in 432 reflected the sentiments he expressed on that occasion, or was written up by Thucydides long afterwards with the benefit of hindsight. There is certainly a good deal of careful contrivance in this speech, in the later speech of the Corinthians, and in the speech of Pericles urging the Athenians to reject the Spartan ultimatum. Echoes, anticipations and answers to others' arguments suggest that Thucydides himself is the controlling mind, though when exactly he wrote up the three speeches remains obscure. But no matter for our purposes here. Whether it was Archidamus in 432 or Thucydides long after who put before the Spartans a dissident, sceptical view of the strategy proposed and an alternative strategy of his own, there certainly was an alternative to which Sparta could turn before they thought of admitting failure.

Thucydides (1.79.2) introduced Archidamus before his speech with the most complimentary word in his vocabulary, 'intelligent' (*xynetos*), and his Archidamus certainly made short work of the strategy Sparta was putting her confidence in. 'For let us not be buoyed up with the expectation that the war will be quickly brought to an end if we ravage their territory. I fear rather that we will leave it for our sons to carry on' (1.81.6). Prescient indeed if Archidamus in 432 actually thought so, for the war was concluded 28 years later in the reign of his son Agis. He declared, rightly, that Sparta lacked the money to equip and train a fleet that could get at the sources of Athenian power, namely their subject tribute-paying allies, and he went on to utter these all-important words:

It is not the case that I am senselessly telling you to let the Athenians harm our allies and not to unmask them as they plan to attack them, but I do tell you not to commence hostilities for the moment, but to send an embassy and make complaint, not too plainly declaring war, nor showing that we will leave them unchecked, and while this is going on to make our own preparations by bringing over allies both Greek and non-Greek, if there is any source from which we will get support, naval or financial. There is nothing objectionable in people who are plotted against as we are by the Athenians getting support not just from Greeks but also from non-Greeks.

(1.82.1)

'Non-Greeks', the Persians, were the nub of his advice. The Spartans finally won the Peloponnesian War because they had the financial backing of the Great King.[13] Of course, a large part (the shade of Pericles might cry a necessary part) was the dreadful loss of power Athens sustained through the Sicilian disaster. The city might have got over that and, indeed, could be said to have been in the process of doing so. It was Persian financial support for Sparta that secured the end of the Athenian Empire and the utter defeat of Athens herself. In advocating appeal to Persia in 432, Archidamus was pointing in the right direction. If Pericles thought that the Spartans would accept that they could not shake Athens' power, and would not do all they could to win Persian support, he was wrong.

'All they could' would not come easily, for seeking Persian support would require of Sparta the most agonising decision. Right at the start of the war they intended to send an embassy to the Great King (2.7.1), and in 430 a Spartan embassy was caught by the Athenians making its way by land to the Great King, 'to see if they could somehow persuade him to provide money and join in the war' (2.67.1). But the price they had to pay was, in those years, too much for their consciences to swallow – as is made clear to us by an event of winter 425/4 (4.50). In that year the Athenians arrested a Persian on his way to Sparta, carrying a letter from King Artaxerxes which said 'I don't know what you want. For although many ambassadors have come, none of them say the same things. If you are willing to say something unequivocal, send men to me with my envoy.' Evidently, Sparta had tried quite often to win over the Great King, but the city lacked a clear and consistent policy, and one can guess what the problem was. In all treaties between Greece and Persia the irreducible minimum on the Persian side was Greek recognition of the King's right to Asia, which included the Greek cities along the coast.[14] To concede as much in the 420s would have been bitter for the Spartans. They had begun the war with a proclamation that they were 'liberating Greece' (2.8.4). If, in liberating Greeks from Athenian rule, they enslaved some of them to Persia, the inconsistency put them in a very queer position. Not only would they be mocked and scorned by the Athenians and denounced to the Greeks at large, but within Sparta itself there would be the most agonised scruples. So for Sparta to face facts, to swallow pride, and to do all that Archidamus' advice entailed would take time.

In time Sparta bit the bullet. We see her in Thucydides' account of the diplomatic efforts in 412 to hammer out a tolerable version of a treaty gradually coming to accept the inevitable if Persian money was to fund the Spartan fleet.[15] They reconciled themselves to this lapse from the high idealism of 432 by privately thinking that it was all only for the duration of the war. In 411, a Spartan admiral reproved the people of Miletus for attacking a Persian fort. He said the Milesians and the rest of the Greeks living within the Great King's territory had to be subject to the Persian satrap and, to some extent, had to court Persian favour until the Spartans settled the war to their satisfaction (8.84.5). Such duplicity was an essential part of getting Persian support. Indeed, the chief proponent and agent of Spartan-Persian collaboration and acclaimed victor and liberator of the Greeks, Lysander, for all his parade of friendship with the young prince, Cyrus,[16] doubtless had such private reservations. Within eight years of the surrender of Athens he was urging King Agesilaus 'to campaign against Asia', as Xenophon put it (*Hell.* 3.4.2). But no matter how much it revolted them, they did it. Archidamus' advice triumphed and so did Sparta. Had the great Pericles been wrong after all?

At this point one enters the world of Tissaphernes, the satrap in Sardis who was also general in charge of all the forces in western Asia Minor (8.5.4), and of his successor in that large command, the son of King Darius II, the prince Cyrus (Xen. *Hell.* 1.4.3). The character and actions of the inscrutable Tissaphernes have been subjected to intense scrutiny, but one cannot have great confidence in what Thucydides endeavoured to make of them.[17] Nonetheless, it does seem clear that he had decided that it was not to Persia's advantage that Sparta should defeat Athens. In a famous chapter

(8.46), Thucydides has Alcibiades point out to Tissaphernes that it was unlikely that if Sparta liberated the Greeks still under Athenian rule, she would not promptly set out to liberate those Greeks who were now under Persian rule. Hence Alcibiades advised a policy of wearing out both sides – which was, Thucydides concluded, very much what Tissaphernes had already decided for himself. Certainly for about four years he played a very duplicitous game (cf. 8.87), promising full financial and naval support, then postponing, pretending all was not yet ready, making every excuse, and finally so disgusting the Spartans that they turned to a rival satrap, Pharnabazus (8.99), who appears to have liked and got on with Greeks as much as Tissaphernes loathed and distrusted them.[18]

Certainly Tissaphernes was a wily, shrewd, and in every way difficult character, but it is important to realise that he was not free to conduct any policy he chose. Herodotus, having described the Royal Road from Sardis to Susa and declared that it was a journey of 90 days (5.52–53), has led many to think of the satraps on the Aegean seaboard as being little controlled by central government. It was not so. The postal system of the Persian Empire was such that a report from Sardis could be before the Great King, and his instructions received in return, within a remarkably short time. Estimates vary. The lowest is seven days for a message from one to the other. Of course, the Great King, like Philip II of Spain in the Escorial, might take his time in replying, but plainly there was no physical obstacle in the way of keeping satraps firmly under control, and it is clear from the events of the 390s that there was indeed constant reference to the Great King from the satraps.[19] Satraps had, like trade union leaders, power to act within stated limits, but they could not thwart the King's purposes without danger of execution. If Tissaphernes dilly-dallied and shilly-shallied with the Spartans, the Great King wanted it that way.

It is generally supposed that with the coming of Cyrus, Royal policy changed from affecting to support Sparta while, in fact, letting the war drag on, to whole-hearted support. Cyrus came down with Spartan ambassadors who declared they had obtained from the Great King everything that they had asked for, and Cyrus carried a letter under Royal seal which declared 'I send down Cyrus as supremo (*karanos*) of the forces that assemble at Castolus' (Xen. *Hell.* 1.4.3). A new phase had begun, which ended in the defeat of Athens.[20] Thus, it might be argued, Archidamus' strategic ideas of 432 were realised and the central weakness of Periclean strategy exposed; namely that Sparta was not without resources, if only she would choose to use them.

It may not, however, have been, and, it is strongly to be suspected, it was not quite so simple. Persia's interests were, indeed, best served by the policy which prevailed before Cyrus came on the scene; if Sparta defeated Athens, she would shortly turn against Persia; the longer the war dragged on, the better. Why should the Great King have changed his mind? Perhaps he did not. He kept Cyrus short of money just as he had kept Tissaphernes, and although Cyrus clearly wanted to do all he could to defeat Athens, the promised fleet never appeared. The fleet would have had to come from Phoenicia, which Cyrus did not control, and the orders for it never came (Xen. *Hell.* 2.1.14, Plut. *Lys.* 9.2).[21] The King, in short, was still up to his same old game, the game so ably played, on his instructions, by Tissaphernes.[22]

Cyrus was different. He was only 15 or 16,[23] but he was vastly ambitious to succeed his father. He had an elder brother, who had been born before his father became King, and Cyrus' claim to the throne rested on his being born in the purple (Plut. *Art.* 2.4). Despite the efforts of his formidable mother, Cyrus was not designated successor, and he must very much have feared that that would be the case. The intention to get the throne by violence if he did not get it by right was perhaps formed early. If he had to revolt and march up-country, he would need a substantial force of Greeks, not only because Greek hoplites were the best infantry in the world, but also because they would be wholly dependent on him and therefore more reliable than Oriental troops. Of Greek hoplites, the Spartans were the best. So whole-hearted support for Sparta and a quick victory over Athens were entirely in his interests. His father hoped to curb his youthful zest by keeping the war ill-supported with money. Cyrus spent vast sums of his own money and got the Spartan victory he needed.

So Sparta won with the help of Persia as Archidamus had forecast would be necessary for victory, but she won only perchance, the strange chance of an ambitious prince who was too grand to be confined to a policy that suited Persian interests and not his own. But for Cyrus, Pericles might not have been proved wrong within three decades. Perhaps Archidamus should have said not that he feared that his generation would leave the war for its sons to finish (1.81.6), but that the war would be inherited by their grandsons.

But was there any alternative to the Periclean strategy? As has already been argued, the Athenians got the chance in 425 of a survival peace, but only because the Spartans made a hideous strategic blunder. Was there any alternative strategy that could have secured the defeat of Sparta?

There certainly was – the strategy of Demosthenes. The late H.T. Wade-Gery remarked in a lecture 40 years ago that 'Socrates was the last of the amateurs'. That was hardly literally correct, but essentially it was true. The development of civilisations is always from the amateur to the professional, from the all-rounder to the specialist, and the classical age of Greek History marvellously exemplifies this. In many ways, fourth-century Athens is the world of the specialist and the professional: in finance, in oratory, in politics and, above all, in military matters. The characteristic Athenian generals of the fourth-century are purely military figures, men like Iphicrates, Chabrias and Timotheus. In the fifth century, Pericles is the great exemplar, orator, statesman, financier, general. Measured against such men Demosthenes was clearly ahead of his time. He had, as far as we know, no part in politics and was frequently a general.[24] We meet him first as general in Aetolia in 427/6 and apart from the following year when after the disaster in Aetolia he was certainly not general, there was not a year until his death when he is known not to have been[25] – a professional soldier indeed. It was he who saw that the light-armed infantry were, in some sorts of encounter, the effective answer to the heavily-armed hoplite. After the Aetolian campaign, he made it his business always to have a strong force of light-armed infantry available (cf. 4.67.2, 7.31.5, 33.4f., 35.1, 42.1). This was an anticipation of the role of specialist arms in the next century, dramatically illustrated in 390 when Iphicrates' peltasts destroyed a division of Spartan hoplites (Xen. *Hell.* 4.5.11–17). Likewise, he displayed an inventiveness and initiative more typical of the generals of the fourth century. Inevitably, one thinks of his decisive and daring action when he arrived at Syracuse, namely, his surprise assault by night on the Epipolae which was nearly successful followed by his firm decision to withdraw which, sadly for Athens, his fellow general, Nicias, obstructed (7.42–47). His strategic vision was large indeed, but what it was for the war as a whole must now be investigated.

That involves some guessing. We have to rely on Thucydides who, for reasons that will be considered in a while, never accorded Demosthenes the chance to explain himself in the way Pericles so fully does. After what we may term a baptism of fire in Aetolia wherein he learned that hoplites were not all in all (3.97.3), there are the three episodes of the fortification of Pylos in 425, the attempt to take Megara in 424 and, shortly after, the planned two-prong attack on Boeotia, himself from the west with a small force and, from Attica, the full Athenian army (4.76.1). Both the latter affairs were unsuccessful, and it might be claimed that with Demosthenes nothing succeeded like one failure after another, that he passed from one bright idea to two other not so bright ideas, that there was no overall strategic vision. Since Thucydides is so terse on the intentions of Demosthenes, such things may be said and cannot be refuted. All that is claimed here is that an overall strategy can be proposed and, equally, its existence cannot be disproved.

The two-pronged attack on Boeotia, had it succeeded, certainly would have accomplished a great deal of good for Athens. In the speech which Thucydides put into the mouth of the Athenian commander at the decisive battle of Delium, it is said:

> Let none of you suppose that we are incurring such great danger in another country when it is no business of ours. We will be contending in our enemy's country for our own. If we win, never will the Peloponnesians invade our land without the support of the Boeotian cavalry, and in a single battle you both win this land and make ours the more free.
>
> (4.95.2)

The effect, in short, would be to tend to confine the Peloponnesian War to the Peloponnese. The same may be supposed for the attempt to take Megara. In the 450s when Megara was in the Athenian alliance, the land of Attica remained free of invasion, and one may suppose that such was Demosthenes' interest in both these plans.

But it was in the Peloponnese that his real strategic vision was unfolded. When he proposed the fortification of Pylos, the generals so little perceived what he was about that they declared that 'there were many unoccupied headlands in the Peloponnese, if he wanted to occupy one and occasion the city expense' (4.3.3). But Pylos, Thucydides says, seemed to Demosthenes special; not only was it provided with a harbour, but the people of Messenia were his old friends, and since they spoke the same language as the Spartans, they could do very great damage from that base. The remark about the language is tell-tale. He did not mean that suitable insults in the Doric dialect could be hurled across the battlefield against the

Spartans. He is thinking of guerilla war waged by Messenians moving around Messenia among their own kind. Demosthenes had put his finger on the real weak point of Spartan power, namely, Messenian nationalism. It is commonly supposed that the real weakness of Sparta lay in her oppressive social system, in the subjection of the Helots. That is not true.[26] In 369 when Epaminondas the Theban invaded Spartan territory for the first time in centuries, with superior numbers against an unwalled city, when it must have seemed that proud Sparta was about to be utterly ended, the Spartan authorities appealed for Helots to come to the city's defence and 6,000 came forward (Xen. *Hell.* 6.5.28). That hardly suggests that the condition of the Helots was the real explosive force. However, Messenian nationalism was. The Messenians had been conquered in the eighth century, savagely suppressed after revolt in the seventh and hence quiescent in the sixth, but from the beginning of the fifth century onwards there was constant danger of uprising. When in 369 Epaminondas liberated the Messenians, Sparta was reduced from being the leader of the Peloponnese to being a mere local wrangler, for the rest of her history hoping for no more than to recover the irrecoverable, and this state of affairs was, one supposes, what Demosthenes sought in the 420s.

In this way, Demosthenes showed the way to unblocking the Periclean stalemate, i.e. to deny Sparta the opportunity to invade Attica and seriously to undermine Spartan power in the Peloponnese. His strategy worked. Although his plans to keep the Spartans out of Attica miscarried, the Spartans obligingly provided the substitute of Spartan hostages from Sphacteria, and his Messenian plan proved most effective in moving the Spartans to seek peace in 421 (5.14.3).

It may be claimed that the effect was only temporary, that although Athens continued to hold the fortification in Messenia, Sparta confidently renewed the war in 413. That, however, was only after Athens had over-committed herself in Sicily. Before that, Pylos continued to be a grave menace. But since Demosthenes' hopes of an all-out Messenian Revolt may be denigrated and doubted, there is another possibility to consider.

The collusion of Demosthenes the soldier and Cleon the politician in 425 has often been remarked.[27] Thucydides took no pains to elucidate it. Rather, it would seem that he sought to obscure it. But he does give a clear enough indication. When Cleon was about to set out on his way around the Peloponnese, he sent a message ahead to Demosthenes saying, in Thucydides' words, 'that he would come with the army which he asked for' (4.30.4). Thucydides did not make clear who 'he' was. If he was referring to Demosthenes, the collusion is plain, for Cleon had declined to take any troops from the city and had contented himself with a motley array of largely light-armed troops (4.28.4) which Demosthenes must have asked for. But if Thucydides was referring to Cleon, the collusion is equally plain. There was no point in sending a message to say he was bringing the army which he, Cleon, had asked for, unless Demosthenes knew what that was.

Now there is a curious passage in the *Knights* of Aristophanes of 424 (465–7) which has often been remarked.[28] The Sausage-Seller says to Cleon: 'Well, what you're at in Argos at any rate doesn't escape my notice' and turning to the chorus, he goes on 'He claims to be making the Argives friendly to us, but in private he's hob-nobbing there with the Spartans.' The joke is the bit about Cleon hob-nobbing with the Spartans to whom he had behaved very badly the previous year. The fact is, perhaps, the part about Cleon being active in Argos. If Cleon was thus active in Argos and trying to persuade the Argives to join the Athenians against Sparta, and if in this Cleon was in collusion with Demosthenes seeking to force Sparta into fighting a major war within the Peloponnese itself, the possibility of Messenian Revolt could have been realised and the whole proud edifice of Spartan power brought tumbling down – a strategy not of mere Periclean survival but of total victory. When the coalition headed by Argos fought Sparta at the battle of Mantinea in 418, it was a close-run thing (5.72.2, 6.16.6). It is not beyond conceiving that Demosthenes was minded to aim a double blow at Sparta, a confrontation with the Spartan army synchronised with a Messenian Revolt.

If he was so minded, he must have been a man of unusual optimism, but at the least it may be claimed that he showed a way out of the Periclean deadlock, and it was a way more viable than the way envisaged by Archidamus. We may therefore not scruple to follow Treu[29] in regarding Demosthenes as 'the most progressive general of the Peloponnesian War', a worthy forerunner of Epaminondas and Philip of Macedon, masters of the art of war.

That, it must be added, was not the view of Thucydides. When both Demosthenes and Nicias were executed by the Syracusans in

413, Nicias was accorded a noble epitaph (7.86.5), but Thucydides omitted to laud or even comment on Demosthenes.[30] As already shown, he did not allow Demosthenes the opportunity to expound his strategy, and on the one occasion when his Demosthenes did speak, he uttered words for which one must suppose Thucydides felt great contempt. The speech he wrote for Demosthenes before the Spartan sea-borne attack on Pylos began thus:

> Men, you who have taken a share in this danger, let none of you in such pressing circumstances wish to be thought intelligent, making calculation of all the terrors surrounding us, rather than with unreflecting optimism go to engage the enemy.
>
> (4.10)

'Intelligent' (*xynetos*) is a key Thucydidean word, accorded to his greatest and best. Anyone who is found in his pages in any sense decrying it must have been for Thucydides a shallow optimist. His view was rather that of the line in Browning: 'Think first, fight afterwards, the soldier's art.' But Thucydides presents Demosthenes as getting what he got by pure luck. 'By chance a storm arose and made the fleet beach at Pylos' (4.3.1). A Messenian privateer just happened to turn up, which carried hoplite equipment, and perchance 40 Messenian hoplites (4.9.1). When the Spartans found themselves cut off on Sphacteria, it happened that fire destroyed much of their cover (4.29.3ff.). Cleon promised that it would be over in 20 days, a mad promise Thucydides declared which happened to come true (4.39.3). Cleon, it seems to us, knew the man he was colluding with and had confidence in him. Thucydides did not. For him Demosthenes was just lucky.

Why, then, did Thucydides not judge Demosthenes more fairly? Some take the view that Thucydides was so fixed in devotion to Pericles and the Periclean strategy that anyone who did not accept Pericles' view of the inevitability of deadlock and stalemate was not to be taken seriously. There may be something in this, but as has been already remarked,[31] there are serious doubts about the historian's military judgement. Perhaps that is why he had so little time or respect for the man so much ahead of his time.

Demosthenes had an alternative strategy which might have succeeded. However, in 425 Athens had the chance to make a survival peace – not what Pericles had foreseen but a peace which could have achieved his end of demonstrating the invulnerability of

Athens and the hopelessness of Spartan liberation of the Greeks. To accept or reject that chance was a matter for political, not military, judgement. Thucydides believed that it was an error not to accept. Anything that the strategy of Demosthenes offered was a hope for the future. Given the uncertainties of war Thucydides was probably right.

4

THUCYDIDES, PERICLES AND THE 'RADICAL DEMAGOGUES'

In his most celebrated chapter, 2.65, Thucydides professed his high opinion of Pericles:

> For as long as he had the leading position in the city during the peace, he showed moderation in his leadership and kept it safe and in his time it became very great; and when the war began his providence regarding the war was still more recognised.

He went on to commend Pericles' strategic judgement and treat the neglect of it as the cause of the disaster. By his outstanding qualities, Pericles kept control of the multitude, whereas those who followed him (*hoi hysteron*) were more on a par with each other and, in the desire each of them had for the leading role, they turned to giving control of affairs to the People just to please them.

It has already been argued in the previous chapter that Thucydides was probably mistaken in his confidence that, if the city had adhered to Pericles' strategy, it could have survived essentially unscathed, although in 425 it could perchance have made a 'Periclean' peace. In this chapter, Thucydides' judgement of Pericles and his successors is to be considered, as far as it concerns those whom we term 'radical demagogues', but it must be made clear that Thucydides was thinking in 2.65 of all the leading politicians who succeeded Pericles, and particularly of Alcibiades, whose prominent part in Thucydides' account of how Athens came to be involved in the Sicilian Expedition seems very much in mind in §§10f. Indeed, the word *dēmagōgos* occurs only once in the whole *History* (as likewise the word *dēmagōgia*), and it seems to be a purely descriptive term and in no sense condemnatory.[1] The word for 'radical' would be *ponēros*. Aristotle (*Pol.* 1304b26) spoke of revolutions in democracies occurring when demagogues 'turned nasty' (*ponērōn engenomenōn dēmagōgōn*), and Thucydides had Alcibiades declaring in his speech at Sparta (6.89.5) that he had been driven out of Athens by those who 'led on the populace to more pernicious measures' (*ta ponērotera*). But in this chapter he had in mind not just demagogues who may or may not have been in his judgement 'radical' – he was also thinking of all the politicians prominent after the death of Pericles.

The chapter sums up the whole history of Athens in the war, ending with submission in 404, and must have been written (or rewritten) after Thucydides' return from exile. However, it is not clear whom he has in mind. If §10 does refer to Alcibiades, §11 does not, for it speaks of 'those who sent out the expedition making further decisions that were not advantageous to those who had gone.' Nor does Cleon leap to mind. Twice he was described as 'most persuasive' (3.36.6 and 4.21.3) and one has the impression that Cleon was not so much led by the multitude as that he misled it – only in *that* sense the opposite of Pericles (§8) – and the speech . which Thucydides put in his mouth in the debate over the fate of the Mytilenians begins by berating 'democracy as incapable of holding power over others' (3.37.1). If anyone was particularly in mind, it was perhaps Cleophon, whose period of prominence Thucydides did not describe, for it was Cleophon whom he might have held especially to blame for Athens squandering the chance to get out of the war before the disaster that confronted Thucydides on his return.

Cleophon is a remarkably shadowy character. This is principally because Xenophon was unwilling to give him the honour of mention. The solitary occurrence of the name in the *Hellenica* (1.7.35) is a casual and, perhaps, inaccurate allusion to his death.[2] So if Thucydides was thinking of him in 2.65, one cannot be sure in what regard. The Aristotelian *Ath. Pol.* (28.3) declares that Cleophon was the first man to provide the 'two-obol payment' (*diōbelia*), but it would appear that the sums distributed were petty and it is unlikely that what was probably a hardship grant would have prompted Thucydides to blame its initiator for bringing Athens to ruin.[3] Much more serious was Cleophon's part in blocking peace with Sparta. There is evidence of three such occasions. First, there is the debate on the peace proposal made by Sparta in 410 after the Spartan naval defeat off Cyzicus (Diod. 13.52.2–53.4, Philochorus F139). Cleophon is said to have opposed the idea of peace based on the principle of each side continuing to retain control of whatever cities it held at the time that the peace was made. It is hard to suppose that Thucydides thought that this was a very seriously mistaken line for Cleophon to take. Byzantium, so well placed to starve Athens if it would, had not yet been recovered, and despite the claim of Endios, one of the Spartan ambassadors, that 'the richest of kings on earth is funding the war' (Diod. 13.52.4), the Persian interest at that time seemed very ambivalent and there was no reason to expect that this would change.[4] Likewise, with the notorious opposition of Cleophon to discussing peace with Sparta after the final disaster of Aegospotami (Lysias 13.8; Aeschines 2.76, 3.150), Cleophon's refusal to face the hard fact that the war was over and irretrievably lost certainly prolonged the suffering of the Athenians, but Thucydides could not have thought that it had any effect on the fate of the city.

It is the other occasion when Cleophon opposed the making of peace that might have seriously affected Thucydides' view of him. According to the Aristotelian *Ath. Pol.* 34.1, after the battle of Arginusae in the summer of 406, the Spartans expressed themselves willing to withdraw from Decelea and make peace on the basis of each party holding what it then held, but Cleophon, 'drunk and accoutred with breastplate', persuaded the multitude to reject the peace, declaring that he would not allow a peace unless the Spartans gave up all the cities of the Empire. If this is indeed what happened, Thucydides may well have regarded Cleophon's response as greatly to blame for the ruin of Athens. It is true that Arginusae was an appalling defeat for Sparta (Xen. *Hell.* 1.6.34), as great as Cyzicus (ibid. 1.1.16 and 18), but this time the Spartans knew that they could count on Cyrus and that their ships would be replaced and shortly operating, as they thought, with the Persian fleet; the chance of peace should have been seized.

But, it may be objected, if Sparta could look forward so confidently to the replacement of what had been lost and if the prospects of victory were so appealing, why did Sparta seek to make peace? Indeed, scholarly opinion is divided on whether the Spartans did so at all after Arginusae; perhaps the source of the *Ath. Pol.* (commonly supposed to be the Atthidographer Androtion) was mistaken about which sea-battle led to the Spartan appeal, and there was only one appeal – namely, that recounted by Diodorus after the battle of Cyzicus.[5] The silence of Xenophon is of no significance; he recounts no Spartan peace-move at all. The silence of Diodorus might seem more serious, but his practices are very fitful, and it by no means follows that his source was silent. The closing lines of the *Frogs* (1532f.) certainly suggest that Cleophon's war-policy was freshly impressed on the Athenians. According to Xenophon (*Hell.* 1.7.2), it was not Cleophon but Archedemos who was, at the time of the trial of the generals, the leader of the People (cf. Ar. *Frogs* 420–5). If the scene referred to in the *Ath. Pol.* was more recent, the references in the *Frogs* are intelligible. The Spartan nauarch, Callicratidas, who died at Arginusae (Xen. *Hell.* 1.6.33) had earlier expressed his disgust with the policy of cooperation with and reliance on Persia and declared that if he got back safe to Sparta, he would do all he could to reconcile the Athenians and the Spartans (ibid. 1.6.7). No doubt there were others so minded[6] and an attempt to end the wretched war would have been likely enough. Dubitable as it is, the story of the *Ath. Pol.* may be accepted. Cleophon did what he could to block the peace and so exposed Athens to the disaster of 405. He must have been in Thucydides' mind as he was writing 2.65.

The one leader of the People about whom one may be confident Thucydides was not thinking was Hyperbolus, who receives a solitary mention of a very dismissive kind (8.73.3). Hyperbolus, to judge by the treatment he received from the Comic Poets,[7] was not only a figure of considerable importance, successor to and on a par with Cleon, but also concerned to advocate policy of a sort that would have discontented Thucydides. It is evident from the *Peace* that, in 421, Hyperbolus was in power with influence comparable to Cleon (cf. 661–92) and that, like Cleon in 425, he had been opposed to making the Peace (1318f. and 918–21), a similarly 'Periclean' opportunity.[8] Perhaps it was Hyperbolus' failure to carry the day that induced Thucydides to regard him as sound and fury, signifying nothing, 'a troublesome fellow, ostracised not out of fear of his power and reputation, but because of his radical politics (*ponēria*) and of being a disgrace to the city.' Thucydides could dismiss him because he did not get his way.[9]

Cleon did get his way, and however largely Cleophon loomed in Thucydides' mind in 404, Cleon must have borne much of the blame for what had gone wrong. So it is to Thucydides' account of Cleon that the present chapter is mainly addressed. (Alcibiades, no less in mind in 2.65, will be discussed in the next.)

It is almost universally believed that Thucydides was so hostile to Cleon that he has painted a quite untrue portrait of him; that he has exalted Pericles and debased Cleon when, in fact, they were very similar; that Thucydides was hostile to Cleon because Cleon had been responsible for his exile or because Thucydides had a snobbish detestation of an ill-born, ill-bred man of the people.[10] All this I hold to be quite wrongly conceived. The truth, it will be argued, is that Thucydides was unfair to Cleon only in so far as he was unfair to Demosthenes, that far from obscuring the similarity between Pericles and Cleon, Thucydides was at pains to present Cleon as one who copied Pericles and copied him badly, with ill consequences for the city.

It has already been argued that Thucydides took an over-optimistic view of Pericles' strategic judgement. Of his leadership of the city during the peace, Thucydides asserted that Pericles 'showed moderation in his leadership and kept the city safe and in his time it became very great' (2.65.5). He does not specify the policies Pericles followed, but the speeches he has Pericles deliver constitute a guide.

Above all, of course, Pericles is the great imperialist. The Funeral Oration is a laudation of imperial Athens by the man so much associated with its creation. He is the man most frequently occupying the office of general[11] through the formative years after the death of Cimon and the commencement of the war; the decision to discipline Samos was taken on his proposal (Plut. *Per.* 24.1); and he seems to have had the leading part in that most typically imperial measure, the implantation of cleruchies (*ibid.* 11.5 and 6).[12] It is no surprise that, in that last speech which Thucydides has him utter, Pericles is represented as proudly proclaiming the magnitude of the Empire (2.64.3).

Second, Pericles was made to include in his Funeral Oration a laudation of democracy (2.37), and proceed (39) to contrast Athens with Sparta, much to the latter's disadvantage. It is clear that he was rightly described by Plutarch (*Cimon* 15.2) as 'favouring the interests of the majority'. Aristotle (*Pol.* 1274a8) linked him with Ephialtes in the reform of the Areopagus and in the introduction of pay for jury service (cf. *Ath. Pol.* 27.3), thought by oligarchs to have had a most deleterious effect on the Athenian character (Plato, *Gorgias* 515e). The Aristotelian *Ath. Pol.* records no changes to the Athenian constitution after 457 (26.2), but it has often been suspected that, in the period of Pericles' ascendancy, the archonship was opened to the *thetes*; if that was the case, presumably it had the blessing of Pericles.[13]

Finally, the great building-programme[14] was undertaken largely on his initiative and must have taken up much of his time. His concern no doubt was to make the city as beautiful as the Empire was great, the visible expression of power (2.43.1), a suitable setting for those 'contests and sacrifices' which provided relief from labours (2.38.1), 'a city admirably provided with every thing and very great' (2.64.3).[15] In Thucydides' eyes, the city was twice as large as life (1.10.2).

It is evident that without the speeches Thucydides put in Pericles' mouth, there would be remarkably little that could be said with assurance about him. Even the nature and the degree of the opposition he encountered is unclear. Plutarch's account of the opposition of Thucydides, son of Melesias (*Pericles* 12.14), often claimed to be derived from a fourth century (if not from a fifth century) source, has been rudely dismissed[16] in recent times as reflecting sentiments inappropriate to the age of Pericles. Thucydides' opposition to the building programme seems to stem from championship of the allies, which, it is argued, is wholly improbable in fifth-century Athens where all sorts and conditions of citizens seem to have made a very good thing out of the Empire. It is true that Thucydides has Pericles speak as if there were those 'who would virtuously have nothing to do with Empire' (2.63.2), but this was in 430 when the war which Sparta had begun, demanding and proclaiming freedom for the Hellenes (1.139.3, 2.8.4), was turning out badly for Athens. Those who wanted peace – a good many to judge by the successful prosecution of Pericles (2.65.3) – must have accepted the idea of at least greatly reduced Imperial power. Up until that moment, he may not have encountered such opposition.[17]

The truth is that we are very ill-informed about Athenian politics during the Pentekontaetea; but we are not completely bereft. The period was not without great political trials, so characteristic of Athenian political life in the fourth century. The young Pericles took a leading part in the unsuccessful prosecution of Cimon, alleging that he had been bribed into not seizing a large portion of Macedonia when he was dealing with Thasos in 465 (Plut. *Cim.* 14f.; [Arist.] *Ath. Pol.* 27.1). Callias was, it was alleged, fined 50 talents, barely escaping sentence of death for his part in the making of peace with Persia (Dem. 19.273).[18] Together with the ostracisms of Cimon and Thucydides, these trials argue that Pericles did not pass his political life in a city of monolithic unity. Whatever was at issue between Pericles and Thucydides, son of Melesias, Cimon was allegedly ostracised for his sympathy for Sparta (Plut. *Cim.* 15.3). A stray anecdote about Cimon's sister, Elpinice (Plut. *Per.* 28.6) suggests that Pericles may have been criticised for his handling of Samos and for not continuing war against Persia. Whether there were those in this period who chose, like Antiphon later, to take the allies' part in contesting tribute assessments (in itself a small matter, but perhaps significant) is unknown.

If one looks at the references to fifth-century political leaders in the Platonic Corpus, one discerns no classification into imperialists and anti-imperialists, and it required the miseries and the final disaster of the War to produce the distrust of imperialism that is to be found in Isocrates and Panhellenist doctrine. Even that took quite a time to flower and was probably of little influence before imperialism brought the city near to bankruptcy at the end of the Social War in 355.[19] However, the seeds of it are to be found in Herodotus[20] and by 411, the date of Aristophanes' *Lysistrata*, it is well enough established to be proposed as the solution of Greece's troubles (1128–34); Greeks are to unite in attacking the Persian.[21] Of course, Cimon's famous appeal to the Athenians 'not to see Greece lame or the city deprived of her yoke-fellow' (Plut. *Cim.* 16.10) must have been uttered in the belief that Sparta and Athens might some time in the future have to share the hegemony against Persia, but it required time for Athenian imperialism to emerge as a threat and for Panhellenism to become a serious alternative. Dissatisfaction with the Empire would not develop until the War had begun, the Delphic Oracle had declared its sympathies, and the Plague had confirmed them.

So, in the end, we have very little idea of how or why Pericles was opposed before the War.[22] What is clear is that by 431 there was very little opposition and the democracy was becoming 'rule by the first man' (2.65.9). The reason was his moderation (2.65.5). The only instance that can be cited is his moderate treatment of the people of Histiaea who, during the revolt of Euboea in 446, had killed all the crew of a captured Athenian ship, about two hundred in all (Plut. *Per.* 23.4). In view of what was later to happen to cities that had merely revolted, the Hestiaeans got off lightly, being allowed under the terms of an agreement (Theopompus F387) to remove to Macedon and be replaced by 2,000 Athenian settlers. Further testimony to the moderation of Pericles' exercise of power can be found in the Xenophontic *Constitution of Athens*. If that tract is rightly dated to the very opening of the War,[23] the author can give no hope of division in the state. Evidently, Pericles had avoided the excesses that by 424 gave rise to talk of 'conspiracy' (Ar. *Knights* 257) and 'tyranny' (*Wasps* 488–507). Finally, judgement of Pericles depends on Thucydides. Undeniably, the city did become 'very great' (2.65.5) in Pericles' time. 'Greatness' is what mattered to Thucydides. Hence his high opinion of the statesman.

In the case of Cleon, Thucydides' judgement is much impugned. There is no doubt that Thucydides thought badly of him. He described him as 'most violent and most persuasive' (3.36.6), with reference to his part in the debate about the people of Mytilene. The latter pejorative term was used again with regard to Cleon's part in the rejection of the Spartan peace offer in 425 (4.21.3). 'Persuasive' (*pithanos*) being the opposite of 'being good at speaking' (1.139.4 of Pericles, cf. 8.68.1 and 4 of Antiphon and Theramenes), Thucydides used it to show that on each occasion Cleon argued for a mistaken policy.[24] Few have gone so far as to seek to defend the proposal to put to death all the adult male Mytilenians,[25] but many have argued that Cleon was right to urge the Athenians to reject the Spartan appeal for peace.[26] That Thucydides took the opposite view is hardly reason for accusing him of unfairness, but it is argued that his antipathy to Cleon was so deep that he was incapable of a fair judgement. It is often claimed that it was Cleon who took the leading part in the exiling of Thucydides (which may or may not be true)[27] and that that is the root of his hostility. Alternatively, it is supposed that Thucydides the aristocrat was repulsed by 'the first of a new kind of politician, vulgar both in origin and in manner'. Whatever the reason, it is generally believed that Thucydides has treated Cleon most unfairly.

A review of Thucydides' account of him must therefore be made. First, however, it is to be observed that Thucydides was not interested in the small change of politics. Cleon's attack on Pericles for not taking action against the Peloponnesian invaders in 431 (Plut. *Per.* 33.8) was beneath his notice, just as politicians like Lysicles or Hyperbolus did not engage him. Again, although Cleon was an important figure all through the Archidamian War,[28] Thucydides introduces him only where the great issue of how to deal with allies that have revolted or the rejection of peace are discussed – apart, of course, from Cleon's military contributions to the war. Thus, having dealt fully with the case of Mytilene, Thucydides does not let on whether there was any debate in 423 when the Athenians, persuaded by Cleon, voted to execute all the male inhabitants of Scione (4.122.6). Likewise, Thucydides did not choose to treat fully the matter of finance. He has been charged with denying Cleon credit for his financial activities,[29] but such matters as the raising of pay for jurors or the adjustment of the interest rate on borrowings from Athena, if indeed Cleon was responsible, were beneath his notice.[30] As to the great reassessment of tribute in 425, consequent on Cleon's success on Pylos and probably enough due to him in some degree,[31] Thucydides could have used it very effectively to illustrate his account of why the Spartan peace offer in 425 was rebuffed. He simply says that the Athenians 'aimed at more' (4.21.2). He could have made play with the severe increases in tribute and the assessment of places, including Melos (portent of things to come), previously not in the Empire, a programme for growth and expansion of the sort mocked by Aristophanes (*Knights* 965, 1087) who plainly makes Cleon responsible as Thucydides does not. His references to 'aiming at more' concern Athens in general (cf. 4.41.4 and 92.2), not Cleon in particular. So he might be held to have missed a golden opportunity, but the truth is that he was not minded to record such matters.[32]

Cleon's part in the Mytilene debate certainly showed him to be 'most violent' (3.36.6). That the punishment he advocated was damaging to Athens' interests has been denied by at least one scholar.[33] However, Thucydides appears to have sided with Diodotus when he argued that revolts would always happen and that if the same penalty was to be meted out to all those involved in a revolt, suppression of revolt would be much more difficult (3.45–7). Thus Thucydides considered that Cleon misled the People – 'persuasive' indeed. Common prudence suggests that Thucydides was right, but even if there is room for the other view, he can hardly be accused of being unfair to Cleon. It is claimed [34] that, by pronouncing Cleon 'most violent and most persuasive', Thucydides was trying to prejudice the reader against him, as if one would not otherwise notice the violence or would take a different view of the policy Cleon advocated. That claim is absurd and, in any case, such introductory descriptions are common enough. Pericles, like Cleon, received a double introduction (1.127.3, and 139.4), and Alcibiades likewise (5.43.2 and 6.15). It is just Thucydides' manner.

Crucial for the assessment of Thucydides' treatment of Cleon is his judgement that Cleon was wrong to urge rejection of the Spartan peace offer. It is almost universally held that Cleon was right, a view most typically expressed by Gomme.[35] Sparta wanted only to recover the men trapped on Sphacteria, it is argued, and once she had done so, would quickly begin the war again. Against this, it may be urged as follows: the Spartans had begun the war with a proclamation that 'they would liberate the Greeks' (2.8.4). Now they were abandoning that righteous cause and nothing could be more cynical than the concluding words of the speech their envoys are said to have delivered (4.20.4):

> and see what advantages are likely to be found in this policy, for if we and you concert policy, the rest of the Greek world, you may be assured, being weaker will pay us the greatest honour.

This was black treachery. Indeed, the embassy was purely Spartan. There is no suggestion that the allies had been consulted as they would be in 421 (5.17.2) and, according to Thucydides, the Spartan envoys refused to hold public discussions lest, if they decided because of their disastrous situation to make some concession, they should be 'slandered to their allies having said it and failed to get it' (4.22.3). In other words, if they got the peace, their allies could resent that Sparta had betrayed them as much as they liked. In 421 their allies did formally agree to making peace with Athens, but even so, the four dissidents caused Sparta a great deal of trouble which came near to destroying Spartan power in the Peloponnese. In 425 it could all have been a great deal worse. Sparta would, of course, have recovered her precious Spartiates, but Athenian power (the growth of which had made her afraid and forced her to war) would have been unchecked and magnified, for now the subject states would have been without hope of being saved by Sparta. Altogether, Athens would have been in a very favourable position.

However, how long would a peace last once Sparta had got back 'the men from the island', her main concern (4.108.7; 117.2; 5.15.1)? The Peace of Nicias lasted until the Athenians ravaged Laconia and gave the Spartans a good reason for renewing the war (6.105.2). That was in 414, even though as early as winter 421/0 there had been those who wanted to end the peace (5.36.1). They had a bad conscience about their part in 431 (7.18.2) and were not likely to invite another disaster like Sphacteria. But even if a peace in 425 had not lasted, the discredit attendant on merely making it would have had a very serious effect on Sparta's leadership in the Peloponnese.

It is unclear what sort of peace the Spartans were precisely asking for in 425, but the final sentence of the Spartan speech (4.20.4) suggests that they sought a return to the Thirty Years Peace of 446 whereby the hegemony of the Greek world was shared. Aristophanes, looking forward in early 421 to the conclusion of the Peace of Nicias, spoke of 'joint rule over Hellas' (*Peace* 1082), and after that Peace there were suspicions in the Peloponnese that 'the Spartans wanted to share with the Athenians in making them subject' (5.29.3). So this was what the noble promise to liberate the Greeks would have come to in 425: Athens and her empire untrammelled and Sparta ever more fearful than before. It was an appealing prospect and it should cause no surprise that Thucydides thought that the opportunity should not have been allowed to slip away, that he considered those who thought likewise 'sensible' (4.28.5) and the man who persuaded the Athenians to think otherwise 'most persuasive' (4.21.3). Thucydides may have been wrong to think so, but there is no reason to think that that he was being 'unfair' to Cleon.[36]

The famous description of the assembly at the end of which Cleon took command of the force going to Pylos (4.27 and 28) has been held to manifest Thucydides' 'unfairness'.[37] Partly, he speaks confidently of Cleon's feelings and motives, of which he cannot have had any knowledge.

> Cleon, realising the suspicion of him (27.3) . . . realising that he would have either to (27.4) . . . realising that Nicias really did want to cede the command (28.2). . . .

So it is claimed that 'Cleon in Thucydides thinks what Thucydides wants him to think', but all political reporters and commentators make such guesses about the motives and intentions of the leading players. Certainly Thucydides was saying what he believed Cleon thought, but that was not necessarily different from the truth or what a great many others present at the assembly may have thought.[38] A good many Athenians are likely to have had their suspicions as to why Cleon had counselled rejecting the peace. Nor is Thucydides to be censured for not censuring Nicias for being 'prepared to hand over an extremely important expedition to the command of a man whom he believes to be incompetent.' Nicias believed the planned attempt on Sphacteria to be military folly and his way of indicating it was to say that if Cleon thought so strongly otherwise, he had better take it over – which was a way of making clear the impracticability of the whole idea and of killing it.[39] The People took up the notion of sending the force under the command of the man who believed in it. To censure Thucydides for not censuring Nicias is absurd (and pompous). Nor is the comment fair that those who had wanted the peace, and whom Thucydides referred to as sensible, 'apparently viewed with pleasure the prospect of a disaster in which, though Cleon fell, many another brave Athenian might die beside him.'[40] Cleon had made a promise that set the Athenians laughing and 'sensible' men who had wanted none of this whole operation made the precise observation that 'they would get one of two advantages; either they would be quit of Cleon, as they rather expected, or if they were wrong in their judgement, they would reduce the Spartans' (28.5). If Cleon failed to keep his promise, he would make a fool of himself and be discredited. They did not want Athenians to risk their lives, but to be rid of Cleon, by whatever means, would be an advantage, and if that is how they thought, it is hardly 'unfair' of Thucydides to say so.

The real doubts raised by the Pylos debate may be deferred until other points in the case of Thucydides' 'unfairness' are examined. First, there is the account of the Amphipolis campaign about which sour things are said. For instance, no colleague is named for Cleon by Thucydides (5.2.1), so that he can be made to be entirely to blame by gullible readers.[41] However, one finds it hard to believe that if Cleon had a colleague in command in the battle of Amphipolis, not a hint of his role would be found or imagined; someone must have been in command at Scione, which remained under siege (5.2.2), possibly Nicostratus, and he and Cleon may have been perceived as colleagues. Again, Thucydides is held to have omitted report of a number of towns captured, petty places which may have been thought beneath notice, but if it was Cleon who recovered them, the omission must be pronounced malign. The whole theory that Cleon did recover them is discredited.[42] As to the capture of Torone (5.3), it was a creditable feat of arms indeed, but Thucydides did not conceal it nor did he emphasise what seems to have been ineptitude in the Spartan command, whether on the part of Brasidas or, as seems more likely, the man on the spot, Pasitelidas. No matter what Cleon did well elsewhere, at Amphipolis he did remarkably badly – if, that is, it is bad to have 600 Athenians killed out of a total of 1,500 (5.2.1 and 11.2), a feat he accomplished by marching his troops within a quarter of a mile of a city with an ample force inside it. Despite the uncertainty about the battle, this is not in dispute. But at two points, Thucydides' *malignitas*, it is held,[43] blazes forth. First, Cleon's army are said to have been 'chafing at the inactivity' (caused by waiting for allied troops) 'and reflecting on the weakness and incompetence of their commander and the skill and valour that would be opposed to him' (5.7.2).[44] It is argued that Cleon's brief military career to date had shown him to be neither weak nor incompetent. The words would certainly be appropriate after the battle, but also it is to be noted that Thucydides is said to have passed his exile at his estate on Mount Pangaeus, at no great distance from the Athenian camp at Eion, and that in view of the difficulties he must have encountered many times already in discovering what precisely had happened, he would in all likelihood have visited the Athenian camp as soon as possible. From such a visit he could well have learned what Cleon 'said' (5.7.3) about his planned reconnaissance, and he could well have got a report of the state of morale in the camp and of what the men where thinking (though such reports may well have been affected by what had happened). So what Thucydides said about it all is not necessarily to be dismissed as merest prejudice.[45] Of course, there are those who are so convinced that Thucydides could not be fair to Cleon that they are minded to call in question, though they dare not deny, the account of Cleon's death.[46] He is said to have run 'immediately and to have been caught up by a Myrcinian peltast and killed' (5.10.9). Cleon had been with the right wing which stood its ground until it was surrounded by the Myrcinian and Chalcidic cavalry, and by the peltasts (5.10.4 and 9). But according to Thucydides, that is not where Cleon was struck and killed. If he *was* on his own, vague phrases about going to get help will not do. If help is needed, commanders send runners with orders; they do not go themselves. It is not to be excluded that Thucydides went into Amphipolis after the battle and talked to Myrcinians himself. It is assuredly desperate to appeal to Diodorus' account (12.74) as evidence that Thucydides is not to be believed. Considerations of Diodorus' methods and style should have prevented such talk.[47]

The burden of this chapter so far is that claims that Thucydides was unfair to Cleon in the passages so far considered are not just. Thucydides certainly thought Cleon's judgement poor and his influence baleful. If one thinks like that of someone, one may well show it by the sort of 'cutting irony' which flashes out when Cleon ran (5.10.9),[48] but on the whole, Thucydides kept his feelings to himself. There is only one point at which his fairness is seriously questioned, and which must now be seriously addressed.

The battle of Amphipolis removed, according to Thucydides (5.16.1), the two men most opposed to the making of peace: Brasidas and Cleon. The latter 'thought that if peace was made he would be more plainly shown up in his wrong-doing and be less trusted in his slanders.' Such notions are no surprise to the reader of Aristophanes. Clearly, Cleon was widely thought of in such terms.[49] But Thucydides could have no evidence for such an explanation of conduct. Cleon himself would not have expressed such sentiments even if he had had them and, indeed, one could readily imagine an *apologia*. Until the end of the Social War when the city was approaching bankruptcy and the imperialist aspirations that had produced such a state of affairs were utterly discredited, all leaders of the People believed that war was the way to increase the prosperity of the city (cf. Isoc. 8.5.6) and Cleon, a rich man himself, could well have claimed to be serving the People's interests, not his own.[50] The explanations Thucydides gave elsewhere of Cleon's political moves (notably in the Pylos debate, 4.27 and 28) were well within the probabilities of political reporting and analysis. This explanation, however, is monstrous and it is the real justification for the view that Thucydides was 'unfair' to Cleon. But is this correct?

The opposition to peace on the part of Brasidas is explained in a similarly extreme way. He was opposed 'because of the success and the honour he was enjoying from the conduct of the war' (5.16.1). Thucydides was even less likely to have any evidence for such a remark, and Brasidas too could well have claimed that his determination to see the war through to the end of Athenian power sprang from the desire to fulfil the promise to liberate Greece which Sparta had proclaimed in 431. That, at any rate, was what he declared to the people of Torone (4.85.1, 86.1), and his principles were to be seen in the distrust he displayed towards his political opponents at Sparta. Before he set out from Sparta he 'bound the authorities with the most solemn oaths' to the effect that any allies he gained would be guaranteed their independence (4.86.1, 88.1). It is astonishing that a Spartiate could demand and secure such an oath and it is testimony to Brasidas' high principles. Thucydides' explanation of Brasidas' opposition to peace was most demeaning. It is one of the harshest things one can say about a military commander, that he is prepared to risk men's lives in pursuit of his personal glory. However, that Thucydides said such a harsh thing about Brasidas is hardly to be attributed to a prejudice against him. He had, in fact, a high opinion of him. Although he judged Brasidas to be not always truthful (4.108.5, 122.6), he spoke of him in the highest terms, according him 'virtue and intelligence' (aretē kai xynesis) and declared that he was regarded as 'in every way good' (4.81.2f.). So why did Thucydides give such an explanation?

It would seem likely that both these sour explanations of opposition to peace are to be understood in the same sense and both derive from the same habit of mind. In Thucydides, there are no starry-eyed idealists. Men either judge well, like Pericles (2.65) or Themistocles (1.138.3), or, if they judge badly, their errors of judgement are explained in personal terms. Thus, although there were critics of Athenian democracy in Socrates, who had no part in politics, and in Critias who was active in 411 as well as in 404 (and who, after 411, became the all-out, starry-eyed Laconiser commending all things Spartan), for Thucydides those who were ready to come to terms with Sparta were prepared to do anything to secure their own safety (8.91.3) – an analysis which sought to explain how they could have misjudged so badly that they were willing, if need be, to subordinate Athens to Sparta. The case of Alcibiades is especially interesting. Thucydides introduced him before recounting Alcibiades' policy as motivated by desire to get his revenge on the Spartans for slighting him, but only partly, for Alcibiades 'thought it was actually better to go over to the Argives' (5.43.2). However, when it came to the great misjudgement of the Sicilian Expedition, Alcibiades' enthusiasm for the venture was ascribed entirely to selfish ambition (6.15.2). The greater the error of judgement, the more extreme the explanation.

That Thucydides thought badly of Cleon's political judgement is plain enough. That he disliked Cleon so much that he was incapable of judging Cleon justly is far from plain. There is, however, a serious question about Thucydides' account. It does not relate primarily to Cleon, but to the general Demosthenes with whom Cleon colluded.

When Cleon got the Athenians in 425 to reject the Spartan offer of peace, he persuaded them to demand in their reply that

the men on the island [namely, Sphacteria] must surrender their weapons and their persons and be brought to Athens, and when they had come the Spartans must return Nisaea, Pegae, Troezen and Achaea which they did not take in war but as the result of the former agreement and which the Athenians

had conceded because of reverses and their special need at
that time for a treaty.

(4.21.3)

On the face of it, this seems like a demand for a return to the Thirty
Years Peace with the Spartiates on Sphacteria as the bargaining
counter. Was that really all that Cleon wanted, or was he masking
other aims with a demand for the trapped Spartiates which he knew
Sparta could not possibly accede to? In Aristophanes' *Knights*,
Cleon is presented as rebuffing the peace embassies so that Athens
'should have empire over all the Greeks' (795–7), declaring to
Demos that he has a 'winged oracle about you, that you become an
eagle and lord it over the whole world' (1086–7), one of those
oracles 'that you must have empire over every land crowned with
roses' (965–6). All this, reminiscent of the large vision of *imperium
sine fine* with which Pericles sought to restore Athenian spirits
during the Plague (2.62.1 and 2), may be mere comic fun, but it
prompts the question of what Cleon's real reason was for opposing
peace both in 425 and in succeeding years.

It has already been argued that Demosthenes may well have had
a large strategy aimed not at a Periclean stalemate, but at the total
defeat of Sparta. Presuming that this was so (admittedly a large
presumption),[51] one may wonder whether the real reason for Cleon's
attitude to peace in 425 and later was his faith in Demosthenes and
his strategy.

Collusion between the politician and the soldier has frequently
been supposed.[52] There is no knowing who was active in securing
that extraordinary permission for Demosthenes (still without office)
to use the ships going to reinforce the squadron in Sicily, under the
command of two generals, for purposes of his own choosing around
the Peloponnese (4.2.4). Thucydides says that Demosthenes himself
asked for it, but Demosthenes was no politician and one would
suppose that someone managed it for him. One would guess it was
Cleon, but there is no knowing. Evidently, Demosthenes had early
formed his plan to attack Spartan power by exploiting Messenian
nationalism, but whether Cleon then knew it must remain unsure.
When it came to the assault on Sphacteria, collusion is very likely.
Demosthenes' plan from the outset was to use light-armed troops
(4.32.4). He assembled an ample force (32.2), partly by his own
efforts (30.3), partly with the forces Cleon brought. These were
Imbrians, Lemnians (presumably hoplites), peltasts from Aenus and

71

400 archers from elsewhere (28.4), and on his way to Pylos Cleon sent ahead a message that 'he would come and with the army which he had asked for' (30.4). Who is 'he'? Presumably Demosthenes, because Cleon had not 'asked for' an army; rather, he had declined to take all that was on offer (28.4).[53] So Demosthenes must have sent to Athens a request for an army, and so, inevitably, an explanation of why he wanted it. Nor can his true purpose have been concealed. Space in the camp at Pylos was already too confined (cf. 4.30.1) and reinforcements of at least 500–600 men would have made conditions intolerable. Clearly, Demosthenes intended a landing. Publicity was inevitable. Mercenaries would cost money and there could have been no summons until the People in assembly had ordered it. Nor was there any danger in the Spartans finding out, once the Athenians had refused to return them their fleet of 60 ships (4.16.1 and 3). No matter how much Sparta learned of Demosthenes' plans, there was nothing that could be done to stop them. So all the world could know and did, including Cleon.

Cleon had had the leading and decisive part in the rejection of peace (4.21) and he also seems to have the leading role in the assembly that debated the dispatch of the army to Pylos. He demanded that the Athenians should 'sail against the men' (4.27.5), and he attacked Nicias for his delay. Unfortunately, the circumstances of the debate are left unclear. It is characteristic of Thucydides that in the great debates he records, he does not feel it incumbent on himself to say what the Council had recommended in its *probouleuma*. Indeed, the existence of the Council emerges in the *Histories* in only two contexts.[54] Since the important decisions really were taken in the assembly, this neglect of the Council is not misleading, but in the case of the Pylos debate more information would certainly have been helpful to us. When Nicias declared himself ready to give up '*the* command on Pylos' (4.28.3), this was not a matter of resigning the generalship, for he is to be found as general in command of an attack on Corinthian territory shortly afterwards (4.42).[55] So the phrase '*the* command' shows that the decision to send the force had already been made, but whether by a decree at an earlier assembly, or in a *probouleuma* that was being considered in the Pylos debate, is not immediately obvious. There is some reason, however, to suppose that there had been an earlier decree and that the Pylos debate was caused by the reports from Pylos.[56] First, although at that debate the Assembly decided to send 'inspectors' to Pylos to test the accuracy of the reports and Cleon and another were actually elected (4.27.4), the Athenians were seen 'to be even more resolved to campaign'; i.e. they had previously decided and Cleon got them to reaffirm their decision. Second, Nicias had been assigned 'the command on Pylos', which was appropriate, while Demosthenes was still not a general. However, by the time Cleon replaced Nicias, that was no longer so (4.29.1). So Cleon took over a command that had been established by an earlier decree, and in the Pylos debate he was active in demanding that Demosthenes be given the army that he had asked for and been actually granted.

In all this, Cleon seems to be Demosthenes' agent, and if it be right that the mover of the great Assessment Decree of 425, Thudippus, was a kinsman, he had a ready instrument to hand in the Council. One cannot be certain, but the collusion is probable from the moment that Demosthenes asked for the troops necessary for a landing on Sphacteria. Yet Thucydides' account is curious. He says that Cleon 'chose to associate with himself one of the generals at Pylos, Demosthenes,' and he did so 'learning that he intended to make the landing on the island' (4.29.1 and 2). Seeing that the plan to land had been Demosthenes' in the first place (4.32,4) and that Cleon's role in taking him the necessary troops was essentially ancillary, Thucydides seems very much to have the cart before the horse. And when did Cleon actually learn that Demosthenes so planned? The moment that Demosthenes' request was made public, everyone including Cleon must have known what was planned. Yet Thucydides' words suggest that 'the learning' was in almost the same breath as the choosing of Demosthenes (4.29.2). More remarkably, Thucydides gives an explanation of why Demosthenes planned an assault on Sphacteria that arouses great scepticism. He gives two reasons. First, 'the troops were suffering from the lack of supplies in the place and being besieged rather than besieging were eager to take a risk' (4.29.2), which is very much of a piece with Thucydides' account of how it happened that Pylos was fortified – an urge on the part of the troops who had nothing better to do (4.4.1). Second, Demosthenes was confirmed in the idea of a landing by the accident of the fire (4.4.2). Anyone who has had experience of jungle warfare must be very sceptical about this. The heavy undergrowth on this previously unoccupied and so pathless island of Sphacteria would have been a serious impediment to hoplites with spears, shields and swords making movement difficult, while the light-armed peltasts and archers would have been able to move much more freely. Only during the landing would the Spartan hoplites been able to strike effectively, but no doubt Demosthenes from the outset intended to effect the landing by surprise. For the rest, the thick cover was much to the advantage of the light-armed. Nor can the fire have been much of a help in revealing how many Spartans there were on the island. In so far as it did not roast or suffocate them, it did not reveal their numbers. Nor can there have been any question of how many there really were. The terms of the truce had prescribed how much each man was to be allowed by way of rations (4.16.1), and during the period of the truce the Athenians must have been supervising deliveries. Thucydides' account of why Demosthenes formed his plan is badly flawed.[57]

One cannot be sure but it is likely that the moment the Spartans made the strategic blunder of putting their troops onto Sphacteria, Demosthenes saw that they could be destroyed or captured. Once he had deprived the Spartans of their fleet, his plan of assault could be set in motion without fear of the enemy seeking to prevent it (for there was nothing they could do). Thucydides, one suspects, could not give him the credit for such strategic acumen. It all happened by luck, he would have it believed, and Demosthenes was no great general. If there is anyone in the *Histories* to whom Thucydides is 'unfair', it is Demosthenes, and if Cleon was indeed in collusion with him all through that momentous year, Cleon was deprived of the credit of backing Demosthenes. No account of what really moved Cleon to oppose the Spartan offer of peace was given. The Athenians simply 'were wanting more' (4.21.2). What that 'more' really was and what was the strategy which might realise it, he did not go into.[58] Thucydides was unfair to Cleon in so far as he was unfair to Demosthenes. If he had been able to appreciate how good a general Demosthenes was, he might have been able to think less badly of Cleon's judgement. In politics we may agree with Thucydides that Cleon did not judge well. Of war, Thucydides' own judgement is suspect.

5

THUCYDIDES, ALCIBIADES AND THE WEST

The same winter the Athenians wished to sail again to Sicily with a larger force than the one that was with Laches and Eurymedon and, if they could, to make it subject, the majority of them having no idea of the magnitude of the island or the multitude of its inhabitants, both Greek and non-Greek, nor realising that they were taking on a war not much less great than that against the Peloponnesians.

(6.1.1)

Thucydides goes on to give an account of the island and concludes:

Such were the races of Greeks and non-Greeks inhabiting Sicily, and against it, so great as it was, the Athenians set out to campaign, desiring on the truest account (*tēi alēthestatēi prophasei*) to get empire over the whole of it, while at the same time professedly wishing to help their own kith and kin and such other allies as they had acquired.

(6.6.1)

How is this second *alēthestatē prophasis* to be regarded?

A *caveat* instantly arises. The decree that was passed as a result of the appeal of their Segestan allies supported by exiles from the Ionian state of Leontini authorised the despatch of 60 ships (6.8.2), precisely the number of Athenian ships in Sicilian waters in 424, not 'a larger force than the one that was with Laches and Eurymedon.'[1] It is hard to suppose that the Athenians could have thought that such a force was large enough to make Sicily 'subject'. The 'larger force' only emerged when Nicias was invited to say what he considered necessary for the task (6.25). Until that moment, the debate was about the despatch of a mere 60 ships and Nicias' first speech (6.9–14) seems curiously inept in so far as it concerned the purpose the 60 ships were to serve. The Athenians are said to 'desire Sicily' (11.5), 'another empire' (10.5, 11.1). Consistently, Thucydides attributes the grandest designs to Alcibiades. In the speech which Alcibiades is made to deliver to the Spartans, he says:

> We sailed to Sicily in the first place to make the people of Sicily subject if we could, after them the people of Italy also, and then to make an attempt on the Carthaginian Empire and the Carthaginians themselves, and if these designs prospered, either wholly, or to a large degree, we intended then to attack the Peloponnese. . . .

(6.90.1–3)

This colourful statement might be thought to have been meant to scare the Spartans, but it is in essence what Thucydides himself ascribes to Alcibiades in his celebrated introduction to Alcibiades' reply to Nicias (6.15.2). 'Alcibiades was most zealous in urging the expedition, wishing to oppose Nicias . . . and being especially eager to be a general and expecting by that means to take Sicily and Carthage. . . . ' For a mere 60 ships, that was large and wild.

Furthermore, in his famous postscript (2.65.11), Thucydides made what has seemed to many a remarkable modification of what he had said at the beginning of Book 6.[2]

> As a result many mistakes were made, as was likely in a large city possessed of empire, and especially the Sicilian expedition, which was not so great an error of judgement with regard to those they attacked as that those who had despatched it did not take the further decisions (*epigignōskontes*) that were of advantage to those who had gone, but through personal attacks over the leadership of the People they made the position in the army more confused. . . .

Careful attention to the Greek[3] makes clear that Thucydides was not saying in this passage (written at the end of the Peloponnesian War) that the Athenians did not make an error of judgement in going to Sicily, only that later decisions were more serious errors. None the less it is a very surprising statement.

It is worth digressing for a moment to inquire what these later decisions were. It is generally assumed that Thucydides was referring to the recall of Alcibiades.[4] That is far from certain but, even if he

76

was, he was not thinking of that alone, for that would have required an aorist participle where he used a present (*epigignōskontes*). Suggestions can be made. Thucydides was not one for underlining points, and what he was thinking of in 404 will not necessarily leap at us from the pages of Books 6 and 7. Nicias in his letter asked the Athenians either to recall the force he commanded or to send out another of no less magnitude and a replacement for himself (7.15.1). Although they might have claimed to have met his request for a new army,[5] they did not recall him, sick as he was, and Thucydides may have considered this an error of judgement. He may also have considered that, instead of reinforcing failure, the whole armament should have been recalled. As to the Athenian ravaging of Laconia in 414 (6.105), he is emphatic; these 30 ships 'most plainly caused a breakdown of the Peace with the Spartans', for the ravaging 'gave the Spartans a good excuse for taking their revenge on the Athenians.' The raid was plainly an error of judgement. What Thucydides did not record in its proper place, namely the Athenian decision to give military aid to the rebel satrap of Caria, Amorges,[6] he may well by 404 have come to regard as a serious mistake. It meant that Sparta had good hopes of securing the Great King's alliance in the war they now felt justified in resuming (cf. 7.18.2 and 3). So no matter what Thucydides thought in 404 about the effect of recalling Alcibiades, there certainly were other matters during the course of the Sicilian Expedition that he could have considered errors which made the position in the army in Sicily more confused (*amblytera*).

One can suppose what Thucydides might have had in mind, serious errors indeed, but could they have in any way eclipsed *the* great error of going to Sicily at all? One has only to read the opening of Book 6 and the opening sentence of chapter 6 to see that, for Thucydides at the moment of writing his account of the Sicilian Expedition, it was a monstrous error, so monstrous as not to be out-topped by later mistakes. The majority did not know how big or how populated the island was. So he tells us and, when he has described it all, he comments: 'such were the peoples both Greek and non-Greek who inhabited Sicily, and against Sicily so great as it was the Athenians set out to campaign.' What stupendous folly! Nothing could make that initial blunder less monstrous, such is the effect on the reader. How then could Thucydides have come to write that palinode?

There was, after all, an excellent reason why Athens should heed the summons of the Segestans and the Leontinan exiles in 416/15. The point was made by the Segestans (6.6.2) that there was a danger of the Syracusans coming to help the Corinthians, of Dorians helping Dorians and colonists helping the metropolis, and Alcibiades is represented (6.18.1) as stating that Athens had made alliances with Sicilian states 'not in order that they should in turn render us military support in Greece, but that they should cause trouble for our enemies in Sicily and so prevent them coming here to attack us' – a view that is echoed in the speech of Euphemus, the Athenian apologist, at Camarina (6.83.4, 84.1). Nicias, however, is made to argue that by going to Sicily, the Athenians will bring on Sicilian involvement in Greece (6.10.1). The possibility of such involvement was declared by Thucydides to be what helped to move the Athenians in 433 to accept the alliance with Corcyra (1.44.3), as the speech he wrote for the Corcyrans makes explicit (1.36.2).[7] Nor was this a matter of Thucydides' imagining. When the Corcyrans appealed to Athens for help in 373/2 (Xen. *Hell.* 6.2.9), they declared that their city's greatest strategic charm was its position 'on the coastal route from Sicily to the Peloponnese'. Even Syracusan minds contained the idea. In seeking to discount the news of an Athenian attack on Syracuse in 415, Athenagoras opined that the Athenians were 'well content that it is not we Sicilians who are going against them' (6.36.4). Certainly, the fear of western help for the Peloponnese was widely felt over a long time.

Indeed, this consideration perhaps best explains Athens' alliances with Sicilian states during the Pentekontaetea.[8] If, as has been argued above, the alliance with Segesta is still best set in the 450s,[9] during the First Peloponnesian War and at a time when Athens was engaged in Egypt, it is hardly likely that Athens was putting out imperialistic feelers and it is unacceptable to argue that the purpose of alliance was commercial.[10] But if Segesta was then at war with Selinus[11] and Selinus was seeking the aid of Syracuse as Syracuse had a few years earlier sought hers (Diod. 11.68.1), it was plainly to Athens' interest that Syracuse should not be allowed to bring a coalition of cities to help the metropolis, Corinth. Alliances with Leontini and Rhegium must have been more directly hostile to Syracuse and it is to be noted that these alliances were renewed in 433/2 (ML 63 and 64), i.e. in Pericles' heyday and after the fateful decision to ally with Corcyra. Of course, there may well have been Athenians who before the war dreamed of the extension of the

Empire to the west,[12] and Pericles himself in his last speech could be represented as offering limitless prospects of naval power once the War was ended (2.62.2). In 432, however, when he saw 'war bearing down on Athens from the Peloponnese' (Plut. *Per.* 8.7), his attitude to renewing alliances with Leontini and Rhegium will have been cautious and prudent.[13] Syracuse had to be distracted from helping the Spartan cause and Sparta's large hopes of the West (2.7.2) had to be rendered vain.

Athens had perhaps exaggerated ideas of what Syracuse could do. Herodotus could picture Gelon responding to the Greek call to arms in 481/0 by offering 200 triremes, 2,000 hoplites, 2,000 cavalry, 2,000 archers, 2,000 slingers, 2,000 light horsemen, and the provision of corn for the whole army, provided he had supreme command (7.158.4, 5). Compared to this, Syracuse's actual contribution to the Peloponnesian cause in the Ionian War, a mere 20 ships (8.26.1), may seem paltry, but after the destruction of the Athenian army in 413 Syracuse began to be itself distracted by political rivalries and was then faced with the threat of Carthaginian expansion.[14] Earlier Syracuse might well have given more ample help, and Athens had good reason to do what she could to prevent it.

If good sense prompted Pericles not to neglect in 433/2 the chance to keep the Syracusans distracted by troubles in Sicily, one might ask why this prudent motive does not show itself in the motivation alleged by Thucydides for the dispatch of the force of 20 ships in 427 (3.86) and of the 40 ships in 425 (3.115). On each occasion he gives a prudent as well as a radical motive, but in neither case is it explicitly stated that the Athenians aimed to prevent Sicilian help for the Peloponnese. Had the Athenians all forgotten the sensible Periclean policy? That was not so. In 427, Syracuse was in no position to help her metropolis, Corinth, other than by sending corn, and the 'sensible' policy is represented in Thucydides' account by the Athenians 'wishing corn not to be imported to the Peloponnese from there' (3.86.4). The great expansion of the Syracusan navy by the building of one hundred triremes, confidently recorded by Diodorus under the year 439/8 (12.30.1), had evidently not been carried out, for the first 20 Athenian ships are in no way checked and seem to move around freely on not very important operations (3.88, 90, 103). But there was a danger that the 20 Athenian ships could be outnumbered and defeated and so Syracuse would be able to help the Peloponnesians. The 'sensible' policy prevented this by despatching an extra 40 ships, and is expressed in the form that the Athenians partly wished to give the navy some training (§4). Thus, it may be claimed that constantly from 460 onwards there was a substantial body of opinion in Athens which favoured a policy of keeping Syracuse distracted and unable to give full support to the metropolis and the Peloponnesian cause.

When in 416/15 there was a joint appeal to Athens for help against the joint forces of Syracuse and Selinus (6.6), prudence should have moved Athens not to stand by and see Sicily united in subjection to the very states that might be called on by the Peloponnesians if the War resumed, and there could be little confidence at Athens that it would not. So a return to the state of affairs that pertained in 424 on the eve of the Peace of Gela was the sensible response. But was there a great deal more to it? Is Thucydides right? Did Alcibiades really have the immense ambitions and the great expectations that Thucydides attributes to him?

Whatever the truth of Plutarch's assertions about widespread and long-held ambitions at Athens for extending Athenian power in the West (*Per.* 20.4; *Alc.* 17.1), it is plain enough that during the Archidamian War a substantial and possibly increasing number of Athenians favoured westward expansion. For both the naval forces sent to Sicily, the prudent cautious purpose is matched in Thucydides' account by a radical imperialist one (3.86.4 and 115.4). By reversing the order he is perhaps indicating that the radical view was gaining the upper hand.[15] Nor is this account merely the fruit of Thucydides' imagination. Whether or not Hermocrates did make the large accusation that Thucydides attributes to him (4.60), the treatment accorded to the generals who both accepted and even commended the making of the Peace of Gela shows the state of opinion in Athens in 424. Indeed, it would appear that Thucydides quoted the charge against them. They were punished, he says (4.65.3), 'since they had withdrawn[16] being persuaded with bribes (*dōrois peisthentes*) to do so when it was possible for them to subject Sicily (*ta en Sikeliāi katastrepsasthai*).' It is the mention of 'bribes' that is strongly suggestive. It emerges from a passage in Hyperides' speech, *For Euxenippus* (29f.), that in certain cases the law required that the charge attribute the conduct complained of to corruption by bribery. So it would seem that these Athenians who voted for condemnation did so because they had wanted the subjection of Sicily. In the *Knights* (1303f.), Aristophanes could make a joke about Hyperbolus wanting to attack Carthage; the reality was perhaps not too far behind. In any case, Thucydides was not exiled until 424/3 and is likely to have been well acquainted with the state of public opinion in these years.

Thucydides may have thought he knew Alcibiades also well enough.[17] It seems probable that Thucydides knew Pericles sufficiently to have encountered the young Alcibiades at his house, but in any case, by 425, he was a well-known figure (Ar. *Ach.* 716). Thucydides may have formed the view that Alcibiades was as wild in his judgement as he was in his ambition and, when in exile he learned that Alcibiades had urged the sending of a force to Sicily, he leapt to the extreme view expressed in his second 'truest cause' (6.6.1).

How then did he come to express the qualified judgement of his postscript (2.65.11)? According to Plutarch (*Alc.* 38.2), after Alcibiades had entered on his second exile, the Athenians regretted the loss of their best general, a view which must have been based on his successes in the Ionian War.[18] Thucydides seems to have acknowledged as much in the passage which is generally agreed to be added to Book 6 at the end of the Peloponnesian War (6.15.3, 4).[19] At what time he began to change his view of Alcibiades is unclear. If the general acceptance of the reading of one manuscript of 8.86.4 is correct,[20] in his account of the cause of the oligarchic revolution of 411.Thucydides was still regarding all of Alcibiades' public acts up until then as of no use to the city – a stance not entirely easy to justify[21] – but there is very little indication of when he wrote that portion of Book 8. However, it is sure enough that Thucydides saw Alcibiades in the course of the collection of material for his account of the Ionian War, that war was for a period Alcibiades' own and the historian was bound to consult the responsible general, especially considering that they were each in exile at opposite ends of Thrace. Indeed, much of Book 8 must have come either from Alcibiades himself or from men very close to him.[22] It is not surprising therefore that Thucydides came to a more tempered view and Alcibiades' explanation of the failure of the Expedition was given credence. In the postscript of 2.65.11, Thucydides made amends.

But how could Thucydides have come to modify his view of the error of judgement 'with regard to those they went against'? Sicily remained large and populous and the original 60 ships decreed (6.8.2), as asked by the Segestans (cf. 6.47.1), ludicrously inadequate. When one stands on the shore of the Great Harbour at

Syracuse and contemplates the military problem of reducing Syracuse, one sees that only by following Alcibiades' strategy (6.48) of attacking Syracuse with a large allied force could Athens with confidence have set about that much.[23] However, the other dissident states would have remained to be dealt with, if Athens was to succeed in 'putting the whole in the empire' (6.6.1). Such a plan would have been quite impracticable.

It is therefore proposed that Thucydides was able to write his postscript only because he came to see that the Expedition was directed against Syracuse and Selinus, no more. In his account of the debate among the generals, which it is to be presumed is a factual report (6.47–9), the strategy of Alcibiades hardly seems to be that of a man to whom such large schemes and ambitions had been earlier ascribed (6.15). It is in essence that the Athenians should seek friends and allies, 'and when they have brought over the cities, and know at whose side they will conduct the war, precisely then' (i.e. and not before) 'they should attack Syracuse and Selinus unless the Selinuntians come to terms with the Segestans and the Syracusans allow the Leontines to dwell on their own territory'. If that happens, we are left to conclude, the Athenian mission would be accomplished and the armada would return home. Again, in Thucydides' version of the letter sent by Nicias to the Athenians, which is so unlike Thucydidean speeches that it sounds like either the actual text or a literary version based on the text,[24] Nicias speaks of 'the Syracusans against whom we were sent' (7.11.2), just as in his contribution to the debate on strategy (6.47) he had spoken of sailing against Selinus, 'our principal objective'. Nowhere in the narrative is there any hint of larger aims. The stated objectives are suitable for a sixty-ship force, unlike the introductory chapters where Thucydides treats the Expedition in the most grandiose way.

Thucydides came to see that his 'truest cause' for the Sicilian Expedition was quite untrue. That is how he wrote as he did in his postscript.

The unwitting villain of the piece was Nicias who, when called on to state what sort and size of force was required, led the city to commit far too many of its forces to the expedition (6.25), who plainly was, although Thucydides did not explicitly say so, culpably dilatory in carrying through the circumvallation of Syracuse,[25] and who, being 'excessively devoted to divination and that sort of thing' (7.50.4), rigorously insisted on the full thrice nine days delay[26] and so ensured the utter ruin of the whole Athenian armament. In

Thucydides' view he did not deserve to come to so miserable an end (7.86.5). Doubtless, to Thucydides' virtue, like 'niceness', was not enough in a statesman. Intelligence, as well as virtue (cf. 4.81.2), was necessary.

The salvation of Syracuse was a 'damned nice thing – the nearest run thing you ever saw in your life.' Just before the arrival of Gylippus, everything was going the Athenian way. Supplies were being brought in to the army from all quarters; many of the Sicels, who had previously been standing by and seeing what would happen, had come to join in the battle; three *penteconters* had arrived from Etruria; the circumvallation was well forward; there were talks inside the city about coming to terms with the Athenians (6.103). Such was the dangerous position of Syracuse (7.2.4). It is not to be doubted that, if Alcibiades had been in charge instead of Nicias, Syracuse would have had to come to terms, and if the purpose of sending 60 ships was to reduce Syracuse, the Sicilian Expedition would have been a glorious success.

Thucydides manifested approval of Lamachus' strategy (7.42.3), but since the force sent to Sicily lacked cavalry and a reliable system of supply, the initial shock on which Lamachus would have relied was bound to fail.[27] In winter 415/14, having gained a victory in the battle of the Anapus (6.70), the Athenians were obliged to withdraw to Catana for the winter (6.71).

> It did not seem possible yet to conduct the war on the spot until they sent for cavalry from Athens and assembled it from the allies in Sicily to prevent their being completely mastered by the enemy horse, and until they at the same time gathered money in Sicily and it came from the Athenians, and until they brought over to their side certain of the cities which they expected would after the battle take more notice of them, and until in general they provided themselves with grain and other necessities, intending in the spring to make the attempt on Syracuse.

In other words, they had to withdraw and put into effect the strategy previously advocated by Alcibiades (6.48).

Alcibiades had been recalled before he had had much opportunity to display his diplomatic skills,[28] but clearly he saw both Athens' need of cavalry[29] and the real weakness of his opponents – namely, the social divisions in Sicilian cities which could be exploited to Athens' advantage. Thucydides has him say in 415: 'The cities are thronged with mobs of mixed origins and they readily change and increase their citizens' (6.17.2), and whether or not Alcibiades did say that at that time, the remark was clearly just. The nature of the divisions in other cities is unclear. We are given no explanation for instance of why some at Catana favoured the Syracusan cause (6.51.2). However, for Syracuse we have quite a lot of information.

Most illuminating is the account given by Herodotus (7.155.2–156) of the manner in which the tyrant Gelon in the 480's made Syracuse the largest and most powerful city in Sicily. Having restored the land-owning class of Syracuse, the so-called *gamoroi*,[30] to their own city, he thought no more of his native Gela but proceeded to concentrate in Syracuse all the Camarinans and the majority of the citizens of Gela. How he dealt with the people of Megara Hyblaea provides the key. The rich citizens of Megara had gone to war against Gelon and, when their city was under siege, had only death and destruction to expect, whereas the *dēmos* which had had no share in the war had no thought of harsh treatment. Gelon took the rich to Syracuse and made them citizens but sold the rest 'for export from Sicily'. He treated likewise the inhabitants of Euboea,[31] a city founded by the Chalcidians of Leontini. The reason Herodotus gave for these acts of what is now obscenely termed 'ethnic cleansing' is that Gelon 'thought a *dēmos* was a very nasty thing to live with' (7.156.3). Clearly, Gelon was not drawing a line between Dorians and non-Dorians. Since the *dēmos* was treated like slaves, one suspects that his purpose was to concentrate in Syracuse all those of Greek descent and expel the rest, but his concern was not just with Greeks; rather, he wanted rich Greeks, the land-owning class, the *gamoroi*, the descendants of the original settlers.

Of course, Syracuse had its own *dēmos* (Hdt. 7.155.2) which may have been a 'mixed lot' in Alcibiades' phrase (6.17.2), but certainly some of them were Greek and minded to aspire to a share of political power. The tyrants assembled mercenaries who were subsequently expelled, but some seem to have remained. After the withdrawal from the city of the mercenaries of the tyrant Thrasybulus (Diod. 11.68.5), there were still 7,000 of Gelon's 16,000 remaining, having been made citizens by Gelon (ibid. 72.3). They would, no doubt, have been Greeks and one may presume that other Greeks had drifted into the city and formed part of the *dēmos*. So the opponents of what Diodorus termed 'the old citizens' (11.72.3) were a mixed lot. In 415 they had their leader in Athenagoras, the arch opponent of Hermocrates whom he accused of dark oligarchic designs. He himself was apologist for democracy (6.36–40). After the defeat of the Athenians, another leader of the *dēmos* emerged in the person of Diocles who certainly took a leading part in the introduction of a more democratic constitution (Diod. 13.34.6, 35.1), as a comment of Aristotle (*Pol.* 1304a27–9) makes clear.[32]

What is special about this conflict of the land-owning class and the *dēmos* at Syracuse is the racial element. As Aristotle observed, 'differences of race make for political division' (*Pol.* 1303a25). Although Syracuse did not hesitate to make citizens of landowners from Chalcidic states, they tended not to stay (cf. 5.4.1–5 for the case of Leontini), and the land-owning class of Syracuse was probably to a large extent ultimately Dorian in origin. As Hermocrates declared, 'free Dorians from the independent Peloponnese' (6.77.1). It was not so, in all probability, with the *dēmos*.

But was the hostility of Athenagoras to Hermocrates merely that of the leader of the *dēmos* (6.35.2) to the leader of 'the old citizens'? Or were there important differences in policy? The exchange of speeches given to them by Thucydides does not encourage one to think that there was anything much at issue in 415, and lack of information about Syracusan politics[33] ought perhaps to compel silence. But it is notable that, in 412, Hermocrates[34] had been 'especially active in urging the Sicilians to join in completing the ruin of the Athenians' (8.26.1) just as in 424 his appeal to the Sicilians as a whole to unite in a peace and get rid of the Athenians had been successful (4.58–65.1). One cannot help wondering whether two important issues of policy are here manifested.

Certainly, Syracuse had established a sort of empire over the Sicels. Nicias is made to allude to 'first-fruits' (*aparchē*) brought from certain non-Greeks to the Syracusans (6.20.4). The sort of system alluded to here is unclear, but since Diodorus (12.30.1) speaks of the Syracusans imposing 'more abundant tributes' (*phoroi*) on the subject Sicels, there was clearly some sort of empire, the extent of which can to some degree be traced in Thucydides.[35] Ducetius had led the defence of the Sicels against this sort of expansion and he was succeeded by Archonides (7.1.4, Diod. 12.8.2). Those nearer the coast were unable to keep free of Syracuse. But, in addition to the Sicels, the Chalcidian cities, Leontini, Naxos and Catana were constantly menaced. It was presumably this which prompted Leontini to make the alliance with Athens, renewed in

433/2 (ML 64). Certainly, the appeal to Athens in 427 was due to the Syracusans attacking the city (3.86.2, 3). Shortly after the Peace of Gela in 424, which ended wars among the Sicilians (4.65.1), 'those in power' at Leontini were sufficiently well-disposed towards the Syracusans to call them in to expel the *dēmos* which 'was planning to redistribute the land'. They then deserted the city and moved to Syracuse in return for citizenship there (5.4.3). By 422 a number of these rich landowners from Leontini had turned against Syracuse and, leaving the city, had returned to the territory of Leontini. Joined by the majority of the *dēmos* whom the Syracusans had assisted in expelling, they recommended war against Syracuse (5.4.4). So it was that by 416/15 Leontini had physically ceased to exist and 'the exiles' (6.19.1; cf. 12.1) joined in the appeal to Athens.

The Greek cities had indeed much to fear, but questions about their relationship to Syracuse arise. First, why did the Sicilians make the Peace of Gela?[36] They had sought a total of 60 ships from Athens and had got them, but instead of exploiting this force, they told them they were no longer needed (4.65.2). Second, according to Diodorus (12.30.1) there was, before the Peloponnesian War, a large increase in Syracusan military forces, including the construction of 100 triremes. What became of these ships? This is the easier question. No such navy challenged the first Athenian squadron of 20 ships of 427.[37] Diodorus records this increase under 439/8 (the year, incidentally, under which he records the beginning of the trouble between Corcyra and Corinth), but such datings of Diodorus are worthless. The reasonable presumption is that the increase was voted in 433/2, and that was why both Leontini and Rhegium appealed to Athens in that year for their alliances to be renewed (ML 63 and 64) and how it was that Sparta looked to Sicily for a large force of ships (2.7.2), but looked in vain. The ships cannot have been built at that time, and it was not until 426/5 that Syracusan naval preparations really began and led to a request for a larger Athenian squadron (3.115.3, 4; 4.24.1).

But why did the Sicilians make the Peace of Gela? There were clearly different views (4.58); but Syracusan behaviour can be largely explained as reaction to Athenian policy. When Athens under Pericles made clear by renewing its alliances with Leontini and Rhegium that it would not in the coming war neglect its policy of countering Syracusan advance in Sicily, the aggressive plans of Syracuse were checked. By summer 427, however, the cost of the war in Greece was becoming ever greater for Athens (3.13.3) and it was not to be expected that she would send help to Sicilian allies. So the policy of expansion was resumed and the people of Leontini sent Gorgias on his celebrated embassy (3.86; Diod. 12.53). Twenty ships were not sufficient to stop Syracuse. Indeed, such naval activities as occurred might have been thought to be to Syracusan advantage (cf. 4.27.6). But when the 40 ships arrived in late summer 425 and joined in the war (4.48.6), it was time for Syracuse to abandon her expansionist policy and make peace. Nor is it really surprising that Athens' allies, the Chalcidic states and Camarina, accepted the peace; they were getting what they had sought, namely their independence guaranteed,[38] and there was nothing more to fight for.

The role of Hermocrates is nonetheless notable. His was, according to Thucydides (4.58), the speech that had the greatest influence in persuading the Sicilians to make peace. The emphasis, if we may trust Thucydides, was on the unity and common interest of all 'Sicilians' (4.61.1–3), 'the single name for the Greeks who, side by side, shared the one sea-girt habitation' (64.3). Now, it is not likely that a man who had in any way been responsible in Syracuse for the expansive policy which had brought the Athenians actively to intervene in Sicilian affairs would have been taken seriously in such calls to unity, and one notes that when next Syracusan expansion prompts Leontinans to appeal to Athens, Hermocrates was not in the office of general, and he recovered it only when the Athenian expeditionary force was in Sicily (6.73.1). So it may be suspected that Hermocrates who, at least in Athenagoras' mind was the leader of 'the few' (6.38.4), opposed the *dēmos* under its leader (6.35.2) in its expansionist policy. If that were so, Alcibiades was not unrealistic in thinking that Syracuse which had given in to pressure in 424 could be pressed in 415 to allow the resettlement of Leontini, as he was reported to have sought in the strategy debate of the Athenian generals (6.48). There certainly were divisions in Syracuse to be exploited.

The other great issue on which Syracuse may have been divided was, of course, whether the city should seek to help the Metropolis, Corinth. The Athenian ambassador, Euphemus, in the speech Thucydides has him deliver at Camarina, treats Syracusan intervention in Greece as a real possibility (cf. 6.84.1), declaring that previously (presumably 427) Camarina had induced the Athenians to come to Sicily by threatening that, if the Athenians did nothing to prevent Camarina being made subject to Syracuse, they would themselves be in danger (6.86.1). There must have been a faction at Syracuse so minded. Who more likely than the descendants of the original settlers, the *gamoroi*, and, if so, who more likely to be their spokesman than Hermocrates? He played a leading part in the Syracusan decision in 412 to join in the utter destruction of Athens (8.26.1), and he may well have wanted so to do earlier. That may have been a policy which Athenagoras would not pursue. In a passage universally despised and rejected, Andocides in 392/1 (3.30) asserted that

> when the Syracusans came with a request, wishing to have friendship in place of hostility, and to make peace rather than war, and demonstrating how much better alliance with them would be, if we were willing to make it, than alliance with Segesta and Catana, we chose war rather than peace, the Segestans rather than the Syracusans.

Thucydides gave no hint of any such thing and, for this reason, the passage is dismissed as rhetorical invention. This may be right, but if Athenagoras who seems to have been in control in 416 had indeed heard of the Segestan appeal of 416/15, it would have been the plainest good sense for Syracuse to seek diplomatic means to prevent renewed Athenian intervention in Sicily, just as it would have been plain good sense for Athens to refuse cooperation; for if Syracusan imperialism and imperialists were left to have their way, there was no guarantee that Hermocrates and his ilk would not sometime regain control and use Syracusan power to help destroy Athens. But whatever the truth about Andocides here,[39] it is likely enough that Syracuse was divided over the issue of help to Greece, and that here too there was opportunity for an Alcibiades.

Even without the diplomatic gifts of Alcibiades, Syracuse came very close to making a settlement with Athens. Just before Gylippus arrived on the scene, the Syracusans were despairing of their prospects and holding discussions on peace terms both among themselves and with Nicias (6.103.3), and they were just about to hold an assembly about putting an end to the war (7.2.1). Gylippus put a stop to all that, though it continued to inspire a misleading confidence in Nicias (7.48.2). Who these people were who could be represented as 'friends of the Athenians' and who sent reports to Nicias about the state of things in Syracuse (7.73.3, 86.4) is unclear.[40] What is clear is that, with Alcibiades in command, the Syracusans could indeed have been forced 'to allow the people of

Leontini to occupy their own city' (6.48), and the expedition would thus far have succeeded. What was nearly done with Syracuse could likewise have been done with Selinus.

Thucydides may accurately enough have divined the mood of the Athenians on hearing Nicias' speech at the second assembly (6.24.3). They may have been thinking of 'endless pay' (*aïdios misthophora*). He may have understood his countrymen all too well. His understanding of Alcibiades is more questionable.

Alcibiades was a controversial figure. When Xenophon recounted Alcibiades' return to Athens from exile, he described the division of opinion, with Alcibiades' apologists receiving a far fuller report (*Hell.* 1.4.13–17). Thucydides would not have sympathised. His Alcibiades of Book 6 emerges as a traitor, a man who went over to his city's enemies and advised them to send a force to Sicily under the command of a Spartiate, to renew the war in Greece and to establish a fort at Decelea (6.91.4–6) and who delivered a cynical defence of himself by claiming that the true patriot is the man who loves his country so much that there is nothing he will not do to get back to it (6.92.4).

Of all the speeches in Thucydides' *History*, the one he ascribed to Alcibiades at Sparta is the least likely to be based on report of what was, in fact, said.[41] Thucydides may have learned that Alcibiades had counselled Sparta to do what they subsequently did do, namely to send a force to Sicily under a Spartiate and to apply themselves to the fortification of Decelea. After all, these were the obvious things for Sparta to do,[42] on which they certainly did not need the advice of Alcibiades. Syracuse could not be abandoned to suffering a siege and Sparta had realised before the end of the Archidamian War that fortification in Attica would indeed be effective (5.17.2). So Alcibiades may have said as much, even though the Spartans took a good 15 months to establish the fort at Decelea (7.18), and they did not do so before Athens, by an act of consummate folly, had given them a good excuse for renewing the war (6.105). It is extremely unlikely that any Spartan would have furnished Thucydides with material for Alcibiades' version of patriotism, which so wonderfully displayed 'the art of words' acquired through a sophistic education but so spurned at Sparta.[43] No doubt, Thucydides enjoyed writing that chapter, but it is very probably a free invention. Likewise, when Alcibiades is made to tell the Spartans how to save the day in Syracuse, his advice corresponds so exactly with what actually happened that it arouses acute suspicion.

Gylippus, the Spartiate, was sent with a force that rowed to Sicily and the rowers turned into hoplites (7.1.3), just as Alcibiades was made to counsel (6.91.4). The Spartans did fortify Decelea and it did do great damage in the very ways Alcibiades had been represented as suggesting it would (7.27–8, 6.91.6 and 7). The correspondence is so nice that one cannot help suspecting that the speech is evidence not so much for Alcibiades' words and conduct as for what Thucydides thought of him.

There is also a curious omission in Thucydides' account, often remarked and often denied. Having crossed from Thurii to Cyllene, Alcibiades is made, it would seem, to go directly to Sparta, summoned by the Spartans (6.88.10). There is perhaps a hint of some lapse of time, but no suggestion of Alcibiades going elsewhere before going to Sparta. In Plutarch's *Life of Alcibiades* (23.1), however, it is asserted that Alcibiades was staying in Argos when the news of his condemnation reached him. The same account is to be found in the speech written for his son early in the fourth century (Isoc. 16.9), where it is also stated that the sentence passed on him 'outlawed him from all Greece', which, if true, put him in a similar condition to that in which an earlier sojourner at Argos, Themistocles, had found himself. Rejected and threatened with the worst by his friends, he had no alternative to seeking asylum with his enemies. But is this whole story to be accepted?[44] Certainly, Argos was the natural place for Alcibiades to go to. His influence there was so strong that the Athenians had found it expedient to require the Salaminian ship not to arrest him in Sicily for fear of upsetting the Argives there (6.61.5). Furthermore, Plutarch (ch. 22) cited the text of the impeachment and described the consequences of the condemnation in absence. It is no longer acceptable to argue that something cannot have happened because Thucydides does not say it did. Plutarch was clearly interested and informed. There is no good reason to reject his evidence.

But why did Thucydides omit Alcibiades' sojourn in Argos? His version has Alcibiades a deserter and Plutarch's a reluctant exile. It makes a very great difference if Alcibiades was driven to do what he did, and one can only suspect that Thucydides was not minded, when he wrote the first version of Book 6, to think well of him. His reader could be left to conclude that, to save his skin, the selfish deserter set out to do what harm he could to spite his country.[45]

One can only wish that one knew when Thucydides wrote his account of Alcibiades going into exile and his sojourn in Sparta. If it was after the events of 412 in which Alcibiades played a leading part in causing revolt in the Athenian Empire (8.14–17), Thucydides may have been greatly influenced in his judgement. But whatever the explanation, it is strongly to be suspected that Thucydides misrepresented the part of Alcibiades in his account of the Sicilian Expedition. His second 'truest cause' was not correct and that is why he wrote as he did in his postscript (2.65.11).

6

THUCYDIDES AND
THE EMPIRE

.

Has Thucydides misrepresented the character of the Athenian Empire? In a celebrated article[1] published in 1954, two years before the Hungarian uprising which began the illumination of the character of another empire, de Ste Croix declared that the truth about Athens' empire was revealed in the speech which Thucydides put into the mouth of Diodotus in the Mytilene debate. That speaker declared (3.47.2):

> As things are now, the *dēmos* in all the cities (i.e. of the Empire) is well disposed to us and either it does not join with the few in revolt, or if it is forced to do so, is hostile from the outset to those who have revolted, and you go to war against the city in revolt having the masses on your side.

Almost 30 years later this same author declared[2] that the fifth-century Empire 'is unique among past empires known to us in that the ruling city relied very much on the support of the lower classes in the subject states.' In between, in 1972, this proud proclamation was somewhat 'sullied o'er'.[3]

> It would be a mistake to exaggerate. Apart from a few leading politicians who might expect great gains from being the recipients of Athenian trust and goodwill, I doubt if many of the ordinary citizens of the subject states felt any real enthusiasm towards Athens: they may rather have seen Athenian domination simply as a 'lesser evil' than being subjected to their own oligarchs. . . . The cardinal fact that under an oligarchy only the propertied classes enjoyed real freedom was bound to drive many of the lower orders in many cities into

reliance, however reluctant, upon Athens, as the evidence shows that in fact it did.[4]

The question is entirely a matter of how Athens's subjects perceived the Empire. As empires go, the Athenian Empire was a good empire. All empires seek to secure peace,[5] and Athens certainly did that until Sparta brought Persia back into Greek affairs. Even then, the age-long evil of the Aegean, i.e. piracy, did not reassert itself until Athens lost her fleet.[6] Further, Athens, like other imperial powers, established and maintained a satisfactory judicial system which provided a fair means of settling commercial disputes between citizens of different member states. Like the Athenian judicial system itself, the imperial system had its dark side – namely 'political' justice which served the interests of the Athenian demos and not impartial justice – but for the most part the system was a matter for pride.[7] Nor were the burdens of Empire, tribute and military service, severe. In 413, the Athenians replaced the tribute with a five per cent tax on imports and exports in the harbours of the allies, 'thinking that by this method they would increase their revenue' (7.28.4), which hardly suggests that the tribute was oppressive.[8] The case was similar with military service. Athens's power was essentially naval and, as the Corinthian speaker in the debate of the Peloponnesian League observed (1.121.3), crews were largely mercenary.[9] Even during the War the call-up of hoplites was probably not very exacting, to judge by the Sicilian Expedition which was a major effort. In all, 5,100 hoplites set out in 415, but only 2,850 came from the subject states (6.43). Whereas Thucydides remarked that the expedition round the Peloponnese in 430 was as large in numbers of ships and hoplites (6.31.2), there were on that occasion, it would seem (2.56.2), no allied hoplites at all. The Milesians seem to have been especially obliged to service (cf. 4.54.1), but in general the military requirements of Empire were slight.[10] But none of this is relevant when considering the attitude of subjects to an imperial power. British India was, in many ways, admirably governed and administered and Gandhi had no expectation that with freedom things would be as good, but he still demanded 'Give us chaos.'

There is another preliminary to be made clear. It is hardly necessary to remark that Athenian imperialism did not cease in 404. In 395 when the Thebans appealed for Athenian alliance against Sparta, they roundly declared 'Of course we all know that you would like to recover the empire which you formerly possessed' (Xen. *Hell.* 3.5.10), and this is the key to Athenian policy down to the King's Peace of 387/6.[11] Indeed, Athens's alliance in 395 with the Boeotians, as it formally was (ML II.101), was a bold move, for Lysander and his army were already on Boeotian soil and the alliance was no mere deterrent. In the succeeding years, Athens made considerable progress in restoring her imperial power, so much progress, in fact, that Persia was moved in 387 to a rapprochement with Sparta and the dissolution of Athenian power and prospects by means of the King's Peace.[12] Again, in 379/8, Thebes appealed at the moment of liberation, and again Athens responded. When Thebes sought to settle with Sparta and so left Athens exposed to Spartan wrath, Athens set about founding the Second Athenian Confederacy – a principally defensive move – but the military aid given to Thebes some weeks before is only to be explained as a return to the mood of 395, a resurgence of hope that, with Thebes to engage Sparta on land, Athens could set about the recovery of her fifth-century Empire.[13] Likewise, at the time of the Social War (357–5), Isocrates is found arguing against imperialist hopes at the start of his speech *Concerning Peace*.

> It was plain to everyone that you Athenians would be more pleased with those summoning you to the war than with those counselling peace. The former led us to expect that we would both recover our possessions in 'the cities'[14] and regain the power which we happened formerly to have, while the latter had no such hope to offer and could only argue that we must have peace and not cherish great possessions we had no right to but that we must be content with what we actually have.
>
> (§§5 and 6)

Later in the speech (§64), he calls on the Athenians 'to give up the desire for naval empire'. At much the same time as Isocrates wrote *Concerning Peace*, Xenophon opened the treatise entitled *Revenues* with a statement of how he had come to write it.

> When some of Athens' leading politicians were declaring that they were as well aware as anyone else of what was right, but because of the poverty of the majority they were obliged to be somewhat unjust with regard to 'the cities', I tried to consider whether the citizens could keep themselves off their own territory . . .
>
> (1.1)

94

So Athenian imperialist hopes lived on even despite the near-bankruptcy of the state at the end of the Social War.[15] But that really was the limit. Near-bankruptcy and then the rise of Philip of Macedon prevented further attempts.

All this is plain enough, but what must be made clear is that, for a decade and a half, the fear of Spartan and Persian reprisals during the 370s and after the elimination of Sparta at the battle of Leuctra in 371 the lingering fear of Persia until the outbreak of the Satraps' Revolt in the mid-360s kept Athens in check.[16] The Second Athenian Confederacy of the 370s was a deliberate abstention from empire. In the Decree of Aristotle (*GHI* 123), the principal features of the fifth-century Empire are renounced. Any state that joins the new league will be 'free and independent' and the meaning of this is spelled out. The state will be free to have any constitution it wishes; there will be no garrison, no governor, no tribute; there will be no 'hangovers' from the past, for Athens renounces all claims to holdings, either by the Athenian state or by individuals, in the territory of states joining the league, and any 'unsuitable' records (i.e. contrary to the terms of the decree) are to be destroyed and, in future, it is not to be possible for the Athenian state or for any individual Athenian to acquire in the territory of a member state either a house or an estate, be it by purchase, by mortgage or by any other means. This thorough-going renunciation of imperial practices and institutions was referred to in 373 by Isocrates (14.44) as 'abandoning your possessions', and in the 370s this self-denying ordinance held. Indeed, as far as the members of the Second Athenian Confederacy were concerned, it continued to hold through the 360s.[17] But the leopard of imperialism had not changed its spots. No new states were added to the league after Leuctra. In 368, Athens began the long and debilitating and vain struggle to recover Amphipolis, the key to empire on the north Aegean seaboard. Then in 365, when Persia was in no position to do anything to stop it, they set about the recovery of the Chersonese. In 365, having intervened in Samos to expel a Persian garrison (Dem. 15.9), they neatly replaced it with a cleruchy, shocking though it was to the Greek world (cf. Arist. *Rhet.* 1384b32–5), and at least one other cleruchy followed elsewhere (*GHI* 146). Finally, Chares, against whose methods Isocrates directed the oration *Concerning Peace* (Arist. *Rhet.* 1418a32), brutally intervened in Corcyra, a member of the Second Athenian Confederacy,[18] and caused such apprehension in the Aegean that Rhodes, Chios and

95

Byzantium, which were the heart of the Confederacy, revolted – a revolt that Demosthenes could describe as due to 'resentment at you recovering your *property*' (15.15). 'Possessions' is the constant theme from the 390s onwards (cf. Andocides 3.15), the profits of empire. Despite a period of enforced propriety from the King's Peace to the Satraps' Revolt, old habits of mind did not die.

Turning to the fifth-century Empire, one instantly remarks that, for good or ill, consideration of Thucydides is central. Quite apart from what various persons are represented in the *Histories* to have said, Thucydides plainly asserted that Athenian rule was greatly resented by the members of the Empire (2.8.4–5; 4.108.3–6; 8.2). What is equally plainly to be asserted is that Thucydides was not in any way hostile to imperialism. One empire might be better than another, and his admiration for the Athenian Empire led him to choose to include the Funeral Oration, that laudation of the imperial city, but in a broad sense he is imperialist. Human nature, which is a constant (1.22.4; 3.82.2), will always move men to seek to have power over others. And since empire for Athens is inevitably naval empire, the rowing class must have its say. So, inevitably, he accepts democracy, the system that best secures that men of political gifts, a rare breed, have a career open to their talents. It is far from sure therefore that Thucydides consorted with and heeded oligarchically-minded men only.[19]

It is a curious feature of the view of the Empire under discussion that it makes Thucydides a man who could not properly understand his own narrative. More than that, in the speech he wrote for Diodotus he expounded the very truth about the Empire (3.47), but must have failed to appreciate that it was the truth. So Thucydides, who is declared[20] mercifully to be 'an exceptionally truthful man and anything but a superficial observer', seems to have been unable to take in the meaning of his own narrative. Was that not stupid? De Ste Croix has read and understood, but not Thucydides, a curious conclusion.

So it would be well to test the evidence adduced from Thucydides. A key role is played by the account of the ending of resistance in Mytilene.[21] Thucydides' account is as follows:

> Salaethus . . . issued hoplite equipment to the people, as he intended to sally forth against the Athenians. When they got the hoplite weapons, they no longer heeded the magistrates, but banding together bade those in power bring out the

corn and distribute it to everyone or else they would, so they said, themselves do a deal with the Athenians and hand over the city.

(3.27.2f.)

This mutiny of the *dēmos* was treated by de Ste Croix as a sign of where their sympathies lay. Others would see nothing other than the straits of hunger to which the siege had reduced the city.[22] Diodotus was made by Thucydides to assert that the *dēmos* 'had no part in the revolt and when it got hold of hoplite weapons, willingly handed over the city' (3.47.3), whereas Cleon asserted the opposite (3.39.6):

Don't let the oligarchs take all the blame and let the *dēmos* off. For all men were equally involved in attacking you though it would have been possible for them to take your side and so now be again in the city. Instead, they thought it of more importance to share the danger along with the oligarchs and so they joined in the revolt.

The Athenians evidently agreed with Cleon since they voted for the death sentence on all adult male Mytilenaeans (3.36.2). This seemed, on reflection, 'savage and monstrous'; it was not said to be unjust. In view of Thucydides' narrative (at 3.27), Diodotus' statement is misleading; it was hunger, not loyalty, that moved the *dēmos*, and it was the oligarchic government, not the *dēmos*, that handed over the city. Since Mytilene was not a democracy, it could of course plausibly be said that the *dēmos* had no share in the decision to revolt, but very plainly, once the revolt had been decided on, the *dēmos* had fully supported it. There was a preparatory period when the harbours were being filled in, when walls were being built and ships constructed (3.2.2). Are we to suppose that this work was being done by 1,000 oligarchs without the aid, or even the cognisance, of the mass of Mytilenaeans? And during the year-long siege was it only the oligarchs who manned the walls and guarded the gates? It is all too probable that Cleon was right. Until the final breakdown of morale, when the military situation was well-nigh hopeless, the people at large must have been whole-heartedly behind the revolt. The case of Mytilene is not one where 'we find only the few hostile'.

The truth is that, in general, the evidence assembled by de Ste Croix does not prove as much as he would have it thought. Sparta had proclaimed that it would 'liberate Greece' (2.8.4). That could only be done by defeating Athens, and prudence must have made cities cautious about joining in the struggle themselves and risking Athenian punishment. Fine words had not saved the Mytilenaeans, and it would hardly be surprising if others were reluctant to risk a similar fate. When Brasidas did encourage Torone and Scione to seize their chance, the people of these cities paid a heavy price. *All* the women and children of Torone were sold into slavery and all the males captured, some 700 of them, were sent to Athens (5.3.4) to be dealt with as Athens chose.[23] In the case of Scione, the women and children were similarly treated, and the adult males slaughtered (5.32.1) as Cleon had persuaded the Athenians to order (4.122.6). It is not surprising that, until the Athenian disaster in Sicily, there were no more revolts and that there was general reluctance to anticipate the liberation which the destruction of Athens would bring.

  · Then, too, Sparta as liberator had proved both bloody and false; liberation from Athens proved to be enslavement to Sparta and the Spartan system. It is very remarkable that Brasidas either himself had so little confidence in how Sparta would behave or was so well aware of how Sparta was in general regarded, that before he set out from Sparta in 424 he bound the authorities of the city 'with the most solemn oaths that whomsoever I win over will be independent allies' (4.86.1, 88.1). That is very surprising. Spartiates had to do what the magistrates ordered, not vice versa. He must have been greatly apprehensive. It would not be surprising if Greeks in general tried to keep themselves free of the hug of the Spartan bear.

  Brasidas was made to assert to the Acanthians:

> I do not come to join in social strife. I do not think I would be bringing real freedom if I paid no heed to the ancestral constitution and subjected the majority to the few or the minority to all. That would be harsher than the empire of others ...
>
> (4.86.4f.)

The fear that revolt would 'subject the majority to the few' must have been a strong incentive to those who greatly feared their local oligarchs. But how greatly did men fear their own oligarchs? Perhaps in time Thucydides would have turned the remarks of Phrynichus which he recorded (8.48.5–7) into a speech which would have excited debate as to whose views were being represented. However, as it is, it seems safe to attribute it all to Phrynichus. So here is an independent opinion that whatever constitution a city had it would prefer liberty to being part of the empire and under a democracy. The suspicion arises that the strife between the few and the many, so vividly delineated by Thucydides (3.82–3), did not completely dominate the political life of Greece. Mytilene plainly had in 428 an oligarchic constitution, yet a leading Athenian politician could assert and as has been argued, correctly assert, that the *dēmos* was as much involved in the revolt as the ruling oligarchs (3.39.6). Of course, where a democracy had to fear Spartan intervention if it revolted from Athens, common prudence would advise putting up with Athens. If one calls that 'popularity', the Athenian Empire was 'popular' – but that is not what most people mean by the word. If one calls it 'loyalty', it was the loyalty of prudent self-interest.

Nor is it evidence of genuine unforced loyalty to Athens that few of the allied contingents in Demosthenes' part of the army in Sicily chose to accept the Syracusan offer of liberty for those who chose to abandon the Athenians (7.82.1).[24] The Dorian Syracusans were a bloody lot, as they were shortly to demonstrate but as was only to be expected, and it may have seemed better to stay with the Athenians. That may have seemed to offer a more likely way of returning to their home states. Similarly, Samos is treated as 'the jewel in the crown', a case of conspicuous loyalty (ML 94). No other state, as far as is known, received a reward so striking as the grant of Athenian citizenship, but Samos had stayed loyal after the battle of Aegospotami, it would seem (cf. ll. 25f.), and Samos alone. Why was Samos so much on her own? One notes that the leaders of the *dēmos* had the blood of 200 Samians on their hands and that there were 400 others in exile awaiting the chance of revenge (8.21). So those in power had no option but to stay loyal to Athens. Also Samos had so constantly been used as a naval base[25] that the Athenian navy must have contributed to prosperity. However, Samos did stand by Athens in her blackest hour, and one would be much impressed if the island's record in the fourth century had continued to manifest more devotion to Athens than it actually did.

All in all, the evidence adduced by de Ste Croix does not prove as much as he supposes. If 'popularity' means that the alternatives to Athenian rule were nastier and so the subject states acquiesced, to say that the Athenian Empire was popular is not saying much.

It is by no means probable that the institutions of the Athenian Empire inclined the subject cities to anything other than resentment, though that resentment may not have been widespread. It is unclear how far the tribute impinged on the lives of most individuals. Rich individuals in each state were appointed to collect the tribute but, to judge by a fragment of Antiphon's speech *On the Samothracians' Tribute*, it may have been a land tax payable by all land-holders, a numerous enough class. Even so, it may well have been the case that the tribute was not large enough to be deeply resented.[26] Similarly with the interference of the Imperial power in the administration of the law in subject cities. As already remarked,[27] the system had its dark side, namely the reference to Athens of cases involving penalties of death, exile, confiscation of property or loss of civil rights. The evidence is very unsatisfactory,[28] but it would seem that, just as within Athens itself the great political trials (e.g. the trial of Pericles in 430 (2.65.3) or the trial in 424 of the generals who had assented to the making of the Peace of Gela (4.65.3)) were decided not on considerations of justice but in accordance with the interests of the Athenian *dēmos*,[29] so too in the Empire at large the conduct in office of leading citizens was assessed by Athenian courts in terms of their usefulness to Athens. This was greatly to Athens's interest. It made sure that men who were out of sympathy with the Athenian *dēmos* had to keep out of politics, for if anyone unsuitable aspired to office, a zealous opponent could easily accuse him of an offence that carried a penalty of death or exile or loss of civil rights and he could be eliminated. No doubt there were many so exiled. There was a band of Thasian exiles living in Peloponnesian states in 411 (8.64.4) and there is no reason to think Thasos unique; charges of 'betraying the Thraceward province' (Ar. *Wasps* 287) or of 'taking the side of Brasidas' (*Peace* 639) could easily catch 'the prosperous and the rich' and have them subjected to the same fate as Dorieus of Rhodes who had, under sentence of death, to go into exile, as had his kinsmen likewise (Xen. *Hell.* 1.5.19; Paus. 6.7.2–6).[30] In this way, dissidence was stifled and a 'correct' or (that favourite word) 'progressive' attitude rewarded. As long as those in power did what suited Athens, they were secure from serious attack in their own courts, for they could appeal[31] to Athens with confident expectation that no Athenian court would find against them. Thus, Athenian interference in the jurisdiction of subject states was a powerful instrument of empire. It may not, however, have been widely resented. Just as men like Antiphon and the young Plato at Athens avoiding the limelight of politics were very much a minority, those throughout the Empire most affected by this extension of 'political' justice may have been comparatively few.[32]

How far the mass of citizens in subject states were affected by military service is unclear. Those members of allied states who rowed in Athenian ships would have been glad to be employed as mercenaries, but in so far as subject states were obliged to furnish men for Athens, it can hardly have been a source of 'popularity'. In small communities, death in Athens' service must have caused widespread grief and resentment. But it is remarkable how rarely the allies are mentioned by Thucydides in his account of operations in the Archidamian War. So probably enough there were not a great number of casualties among contingents of allies after the cessation of war with Persia, and one must not think of military service being more than an irritant.[33]

But irritants do irritate, and there were plenty of others. According to our text of the Aristotelian *Athēnaiōn Politeia*, there were 700 'overseas officials' (24.3), a figure one hesitates to trust since precisely the same figure is given in the preceding line for 'home officials',[34] but it is unlikely to be much too large. There were over 200 cities,[35] and although the evidence for garrisons and garrison commanders, for 'overseas magistrates' (*IG* 13 156), for the *episkopoi* (who appear to have moved around, like bishops round a diocese), and for heralds and the like, is all very scattered and incomplete,[36] there is sufficient to make plain that all the cities of the Empire were under the supervision of some Athenian official. In the Clinias Decree (ML 46), probably correctly dated to before the battle of Coronea (447/6), it seems that all the cities of the Empire either had an Athenian *archōn* or were under the supervision of an *episkopos*.[37] Of course, at that date there may have been comparatively few cities with Athenian *archontes*; if Potidaea was still receiving annual magistrates from its metropolis, Corinth (1.56.2), as late as 432, there were probably many free cities, and it is not possible to say how much Imperial officers were making themselves felt at different times in the Empire's history. But any sort of restrictions must have been irksome, and there is an indication of how far things had gone by the 430s. If cities found it expedient to assess themselves tribute and if in some cases individual citizens undertook to pay for their cities, Athenian control of maritime traffic, to which the Old Oligarch alludes (2.12), must have been comprehensive. 'Protection rackets' do not make the 'protectors' popular and it would not have been only the rich in the allied cities who would have felt resentment. Inevitably, the cost to them would have been passed on to their citizens. If it was necessary to pay a tithe on cargoes brought through the Hellespont (ML 65 34–41, 58 A 7), prices would be at least that much greater. Such pin-pricks certainly stung.

Some things were more than pin-pricks, none more so perhaps than the take-over of allied land. The evidence for cleruchies is not good and it is impossible to say in how many states they were established.[38] That they were felt to be an evil is plain from Isocrates' bland words on the subject (4.107) and from the fact that, in 377, Athens passed a law formally abandoning any claims to past (or aspirations to future) cleruchies, as the Decree of Aristotle (*GHI* 123) shows. But this decree of March 377 is much wider in scope. Not only does it promise that there will be no more cleruchies, but it forbids any land-holdings by Athenian citizens in the territory of members of the new league. Again, the evidence is scrappy, to be found largely in the so-called Attic *stēlai* which record the sale in 414 of the confiscated property of the Profaners of the Mysteries and the Hermocopids (ML 79),[39] but it is suggestive – one case particularly so. An Athenian owned an estate in Thasos (B 55); since there is no reason to suppose that Thasos, which had been dealt with after revolt in the mid-460s, had ever received a cleruchy, this estate had in all likelihood been acquired by private initiative. Indeed, when Andocides in 392 (3.15) alluded to the fifth-century Empire, he spoke of 'the colonies and the properties (*engtēmata*) and the loans (*chrea*)'. That is, there was a considerable amount of investment in the cities of the Empire and that is why, in Xenophon, we encounter men who have lost their overseas property (*Symposium* 4.31; *Memorabilia* 3.8.1). Such landlords, whether absent or present,[40] are not likely to have endeared Athens to the citizens of the subject states, and the law of 377 shows it.

> From the archonship of Nausinicus (i.e. 378/7) it is not to be possible for any Athenian, either privately or publicly, to acquire within the territories of the allies either a house or an estate, whether by purchase or by mortgage or in any other way, and if anyone buys or acquires or controls in any way such real estate, any ally who so chooses may denounce him to the council of the allies . . .
>
> (*GHI* 123 35–44)

Such things could hardly have endeared Athens. Nor would it be only those whose land had been taken over who would have resented the loss. Not only do debtors not love their creditors, but also nobody wants to have the best land of his city exploited by citizens of another.

It is otiose to go further. In a world where freedom was so highly valued, the Athenian Empire, excellent as it was and highly worthy of a Funeral Oration, could not have been in any sense popular. All its institutions, all its methods of stopping the allied states getting their independence must have been resented.

The history of the fourth century says the same. In 378, Athens founded the Second Athenian Confederacy. Spartan power had, since the end of the Peloponnesian War, been exercised most bloodily and defence was needed. The fullest extent of the Confederacy was 75 cities, of which the names of about 50 are known to us.[41] Of these 50, eight were mainland or western Greek cities which were never included in the fifth-century Empire. If the same ratio applied to the whole 75, something like 50 members of the fifth-century Empire joined the fourth-century Confederacy. Where were the 90 and nine? They did not rush back. Where was Samos, the jewel in the crown?

The Confederacy had a faltering beginning. In the first year of its existence a mere half-dozen joined (including Thebes which had not belonged to the fifth-century Empire) and it was only after Athens had passed the law promising that there would be no more public or private Athenian occupation of members' territory that the Confederacy began to grow, and even then only slowly.[42] Owing to the condition of the stone recording the Decree of Aristotle to which names of states joining the Confederacy were added, one cannot be sure, but it looks as if no more than 23 states joined before Athens so re-established herself in the Peace of 375 that there was a rush of 29 new states in the autumn. There was clearly advantage in securing the guarantees, for what they were worth, of freedom from the evils of the fifth-century Empire. In this way, the fourth century passed judgement on the fifth.

When in 380 Isocrates in his *Panegyric Oration* spoke of the Athenian Empire (§§100–19), the *apologia* is comic:

> Some declare against us that when we took over the Empire, we became responsible for many evils for the Greeks, and they cite against us the enslavement of the Melians and the destruction of the Scionians, but I think first that it is no proof that our empire was bad, if some of those who made war against us are shown to have been severely punished . . .

Melos was not at war with Athens when she was attacked in 416; whatever she had done during the Archidamian War was not relevant during the Peace of Nicias.[43] Scione, of course, did revolt (4.120.1) and if revolt was war, she was at war with Athens. In both cases the same punishment was meted out, namely the execution of all adult males and the enslavement of all women and children (5.32.1, 116.4). Thucydides in neither case chose to recite the arguments of the Mytilene debate; frightfulness and terror had become the normal way. Isocrates elsewhere (12.63–6) sought to excuse Athens by declaring that whatever Athens had done, Sparta had done worse. Whatever the truth of that, in no sense could Athenian actions have engendered other than hatred, that abiding hatred to which Isocrates' shabby arguments testify. What Athens was capable of, she showed in the vote at the first Mytilene debate, and realised in her treatment of the captives of Torone, Scione and Melos. To speak of such a power being popular can hardly be right. Empire was empire, in some degree a reign of terror.

In the last analysis, the Athenian Empire depended on Athens' naval power and that is why Pericles was so emphatic about the maintenance of it (2.13.2, 2.65.7). There were, of course, all the ancillary institutions like garrisons, *archontes* and so on. One is of especial interest: the *proxenoi*, a well-established institution in the Greek world, but one of peculiar usefulness. It is not attested that there was a *proxenos* of Athens in every city, but it is probable that there was at least one and perhaps several in large states.[44] Whereas in general there was no necessity that a *proxenos* did any more than represent the interests of another state and accommodate visiting envoys,[45] in the case of the Athenian Empire they seem to have more actively supported Athens by informing on suspicious developments. This, at any rate, is what happened at Mytilene in 428 (3.2.3), and the decree in honour of Oeniades of Sciathus (ML 90) suggests that exceptional services could earn a man the title. He had shown himself 'a good man with regard to the city of the Athenians and eager to do what good he can . . . ', a useful tool of empire and a species to be protected. Thus, when the *episkopos* arrives in 'Cloudcuckooland', his first demand is 'Where are the *proxenoi* (Ar. *Birds* 1021)?', as if they are Athens's political agents,[46] and one cannot help wondering how important the part individuals played in the continuance of empire was.

In a celebrated passage of Plato's *Seventh Epistle* (331d–2d), Dionysius' failure to secure his power by 'acquiring faithful friends

and companions' is contrasted first with Darius I's success in his use
and treatment of the six other conspirators in the murder of
Smerdis and the rule of himself, and second, with the Athenians
preserving their Empire for 70 years 'by having acquired friends in
each city'. This has been abruptly dismissed.[47] 'Since Plato gives this
as the one sufficient reason, it will hardly be maintained that he is
merely referring to a handful of pro-Athenian individuals of note,
such as those who received Athenian *proxenia* and were evidently
expected to act as Athenian watchdogs.' If this comment were
correct, Plato could hardly have made himself less clear. Could he
really have expected his readers to suppose that a people in control
of its state, a *dēmos* in a democracy, was comparable to the seven
eminent Persians or to the handful of 'friends and companions'
whom Dionysius should have used as partners in power? It would
seem rather that Plato certainly was thinking of the role of 'pro-
Athenians of note' in the preservation of Athenian power. He may
have been wrong but that is what he appears to say.

There are signs that Plato was on the right lines. Methymna had
a long record of loyalty to Athens. In 428, the city declined to join
in the revolt of Lesbos (3.2.1, 5.1) and was still to be classed as
'autonomous, ship-contributing' in 415 (6.85.2; 7.57.5). She joined
the general revolt in 412 (8.22.2) when a Peloponnesian force sailed
in, but was quickly recovered (8.23). The city was, for whatever
reason, reliable. It is noteworthy, however, that when it was captured
in 406 by the Spartan nauarch, Callicratidas, Xenophon recorded
the event (*Hell.* 1.6.13) thus: 'Since the Methymnians were not
willing to come over but there was an Athenian garrison and those
in control of the government were supporters of Athens, he
attacked and captured the city by force.' If the Methymnians 'were
not willing', what was the point of the remark about 'those in
control'? It is at least to be suspected that it was this group of
individuals that really counted. Likewise with Chios, which appears
to have been an oligarchy of some sort. Apart from arousing
Athenian suspicions in 425/4 by erecting 'the new wall' (4.51), Chios
remained loyal until 412, most notably at the time of the Samian
Revolt (1.116), when a danger (cf. 8.76.4) might have turned into a
disaster if the Chians had not sided with Athens. At that time Chios
was presumably under the control of Ion and similar friends of
Athens just as the party of Tydeus had to be put to death in 412/11
for their support for Athens (8.38.3). The policy of this oligarchical
state depended on the politics of the controlling group, which

remained pro-Athenian until the general upheaval of 412. Indeed, one may be sceptical about these labels 'oligarchic' and 'democratic'. Politicians then, as always, knew on which side their bread was buttered. In 412 there occurred in Samos 'the uprising by the *dēmos* against those in power (*hoi dynatoi*), resulting in the murder of the two hundred most powerful citizens, the exiling of four hundred others and the seizure of their land and houses' (8.21). Within a year 'the most powerful of the Samians' (8.63.3) were being urged by the Athenian of the hour, Pisander, to try and turn Samos into an oligarchy. He succeeded, for shortly afterwards 'those of the Samians who had formerly risen up against those in power and being a *dēmos* changed again' and so there were 'about three hundred who joined in conspiracy and intended to attack the rest on the grounds that they were a *dēmos*' (8.73.2). The titles did not mean much. It was the politicians who counted. Perhaps Plato was right and Athens kept her empire in part because it was to the interest of politicians that the Empire should be kept. Certainly, Plato's remark should not be used to corroborate the view that in the Athenian Empire 'the ruling city relied very much on the support of the lower classes in the ruling city'.

As to the attitude of 'the ordinary citizens', Phrynichus gave his opinion. 'They will not wish to be subject, whether under oligarchy or democracy, rather than to be free under whichever system they happen to live' (8.48.5). This seems to be much the same as the view of Thucydides who, despite having written his essay on *stasis* (3.82–3), judged that 'the sympathies of mankind were largely on the side of the Spartans, especially since they proclaimed that they were liberating Greece, and every individual and every city . . .' and so on (2.8.4). The argument adduced for thinking him mistaken is not valid. Empire is always empire. Only where the subject peoples are inspired by awe of what seems a more advanced and superior civilisation do they put up with subjection and, even then, not permanently. That was not how the rest of the Greeks viewed Athens, and they simply wanted freedom.

APPENDIX 1

A note on the so-called 'Financial Decrees' of Callias, *IG* 1³ 52 (= ML 58)

Of the two decrees cut by the same hand[1] on the two sides of the one slab of stone, it would appear that Decree A, the one with the full prescript and giving the name of the proposer Callias, was prior to Decree B, the one with a very scrappily preserved prescript. In A, there is provision for establishing for the first time[2] a board of Treasurers of the Other Gods (l.13 *tamias de apokuameue[n]*) who are to look after the money of these gods in the Opisthodomos, whereas in the second it is prescribed exactly where in the Opisthodomos the treasures of the Other Gods and the treasures of Athena are to be kept – clearly, a later provision. This does not mean that both decrees could not have been proposed to the People on the same day, for they may have been put before the Council at different meetings, but put before the People at the same assembly. Indeed, the demonstration by Kallet-Marx,[3] following Pritchett,[4] of how insecurely based is the general opinion that B bore the same prescript as A, makes it less incredible that both decrees were presented on the same day, for if there was a different proposer it is less surprising that the dative plural should be differently spelt in the two decrees, that B should use the term *akropolis* (l.11) which A does not (ll. 4, 15, 21, 30), that A should speak of *hoi theoi* and B of *hoi alloi theoi*. So A is prior to B, but not necessarily by more than a few days. (One might compare the two decrees concerning Chalcis (ML 52) presented to the People on the same day; the decree of Antikles prescribes what sort of oath is to be sworn and the decree of Diognetos spells it out, presumably at a later meeting of the Council.)

Decree B was passed in the first year of a Panathenaic quadrennium (cf. l.25). According to Kallet-Marx, it cannot be earlier than 430–29, for she insists that Decree A must come after the situation envisaged in Thuc. 2.13.3–5. There Pericles, enumerating Athens's resources for fighting a war, seems to contrast the 6,000 talents on the Acropolis with *ta ek tōn allōn hierōn chrēmata*, for which he does not give a figure. So she presumes that the outlying treasures had not yet been concentrated and counted. But *ta ek tōn allōn hierōn* are not *en tois hierois* (to quote Decree A l. 19). Taken literally, it shows where the treasures have come from; i.e. they have already been moved. These treasures may well no less be on the Acropolis than the gold plates attached to the statue in the Parthenon which he proceeds to mention, and the reason why Pericles did not give a total for the wealth belonging to the Other Gods may be not that it had not yet been counted and totalled, but that at that stage, before the full cost of the revolt of Potidaea (2.70.2) had been realised, Pericles thought the resources of Athena would suffice for his purposes.[5] Alternatively, Thucydides may simply have failed to record it. So Kallet-Marx's inference from 2.13.5 is not as sure as she supposes, and in any case her theory suffers from a not inconsiderable disqualification. Thucydides has Pericles make his speech when the Peloponnesians were 'assembling at the Isthmus and were on their way' (2.13.1) and this would seem far too late for the Athenians not to have taken the precautions provided for in Decree A. They had known for a good part of a year that the Peloponnesian League had voted for war (1.125), and it must have been evident through diplomatic exchanges (1.126.1) that there would in all likelihood be war. The very eve of the invasion was far too late.

It is unhappy indeed that Decree B is in such a state that we are prevented from knowing what the opening clauses were about, but the supplementation of *PRO* in lines 3 and 9 seems likely enough, and one can with reasonable confidence assert that the first part of the decree was a proposal that concerned the Propylaea. In line 4 one finds: . . .] *ethēi pantelōs* and one automatically thinks of the fragment of the antiquarian Heliodorus (*FGH* 373 F1) edited by Harpocration s.v. *Propylaia tauta . . . En etesi men gar e´ panteōs exepoiēthē* –.[6] Did the opening of Decree B order the 'completion', which was in fact the curtailment, of the Propylaea? And did it in line 9 require 'the architect of the Propylaea' to produce 'a drawing' (a *gramma*, of which only *MA* remains for us to read) of the work in its curtailed shape? Certainly one would expect 'the Acropolis' (l. 5) to be tidied up and a sum set aside for building maintenance (ll. 7, 11, 15) when the original plans were being abandoned.

Heliodorus would seem to have been a later Hellenistic writer,[7] but if he did indeed fill 15 books on the monuments of Athens, he had time and need for careful research and it would be no surprise if his researches had included inscriptions touching the Propylaea. There seems no reason why his 'in five years' should not be accepted (and the same figure is found in Plutarch *Pericles* 13.12). That means that the building was 'completed' in 433/2 and the decision to complete it by curtailing it could have been taken late in the Panathenaic year 434/3.

If Decree B was passed in 430/29 or in the first year of some later Panathenaic quadrennium, it was concerned merely to tidy up the Acropolis, including the Opisthodomos where, for some time, the Treasurers of Athena and the Treasurers of the Other Gods must have been muddling along – a situation one would hardly expect to have lasted more than a very short time. But if, as is to be suspected, the decree was the instrument of cutting short the work on the Propylaea, it must have been passed in 434/3.

Supposing then that Decree B belongs to 434/3, where is Decree A to be placed? If the two decrees cannot be shown to have been passed on the same day, Decree A could in theory belong to any year after the completion of the Parthenon,[8] but the objection made by many[9] (that a war-budget before the Corcyra debate would make Thucydides' report of it misleading) urges one to inquire whether both decrees can be set in the period between the debate and the end of the Panathenaic year, 434/3.

There is no suggestion in Decree A that the outlying treasures are to be assembled only when the new board of Treasurers has been chosen by lot, and there is no suggestion that the appointment of Treasurers is to be delayed until the appointment of the rest of the magistrates. But when did that occur? ML (p. 158) rightly places it 'shortly before the elections', but add '(? in the spring)'. There is no precise evidence as to when exactly the elections were held, but the *dokimasia* of archons could be very late in the civil year; the eponymous archon of 382/1 was under inquiry on the second to last day of the year, and such lateness was not without precedent (Lysias 26.6–8), even though it would seem that the man under scrutiny had contrived to delay the process.[10] How much time was allowed for the *dokimasia*? Hansen[11] envisages that 'it must have taken the Council several days and a section of the court several weeks to get through' but, as he remarks, 'in most cases it was a mere routine'. So far from it being a case of 'only a few minutes per candidate' it is far more likely that it was a case of 'only a few minutes per list' for most of the minor magistracies. It is therefore not unreasonable to posit that the new board of Treasurers of the Other Gods was chosen by lot in the last month of the civil year, Scirophorion, and fairly late at that.[12]

When was the Corcyra debate? The first squadron sent to Corcyra drew money from the Treasurers of Athena on the thirteenth day of the first prytany of the conciliar year of 433/2 (ML 61). According to the calculations of Meritt,[13] the conciliar year 433/2 did not begin until the seventh day of the civil year 433/2. How long an interval elapsed between the debate and the first squadron drawing money? Thucydides says that the despatch of the ships was 'not long after' the debate and the departure of the Corinthians (1.45.1). 'Not long after' is a subjective term. Athens may have waited at least until she ascertained Corinthian intentions and even proceeded at a leisurely pace if she knew that Corinth was calling on others to assist her (1.46.1). If 'not long after' were a full month, it could well have been the case that Decree A was passed in the course of 434/3 after the Athenians had made their fateful decision about Corcyra. Decree B could have followed at no great interval, as indeed one would expect, for once the new board of Treasurers had begun to share the Opisthodomos with the Treasurers of Athena, the ruling of B ll. 23–5 would have been quickly needed (if, indeed, it had not been made in advance).

There are many uncertainties. Suffice it to say that if Decree B belongs to 434/3, Decree A need not be placed before the Corcyra debate and, in view of the tone of that debate as reported by Thucydides, one may reject the notion that Athens passed a war-budget before she responded to the Corcyran appeal.

APPENDIX 2

The Megara Decrees of Plutarch, *Pericles* 30

Plutarch, *Pericles* 29 records *the* Megarian Decree but, in the following chapter, records two further decrees. First, a decree of Pericles (§2) which he describes as 'reasonable and courteous', providing for a herald (*kēryx*) to be sent to both Sparta and Megara to denounce the Megarians; second, after this herald, Anthemocritus, had been murdered by the Megarians, a decree of Charinus (§3) containing four provisions:

1 that there should be enmity without truces and without heralds (*aspondon kai akērykton echthran*);
2 that whoever (of the Megarians) sets foot on Attica should be punished with death;
3 that whenever the generals swear the traditional oath, they should swear in addition that they will invade Megara twice every year;
4 that Anthemocritus should be buried by 'the Thriasian Gates'.

What is the relationship of these two decrees to *the* Megara Decree?

The Megara Decree was passed before the meetings in Sparta of 432/1 recorded by Thucydides, perhaps in autumn 432. De Ste Croix,[1] who is dismissive of the chronological sequence of Plutarch's narrative, is persuaded that the 'courteous and reasonable' decree of Pericles must have preceded *the* Megara Decree because he finds it an unacceptable order for courtesy and reasonableness to come after the abrupt and discourteous exclusion decree. This ordering is rightly rejected by Brunt:[2] 'the fact that the herald was to go to Sparta as well as Megara makes it natural to put his mission after the time when the Spartans had taken up the

Megarian cause.' To that consideration, it may be added that it would have been a queer opening of negotiations to send a *herald*[3] denouncing the conduct of Megara and to send him not only to Megara, but also to Sparta. Surely the normal embassy would have been more appropriate? As to whether the 'courteous and reasonable' decree must come first, a man may 'smile and smile and be a villain', and if Pericles chose to coat a sour announcement with sweet words[4] when his earlier decree was blunt, there may be an explanation, to wit that what Plutarch calls *dikaiologia* (30.3), and we would call 'legalities', was no part of the original measure, that it was only when the Spartans, seeing the Megara Decree as the plainest case (cf. *malista ge pantōn kai endēlotata* 1.139.1), came demanding its repeal that Pericles knocked them back with the *dikaiologia* about sacred land and runaway slaves (1.139.2). The 'courteous and reasonable' language of his second decree was part of it. So Plutarch is not so lightly to be dismissed. His order of decrees is correct.

The Charinus decree provided for the burial of the murdered herald. So it came last, but when exactly? The decree ordered generals to swear that they would invade Megara twice every year, and Thucydides recorded (2.31) the full-scale invasion led by Pericles in autumn 431, adding that there were 'further invasions thereafter during the war ... until Nisaea was taken by the Athenians.' At 4.66.1, introducing the operations that resulted in the capture of Nisaea, he remarked that the Megarians in the city had been 'having a hard time of it with the Athenians constantly twice a year invading the land in full force.' Curiously, he makes nothing of these invasions,[5] but clearly they are the effect of the Charinus decree. But when was it passed? The first generals to be bound by the addition to the generals' oath must have been those who came into office at the start of 431/0, and the invasion of autumn 431 is the first possible, but that does not help us to know when exactly the Charinus decree was passed.

According to the *Letter of Philip* ([Dem.] 12.4) the murder of Anthemocritus led the Athenians to exclude the Megarians from the Mysteries. His statue, as ordered by the decree of Charinus, was placed at the Thriasian Gates (later known as the Dipylon), the start of the route to Eleusis. Pausanias (1.36.3) says that those going to Eleusis by the Sacred Way passed the memorial.[6] The first invasion of Megara was according to Thucydides (2.31.1) in the autumn, i.e. just about the time when the Greater Mysteries were celebrated in the month of Boedromion.[7] These facts led me to propose that Anthemocritus was one of the heralds that went out twice a year to proclaim the Sacred Truce, for the Greater and Lesser Mysteries, that his murder excited Charinus to propose his decree shortly after the Lesser Mysteries of 431, that the twice annual invasions were made either shortly before or shortly after the Mysteries.[8] The hypothesis was pronounced by de Ste Croix 'unacceptable'.[9] I still hold it and will try again.

We are informed about the truce-making heralds (*spondophoroi*) principally by what Aeschines says about the events of 346; 'the Phocians were the only Greeks who did not make a truce with the *spondophoroi* who were proclaiming the truce for the Mysteries' (Aeschin. 2.133). (Athens was, at that time, an ally of Phocis and of Sparta in the Sacred War against, principally, Thebes and Thessaly. So the *spondophoroi* must, it would seem, have gone to friend and foe alike.) We meet them also in an inscription of 367 (*GHI* 137). Two of those who had in that year proclaimed the truce for the Mysteries to the Aetolian *koinon* which had accepted it, had been subsequently arrested by one of the peoples of Aetolia, and a herald was sent to the *koinon* to demand their release. That is effectively all we know, but one cannot help wondering whether Anthemocritus was a *spondophoros*. Such an idea de Ste Croix politely declares 'worthless', because he can see no reason why Athens should 'make an exception in 431 not merely of Megara but of Sparta which had offended in no way the Two Goddesses.' But of course there was a very good reason, if de Ste Croix is wrong in supposing that the 'reasonable and courteous' decree preceded *the* Megara Decree. If the order of decrees was as Plutarch gives it, by the time the 'reasonable and courteous' decree was passed, Sparta had supported Megara in her pretended wrong-doing and was to be joined with Megara in exclusion from the Mysteries.[10]

If Anthemocritus was one of the *spondophoroi* for the Lesser Mysteries of 431, the decree of Charinus may belong to the assembly held in the theatre of Dionysus at the end of the festival when impieties connected with the festival were dealt with (Dem. 21.9).[11] One would certainly expect the decision about where Anthemocritus was to be buried to be taken at no great interval after his death and the provisions of Charinus' decree seem to be very apt when considered in relation to the Dionysia. There is to be 'enmity' (*echthra*) 'without truce' (i.e. Megara will not be able to share in the truce for the Mysteries) and 'without herald' (i.e. no *spondophoros* will go to Megara), and if any Megarian should be found attempting to attend the Mysteries, he is to be punished with death.[12] The Megarians are to be punished with spring and autumn invasions roughly at the time of the Mysteries, and Anthemocritus is to have an honoured place of burial which all Athenians who attend the ceremony will pass.

The hypothesis cannot be proved, but also it cannot be disproved. What is important is that the order of decrees given by Plutarch be accepted as the right one. The origin of the Megara Decree was not necessarily anything to do with Megarians encroaching on sacred land.

APPENDIX 3

Military service in the Athenian Empire[1]

The starting point must be Thucydides' listing of the allies involved in the Sicilian Expedition (7.57), since forces were assembled there from every source on which Athens could draw. The fleet was as large as any Athens had ever dispatched (6.31.2, 43) but, more than that, the reinforcements which Demosthenes took out in 413 seem to have scraped the bucket. The Athenians 'decree the sending of a further force, both naval and land, consisting of Athenians off the muster-roll (*ek katalogou*) and of the allies' (7.16.1). Demosthenes prepared for the departure in the spring, 'sending to the allies for troops (*stratian*) and getting ready in Athens both money and ships and hoplites' (17.1). At the beginning of spring the Athenians despatched him with 60 Athenian and five Chian ships; and 'off the muster-roll 1,200 Athenian hoplites, and of men from the islands (*nēsiōtōn*) as many as it was possible to use from each place, and having provided from the other subject allies whatever they had suitable for the war' (7.20.2).

Evidently, military service involved both service in the army and in the navy. In the armada of 415, there were 2,200 Athenian hoplites and, it would appear, 2,150 hoplites from the subject allies (6.43). This is no surprise since Thucydides, listing the allies of Athens in 431 (2.9.4f.), remarked that the Chians, Lesbians and Corcyrans provided naval forces 'but the rest infantry (*pezon*) and money'. In fact, through the whole history of the Delian league, allied military service was not confined to providing and manning ships. At the battle of Tanagra in 457 Athenians fought 'in full force' (*pandēmei*), but the total army was 14,000 (1.107.5), a figure which, even allowing for the 1,000 Argives present, is possibly twice as large as the Athenian army 'in full force'.[2] So 'the other allies' that Thucydides speaks of were present in large numbers, and it is clear that they were from member states of the Delian League. The epigram on the shield offered up to Zeus at Olympia (ML 36, Paus. 5.10.4) spoke of victory over 'Argives, Athenians and Ionians', which was presumably Peloponnesian shorthand for the Delian League. The casualty lists similarly record allied deaths. The dating is insecure, but a list judged to belong to 464 records Madytian and Byzantian casualties (*The Athenian Agora* XVII 1 ll. 34 and 118) and other lists, to judge by the names, record the deaths of non-Athenians (ibid. 8, 9).[3]

It would seem wholly unlikely that military service was not on a regulated basis, though very little positive can be said. Unlimited liability would have been quite unacceptable in the first three decades, when one might guess that the total of all the allied contingents matched the Athenian, indeed that the phrase *apo tou isou* (1.99.2, 3.10.4) meant literally equal contributions by Athens on the one hand and the allies as a whole on the other.[4] By 431 such parity was long forgotten, but some sort of regular service is implied by Thucydides' remark about the 10 Mytilenian ships which were seized by the Athenians at the start of the Mytilene revolt (3.3.4) – 'they happened to be there on service (*boēthoi*) in accordance with the role of ally (*kata to xymmachikon*)' – or, perhaps, 'in accordance with their obligation as allies' – and the same has been suspected for 'the seven ships of the Chians' found operating with the Athenians in 412 (8.10.3, 15.2). Some sort of system is to be presumed, but we are in no position to discern it.

It must also be remarked that for much of the time, to judge by what Thucydides records of the Archidamian War, Athens chose not to use the allies. The greatest expedition (cf. 6.31.2) was the large force sent round the Peloponnese in 430 (2.56.2), and it included not only Chian and Lesbian ships, but also allied land-troops.[5] However, the large expeditions of 431 (2.23.2, 31.2) seem to have involved no allies at all, despite the fact that the Athenians were 'collecting allies' (2.17.4), and on numerous subsequent occasions there is no sign of either allied ships or allied land-forces being involved. The notable exception is in later 425 when Milesians, Andrians and Carystians were included in the force attacking Corinthian territory (4.42.1) and in the early part of 424 when 'of the allies Milesians and certain others' (4.53.1) were involved in the assault on Cythera. Most surprisingly there were '2,000 Milesian hoplites' (4.54.1), matching the 2,000 Athenian hoplites. But for the rest, the allies seem not to have been used regularly. Of course, allied ships may have been used routinely on such duties as the guard of the Hellespont, of the very existence of which we would have no inkling were it not for the Methone Decree of 426/5 (ML 65 l. 39) and the squadron commanded in 424 by one of the two generals in charge of 'the Thracian area' (*ta epi Thrāikēs* 4.104.4f.), Thucydides himself. Certainly, strategic considerations dictated that there be such ready forces, as much in the fifth century as in the fourth; the Etesian winds were a constant in Aegean naval strategy.[6] There is, however, no reason to suspect that Thucydides made a habit of omitting to notice the share of the allies in the expeditions he recorded, and clearly the allies were employed very much less than the Athenians themselves. The burden of military service was probably not great.

Yet the allies did serve. 'A large number of the allies' joined the Athenian forces attacking Potidaea in 432 (1.61.4; cf. 62.4), including Sermylians (1.65.2). In 430, the force sent to raise money in Lycia was 'an army of the Athenians from the ships and of the allies' (2.69.2); i.e. the allies were land-troops. In 428, allies were summoned to help deal with the Mytilene Revolt (3.5.1, 6.1), as also in 428 the force sent to Mende included 'others of the local (*autothen*) allies' (4.129.2), and in 422 Cleon's army in Thrace had in it more allies than Athenians (5.2.1).

An explanation may be proposed. In the Brea Decree of the mid-440s (ML 49) the clause occurs: 'And if anyone attacks the territory of the colonists, the cities are to lend military aid as quickly as possible in accordance with the regulations (*syngraphai*) which were established in the secretaryship of ... concerning the cities in the Thracian area' (ll. 13–17). Evidently, there was a system of military aid within the Thracian area of the Empire, and this explains the role of the allies including the Sermylians in 432, of 'the local allies' in 428, and of the preponderance of allies in Cleon's army in 422. Did similar systems of regional defence apply elsewhere? Such a theory could perhaps explain the role of the allies in the Mytilene Revolt.[7]

It is striking that 'the islanders' should have such a prominent part in the Sicilian Expedition. When Athens was scraping the bucket to send as ample reinforcements with Demosthenes as she could muster, why were 'the islanders' singled out for special service or for special mention (7.20.2)? It is true that having said they sent 'as many islanders as it was possible to use from each place', Thucydides added 'having provided from the other subject allies whatever they had suitable for the war', but that would be a very odd expression if the other subject allies were in the same condition as the islanders and having to send troops. It is much more probable that Thucydides is referring to troops like the slingers and javelineers Demosthenes assembled from Acarnania (7.31.5) or the Thracian peltasts who arrived too late (7.27.1), mercenaries all, as were, no doubt, the 80 Cretan archers and the 700 Rhodian slingers[8] whom Nicias had taken with him (6.43; cf. 6.25.2), or the peltasts from Aenus (cf. 7.57.5, 4.28.4). So why were the islanders singled out by the Athenians in 413 in this way? Likewise, one wonders why did Gylippus and the Syracusans call on the islanders in particular to abandon Demosthenes (7.82.1).

The answer suggested is that mainland members of the Empire had been covered by the sort of *syngraphai* we hear of in the Brea Decree, one set for Thrace, as the Brea Decree shows, exemplified perhaps in the forces attacking Potidaea in 432 and in the defence of Mende in 422, another set for the Aetolian cities exemplified in the forces assisting Athens against the revolt on Lesbos in 428, another set covering the Carian district, seen in the army in Lycia in 430, etc. That was perhaps the limit of their military obligations, but there had never been any question of defence of the islands. The supreme Athenian navy saw to that, and so the original military obligations could still be applied or re-applied in that district of the Empire.

But the really striking thing about Thucydides' list of Athens' allies before Syracuse (7.57) is not merely the special role of the 'islanders'. It is the very small number of 'islanders'. The authors of *The Athenian Tribute Lists* (I, 1939: 457) list 39 names of island states. Not all of them were still in that category in 415, and four were listed separately by Thucydides as being akin to the Athenians (7.57.2). But where are the rest? Of non-ship-contributing 'islanders', there are the four Euboean states (Eretria, Chalcis, Styra, Carystus), the Keans, the Andrians, and the Tenians. But why are the rest not there?

We know at what date and in what circumstances the Euboean cities obliged themselves to military service. In 446, the whole of Euboea revolted and a settlement was made with each city, apart from Histiaea where the inhabitants were expelled and a cleruchy installed (1.114). The oath of the Chalcidians in the Chalcis Decree (ML 52 ll. 21–32) shows that the Chalcidians swore to be as good and as just allies as they could be, and this was precisely what the Eretrians had sworn (l. 42). Similar treatment for the other rebel cities, Styra and Carystus, is to be presumed.

We know nothing of the histories of Keos, Andros and Tenos which could explain when and why they were singled out. All are close enough to Euboea to make one wonder whether they were caught up in the revolt of 446, but speculation is fairly pointless. More to the point is to wonder why Paros, Naxos or Cythnos, for instance, were not called on to serve in Sicily when these others were. Military service had been demanded of the allies at Tanagra in 457 (1.107.5). Why was it that in 415 not only were the 'islanders' singled out, but also of the islanders these few particular states?

A solution may be proposed. When Athens concluded the Peace of Callias and perhaps summoned a congress to discuss 'how all might sail the seas free from fear and carry on the peace' (Plut. *Per.* 17),[9] relations with the allies were at a delicate point. The Missing Year on the Tribute Lists[10] shows as much. I suggest that, at this moment, Athens revoked all her earlier arrangements for military, as opposed to naval, service. The need for naval patrolling continued – to deal with piracy[11] if not with Persian armaments – but there was no longer a need for the sort of military system that had obtained. All that was necessary was provision for common action within districts of the sort the Brea Decree acquaints us with. The islands were secured by the fleet. So there was indeed a brief period when those words attributed to Pericles in Plutarch (*Per.* 12.3) were apt for all but the remaining autonomous, ship-contributing allies – 'the allies contribute not a horse, not a ship, not a hoplite, but merely money'. The revolt of Euboea changed that for the four Euboean states we meet at Syracuse and, it may be guessed, for the three Cycladic islands, Andros, Tenos and Keos. For the rest of the cities of the Empire the new deal of 448/7(?) held and that is why, when all possible forces were mustered for Demosthenes in 414/13, the list was so short.

There is, of course, the problem of Miletus. In 425/4 the Milesians are twice especially named as rendering military service. In the attack on Corinthian territory in 425 'Milesians and Andrians and Carystians' were named as the attendant allies (4.42.1) and, in 424, 'of the allies, Milesians and certain others' were in the assault on Cythera (4.53.1), '2,000 Milesians' indeed, as the narrative reveals (5.4.1), but there is no other mention of them before the expedition of 415 (7.57.4). The very figure 2,000 is surprising and questionable. How was such a large force of hoplites transported across the Aegean? Perhaps the numeral is corrupt.[12] But, above all, how and why were the Milesians rendering military service in 425/4? Were their obligations new or had they been long-standing but not enforced earlier in the War? As already pointed out, the number of expeditions in the Archidamian War that involved Imperial land forces is surprisingly small, and it may be that Miletus could have been called on annually but was just not, save in 425/4. It is nonetheless hard to resist connecting Milesian service in that year with those clauses of the Miletus Decree (*IG* 1³ 21) which seem to deal with military service.[13] The decree is dated to the archonship of Euthynus and, in 426/5, the archon was indeed of that name. The special role of Milesians in the operations of 425/4 can thus be readily explained. That Thucydides makes no mention of troubles in or with Miletus in 426/5 is hardly decisive. He makes no mention of trouble in Euboea in 424/3, under which year Philochorus recorded an expedition to that island (F130). But if the true date of the decree is 450/49 as many have believed,[14] what becomes of the theory that the Peace of Callias resulted in a general reordering of the military obligations of the members of the Empire? This objection is not, however, decisive. Miletus, in a settlement at the end of the revolt, could have been given special obligations in 450/49 which were shortly cancelled after the Peace of Callias. Similar, if not identical,[15] obligations could have been laid on her at some later date. One notes that whereas in the 430s the name *Milesioi* stands on its own in the Tribute Lists, in the 420s it is accompanied by *Leros* and *Teichioussa*, an indication that something had happened which prompted a return to the system established before the Peace of Callias.

To conclude, explanations advanced for the remarkable shortness of the list of allies before Syracuse in 413 may or may not be correct. What seems beyond dispute is that military service in the Athenian Empire was not burdensome.

NOTES

1 THUCYDIDES

1 Cf. Davies (1971: 233–6). The only reliable evidence outside the text of Thucydides is furnished by Plutarch, *Cim.* 4.2–3, where it is stated that his remains were buried among the relatives of Cimon, beside the grave of Cimon's sister Elpinice; presumably this comes from someone's having inspected the graves. Other alleged facts are probably based on guesswork from the text; e.g. the statement that Cleon was responsible for Thucydides being exiled (Marcellinus, *Life* §46), not improbable in itself, appears to be guessing, for the reference to 'madness' and 'lightness' seems to derive from 4.39.3 and 4.28.5. The Cimonian connection is clear enough from the patronymic Olorus, coupled with the right to work gold mines in Thrace (4.104.4, 105.1); Olorus was the name of the Thracian king whose daughter, Hegesipyle, the father of Cimon married (Hdt. 6.39.2). Thucydides himself tells of his unfortunate generalship in the north Aegean in 424/3 (4.104.4) after which he was in exile for 20 years (5.26.5), i.e. he was able to profit from the Spartan peace which made the exiles free to return in 404 (Xen. *Hell.* 2.2.20). He was certainly in Athens in the early part of the Archidamian War, when he caught the Plague (2.48.3). He claims to have begun to compose his history at the beginning of the war (1.1.1) and exile enabled him to gather his material from the Peloponnesians as much as from their opponents (5.26). (One would have expected him to attend the Olympic Games as did many a rich Greek, but his account is too impersonal to betray it in his account of 420 – cf. 5.50 – or in his allusions to 416 – 6.16.2 and 15.3 – where Alcibiades would have made a far from pleasing impression on him.) Some have argued that 2.100.2 shows that he outlived King Archelaus of Macedon who died in 399. Marcellinus (*Life* 19, 25, 47) probably correctly sited his exile at Skapte Hyle (cf. Plut. *Mor.* 605c), where Herodotus (6.46.3) tells us the Thasians had mined gold, perhaps on the same terms as Thucydides. Certainly, Thucydides manifests some familiarity with Amphipolis (4.103.5; 5.10.6, 11.1). Whether he met a violent death in Thrace (Plut. *Cim.*

4.3), on his way back to Athens (Paus. 1.23.9), or in Athens (Marcellinus §32) is unclear.

2 The argument is set out by Andrewes (1959: 232n6). For Alcibiades' age when he first became general, see Andrewes on Thuc. 5.43.2, and for the date (421/20) see Develin (1989: 140).

3 According to Demosthenes 19.273f., Callias was heavily fined for allegedly taking bribes. There is no good reason to doubt this. Presumably, the Peace was promptly followed by the summons to a Panhellenic Congress (Plut. *Per.* 17) and there is a curious delay before work began on the Parthenon in 447/6. Pericles' policy may have been under fire.

4 Diels, *VS* no. 88 B25. For atheism in fifth-century Athens, see Guthrie (1969: 235–44).

5 Cf. Derenne (1930).

6 'When Crates asked Stilpo (of Megara) whether the gods delight in worship and prayers, it is said that he replied "Don't ask me about it in the street, you silly fellow, ask me when I'm on my own" ' (Diog. Laert. 2.117).

7 Cf. Dover (1988: 65–73).

8 Most of the Athenians with Nicias in Sicily took the eclipse as a divine sign (Thuc. 7.50.4). When Xenophon was addressing the Ten Thousand and someone sneezed, the soldiery with one accord fell to their knees before the god (Xen. *Anab.* 3.2.8).

9 Cf. Macan, R. W. (1895) *Herodotus IV–VI*, London: Macmillan, vol. 1, Introduction, pp. cx–cxiii.

10 E.g. the oracle given to the Spartans at 1.66.

11 *Pace* Marinatos (1981: 140).

12 Cf. Syme (1962: 52), a view echoed by de Ste Croix (1972: 19f).

13 Cf. Parker (1983: ch. 9).

14 Sceptical remarks could be made in drama; e.g. the messenger in Euripides' *Helen* 744f. expresses contempt for divination, and Critias' Sisyphus in the play of that name treats the gods as human invention (Diels, *VS* II no. 88 B25) and comes to a bad end. Diagoras of Melos, outspoken in his contempt for the Eleusinian Mysteries, had to flee from Athens with a price on his head (*FGH* 326 F3).

15 Thucydides mentions, but seems not to accept, the story that Plataea was saved from total conflagration by a timely downpour (2.77.6). His explanation of why those breaking out of Plataea wore only one sandal each, namely to stop them slipping in the mud (3.22.20), is weak and it has been suggested that the true explanation was religious (cf. Hornblower ad loc.).

16 Cf. Hornblower ad loc.

17 *Pace* Hornblower (1987: 160).

18 Thuc. 1.93.4 and 7; [Arist.] *Ath. Pol.* 25, where his alleged association with Ephialtes must have arisen from a similarity of attitude to democracy.

19 Hornblower (1987: 161f). would have it that Thucydides at 8.24.4 manifests a sympathy for Spartan oligarchy: 'the Chians were the only people I know of who at the same time flourished (*eudaimonēsan*) and

had moderation', 'moderation' (*sōphrosynē*) being a word for oligarchy (cf. 8.64.5). There must have been more than two enduring oligarchies in fifth-century Greece, so he clearly did not think that oligarchy produced *eudaimonia*. Nor did he think that democracy necessarily precluded it (witness the Funeral Oration). That speech shows how poorly Sparta compared with Athens (cf. 2.39) and, quite apart from that, Thucydides remarks that Brasidas was exceptional (4.81) and considers that most Spartiates abroad misbehaved themselves (1.95.7; 3.32.2; 3.93.2; 5.52.1). He may have admired Spartan military prowess on land – who in the Greek world did not? – but Athenian naval might was equally to be admired as the proud farewell of 6.32 suggests. When in 2.65.5 Thucydides remarks that as a result of Pericles' leadership the city became very great, one thinks of 2.64.3.

20 It may be doubted, however, whether these words carried a pejorative sense for Thucydides. *Ochlos* occurs 25 times in the *History*; of these only two or possibly three instances may be contemptuous (4.28.3; 7.8.2; and perhaps 6.63.2), while of the 16 uses of *homilos*, only two may reflect contempt (2.65.4; 6.17.2). To translate by 'rabble' and 'mob' is misleading; those words never have a neutral sense for us.

21 'Thucydides may be something worse than an oligarch: an enthusiast enamoured of intelligence and power, not interested in forms of government' (Syme 1962: 51). 'Thucydides may have agreed with Pope: "For forms of government let fools contest; /Whate'er is best administered, is best" '(Adcock 1963: 55). Whatever the truth about that, Thucydides was certainly not the puppet oligarch he is often made out to be.

22 Anyone minded to tangle with the problem of the composition of the *History* had best begin on the *inextricabilis error* by studying the appendices of Andrewes and Dover in *HCT* V 361–444.

23 At 1.51.4 a name is omitted and one name incorrect, as ML 61 shows (the error *may* be due to early corruption of the manuscript). At 2.34.1 the claim that the public burial and funeral oration was due to 'ancestral custom' (*patrios nomos*) has been hotly denounced and defended. 4.8.6 (and other passages in his account of Pylos) shows that his notion of the topography of Pylos was faulty. 5.38.2 seems to conflict with the account of the Boeotian constitution given by the author of the *Hellenica Oxyrhynchia* (ch. 16 in Bartoletti's 1959 Teubner edition; ch. 19 in Chambers' 1993 edition). At 8.67.1 he speaks of 10 *syngrapheis autokratores* which has generally (but perhaps incorrectly) been denounced in view of [Arist.] *Ath. Pol.* 29.2. For all these passages, see the commentaries of Gomme and Hornblower. The list is astoundingly brief and the only certain error, concerning the topography of Pylos, was in an area presumably not open to autopsy. (Thucydides is argued to have erred mightily in his estimate of Spartan numbers at Mantinea (5.68.3), against which I have argued in Cawkwell (1983) and cannot even list it as an error.)

24 8.18, 37, 58.

25 Cf. Cawkwell (1983: 389).

26 The concourse at Olympia must have been large. The 20,000 exiles who assembled in 324 (Diod. 18.8.5) were perhaps exceptional, but they show the capacity of the ample site and the pavilions (*skēnōmata*) erected for the festival (Xen. *Hell.* 7.4.32). The spectators were interested in more than athletic contests; Hippias of Elis would display his wondrous powers of memory and his vast range of knowledge (Plat. *Hipp. Minor* 363c, 368b) and Gorgias call on the Greeks to unite against Persia (Diels, *VS* 82 B8a); Lysias in his *Olympic Oration* (33) attacked Dionysius the Elder, who had sent rhapsodes to recite his poems (Diod. 14.109). Isocrates in the *Panegyricus* (§§1, 2) affected to be delivering it at Olympia, beginning with a complaint about a lack of prizes for others than athletes, but showing in §§41–6 that the great concourse at the national festivals made them suitable and likely places for Thucydides to meet the sort of people who could have greatly aided his collection of evidence. Was he at Olympia when Sparta was denied official representation and Spartan military intervention was feared and a notable Spartiate was whipped in the sight of all the Greeks (5.50, Xen. *Hell.* 3.2.21)? And did he see for himself the great splash made by Alcibiades in 416 (6.16.2, Andoc. 4.25ff., etc.)? He could even have been at Olympia in 428, when there were observations to be made (3.8.1), for it is by no means clear that war meant that enemy states were not included in the Sacred Truces (as they appear to have been in the fourth century – cf. Aeschin. 2.134). For the non-athletic side of Olympia, see Gardiner (1910: 139f).

27 For autopsy at Mantinea, cf. notes on 5.64.5 and 74.1 by Gomme and Andrewes in *HCT* IV. Whether Thucydides had inspected Syracuse is debated (cf. Dover's Appendix in *HCT* IV 466ff.). Error in his account of Pylos is generally admitted (see n. 23 above).

28 Dionysius (ch. 8) comments on Thucydides' remark at the end of 1.22 thus: 'Witness in support of Thucydides is given by all, certainly most, philosophers and rhetoricians (*rhētores*), that he paid the greatest regard to truth of which history is the priest . . .'.

29 Cf. Woodman (1988: 1–69).

30 Cf. Hdt. 8.65.1 and 6, Thuc. 4.34.2 and 44.4, Xen. *Anab.* 1.8.8 and *Cyrop.* 6.3.5, Polybius 3.65.4, 5.85.1 and 12, etc.

31 Wallace (1964: 258f.) remarks on Thucydides' silence about his sources, and Woodman (1988: 22f.) concludes that

> Thucydides' narrative cannot be as accurate as is usually thought. What seems to have happened is that Thucydides has eliminated almost all traces of the difficulties he encountered and in so doing has created an impression of complete accuracy . . .

This may be sensible and salutary. Who can tell, however, how oft Thucydides offendeth? Are we, because Thucydides wrote as he did, to abandon the subject? One can only proceed in the hope that we are not gravely misled.

32 Cf. Woodman (1988: 31).

33 Cf. *HCT* IV 323.

34 If Plato read Thucydides, he was not persuaded (*Hipparchus* 228b).

35 The main difficulties are:

1 that, although the letters exchanged with Xerxes are presented as genuine (note that each is introduced by *tade* 1.128.6 and 129.3), it is most improbable either that Thucydides obtained a copy of the letter sent to Xerxes or that Pausanias did not promptly destroy such incriminating material;

2 that the whole story of the Argilian man in chs 133 and 134, presented merely as a story (cf. *legetai* at 132.5 and 134.1), is frankly incredible; and

3 that he speaks of negotiations with the helots as if there was something akin to a Trades Union with which to negotiate (1.132.4), which there was not. Cf. Cawkwell (1970: 49–53).

Westlake (1989: 1–18) argued for a literary source for Thucydides' account of Themistocles and Pausanias, but even if that is correct, it makes no difference for Thucydides' credit whether he took the story over from someone else or not. If it was a youthful essay to which he was much attached, he may have intended to give it mature reconsideration and was forced by age, illness, or other preoccupations to leave it as we have it. Presumably, he would have preferred to complete the excursus on the Pentecontaetea.

36 If the second day's assembly had been provided for by the Council, as had been the case in 433, with the debate on the Corcyran alliance (1.44.1) and was, perhaps, to be the case in 415 with the debate on the Segestan alliance (6.6.3 *en tais ekklēsiais*), this argument can only stand if it had been arranged, as it would be in 346 (Aeschin. 2.67), that on the second day there would be no speeches, only the vote.

37 In 392, Andocides and his fellow ambassadors were fully empowered to negotiate (*autokratores*), but still deemed it necessary to refer the agreed terms back to the assembly (Andoc. 3.34).

38 Because Thucydides did not berate Herodotus for his fantastic numbers for the Persian expedition of 480, he has himself been berated (cf. Hornblower 1987: 108). The second passage noted in the text shows that he was indeed aware of the truth.

39 At 6.13.2 Nicias is made to say that since the Segestans began war against the Selinuntians in the first place without the consent of the Athenians (*aneu Athēnaiōn*), they should settle it on their own (*meta sphōn autōn*). At 6.18.1, Alcibiades is made to say that Athens is obliged to her allies in Sicily (*pros tous ekei xymmachous*): 'what excuse could we make for not sending military aid?' (Cf. 6.19.1 where it is unclear whether reference is to oaths made to just the Leontinans – as the echo of *anamimnēskontes* at 6.6.2 suggests – or to the Segestans as well.) Such remarks are consistent with the Segestans having sought to revive an alliance dormant for decades. Hence, in 416 they 'reminded' the Athenians that they were obliged from recent times to help the Leontinans 'and their crowning argument was that if the Syracusans got off scot-free after *both* uprooting the Leontinans *and* destroying Athens' still remaining allies, there was a danger . . . '

(6.6.2). The Segestans concluded by declaring 'that it would be sensible to join with their still remaining allies in resisting the Syracusans.' That is, no new alliance was formally necessary; the old one stood, though it was necessary to 'remind' the Athenians of the recent one made with Leontini during a war in which Segesta had played no part, whereas recently acquired allies were hardly to be referred to as 'still remaining'. At 6.10.5, Nicias is made to say 'We quickly go to help the Segestans who are our allies...' which is suitable for a long-standing alliance, but hardly for a very recently formed one.

40 See Chambers, Gallucci and Spanos (1990: 38–63).
41 I owe this observation to Professor P. J. Rhodes. Cf. Henry (1992) for a sceptical view of the arguments advanced by Chambers; also Henry (1995) against Chambers (1992; 1993).
42 A serious onslaught on Thucydides has been made by Badian (1993), especially in chs 4 and 6, where Thucydides appears as the devious apologist for Athenian *Realpolitik*: 'Thucydides has consistently tried to disguise this *Realpolitik* by selective omission and disinformation, and by delivering his own interpretation of motives and intentions under the guise of facts' (1993: 184). I postpone discussion of this to the next chapter.
43 For Cleon and finance, see below p. 64.
44 For Hyperbolus and Cleophon, see below pp. 57–9.
45 I adhere to the views that the two decrees described in Plut. *Per.* 30 and directed against the Megarians were subsequent to the exclusion decree (cf. Thuc. 1.67.4); that the decree which sent Anthemocritus to Megara (and, as it turned out, to his death) was concerned to deny Megarians access to the Lesser Mysteries at Eleusis of spring 431; that the decree of Charinus which required the generals to swear that they would invade Megara twice a year was responsible for the first invasion at the time of the Greater Mysteries of autumn 431 (Thuc. 2.31); that the twice-annual invasions which continued until Athens took Nisaea in 424 (Thuc. 4.66.1) followed the Mysteries (for the dates of which see *IG* 1^3 6) and were reprisals on behalf of the Twin Goddesses of Eleusis. The matter is discussed more fully on pp. 111–14.
46 See below p. 127n.5.
47 Cf. *CAH* V^2 465. Westlake (1989: 103–13) rejected the evidence of Andocides and explained the Persian hostility to Athens in 412 as exploitation of Athenian weakness after the Sicilian disaster. Even if he was right, some explicit account of Athens' dealings with Amorges should have been furnished by Thucydides and some explanation of the Great King's change of policy given.
48 See below pp. 63–74 for Cleon, pp. 89–91 for Alcibiades, and pp. 71–4 for Demosthenes.
49 For Lamachus' generalships, see Develin (1989).
50 Cf. Liebeschuetz (1968: 300f.).
51 Cf. Dover ad loc. in *HCT* IV 419f.
52 See below p. 50–4 for Thucydides' treatment of Demosthenes.

2 'THE TRUEST EXPLANATION'

1 De Ste Croix (1972: 214–20) adequately dealt with the theory that the War was due to commercial rivalry between Athens and Corinth. The theory originated in the conviction that the Archidamian War was essentially Corinth's war; since Corinth was very much a commercial state, the cause must have been commercial rivalry. There is no evidence for such rivalry; measures of blockade during the war (cf. 3.86.4, 1.120.2) do not argue rivalry earlier. In the sixth century when Athenian pottery was ousting Corinthian in the west (cf. Heichelheim 1964: 41), there was 'special friendship' on the part of Corinth for Athens (Hdt. 6.89). Commercial rivalry would have taken time to develop, but in 440 Corinth took Athens' part in the debate in the Peloponnesian League (1.40.5). Trade and politics were separate (cf. Hdt. 7.147.2 and Woolley (1938: 22) for uninterrupted trade with the Persian Empire during the Persian Wars). Trade was also conducted by individuals and on a small scale. Merchants had little influence on political decisions. The only treaty of alliance involving commerce known to us from the classical age is in the treaty of alliance between King Amyntas and the Chalcidians of Thrace (ML no. 111), and that is the exception that proves the rule; i.e. it concerns the exceptional case of a king who was both head of state and a large timber-exporting landowner.

2 De Ste Croix (1972).

3 Badian (1993: 125–62).

4 Andrewes (1959).

5 Hellanicus, to whom Thucydides refers in 1.97.2, recorded in his *Atthis* an event of 407/6 (*FGH* 323a F26), and this indication of 'late' composition is supported by what he says about the construction of the walls of the Piraeus (1.93.5). If the walls had not been demolished as they were in 404 (Xen. *Hell.* 2.2.23), he would not have said – *pace* Gomme (1962) ad loc. – that the thickness of this was 'still now' plain. If the wall still stood when he wrote, the thickness would have been plain *tout simple*, but he must mean that it was 'still now' plain because the foundations, and only the foundations, remained. So a 'late' date for the Excursus is indicated. (The claim made by Jacoby on p. 5 of his commentary on *FGH* 323a that only the sentence about Hellanicus was 'late' is to be rejected. It would have been absurd for Thucydides, having said that all his predecessors had omitted the Pentekontaetea, to have added 'and the man who actually dealt with it, Hellanicus, did it badly.' He could have made his addition sensibly by saying 'except for Hellanicus'. The point is that Thucydides is contrasting his predecessors (*hoi pro emou*) with his contemporary (*ho ep' emou*).) However, the indications of 'late' composition apply only to the first eight chapters at the end of which he seems, as it were, to rule off his 'late' work by explaining in 97.2 why he has written the excursus. After that, he becomes very much more sketchy. In 89–97 (5½ pages of *OCT*), he covered about 18 months, whereas in 98–115.1, a mere nine pages, he covered over 30 years, and it might be thought that having written an *Ur*-Excursus of a sketchy sort, he

began to replace it with a very full version, but got no further than chapter 97. In this way, it might be maintained that such difference between the two parts suggests that the original of Book 1 did indeed cover the Pentekontaetea but did so unsatisfactorily, and that after return to Athens from exile Thucydides began to rewrite it, but got no further than the end of summer 478.

Against this must be urged the incompleteness of the Excursus. The only event treated after the Thirty Years Peace is the revolt of Samos (1.115.2–117.3, covering 1½ pages of *OCT*) with a fullness characteristic of the opening chapters rather than of the central part (cf. 1.100 where the battle of Eurymedon, which was Salamis and Plataea on a single day, and the revolt of Thasos are dealt with much more sketchily). He could have properly dealt with the foundation of Amphipolis, the importance of which he was well aware of (4.108.1), and must have done so in any 'original' Excursus, no matter what else he would or would not have chosen to include. So the incompleteness argues for there being no such 'original' version.

The Excursus was 'late', i.e. after 404. He began to do it with a thoroughness more demanding of his time (and perhaps of his health) than he could maintain. So at 1.97 he broke off and resorted to doing no more, perhaps, than ordering the chronologically inaccurate account of Hellanicus, which he had criticised on that score, but also for its brevity. But what could be briefer than Thucydides' account at various points? So he tidied up Hellanicus and planned to treat the whole as he had begun, but beyond properly covering the Samian Revolt (during which he had perhaps done military service), the last years of the Pentekontaetea remained unwritten.

6 *Ton de polemon, di' honper chrēsimoi an eimen, ei tis humōn mē oietai esesthai, gnōmēs hamartanei kai ouk aisthanetai tous Lakedaimonious phoboi tōi humeteroi polemēseiontas.*

7 Cf. Scholiast's *pros tous Argeious.* Defeated by Sparta in the Battle of the champions in 546, the Argives (Hdt. 1.82) cut their hair short (as the Spartans took to growing theirs long, for in Greece the strongest were the longest and 'to set your cap at tyranny' was *komān epi tyrannidi*). Why Sparta chose to attack Argos in 494 is unclear. It may have been that a fifty-year truce after the Battle of Champions, a hypothesis for which there is no evidence, had expired, or it may have been that Sparta feared that Argive ambitions were reviving. The crushing defeat at Sepeia turned Argos to alliance with Persia (cf. Hdt. 7.152.3, 9.12.1) which endured for a generation (Hdt. 7.151), but is no more heard of after Argos came to terms with Sparta in 450 (5.28.2). By 424, Athens perhaps began to hope that Argos would be useful (Ar. *Knights* 465–7; also see p. 53) and after the Peace of Nicias Sparta's disaffected allies began to exploit her for all she was worth. Corinth called on the Argives 'to save the Peloponnese' (5.27.2), 'the Peloponnese' being an emotive term (cf. Xen. *Hell.* 7.5.1 and 4.35; Plut. *Cim.* 4.5, preserving Stesimbrotus' comment that Cimon was in his inner self 'Peloponnesian'). In this period, Argive ambitions to have the hegemony of the Peloponnese (5.28.2, 40.3) burgeoned, and

before the battle of Mantinea in 418, the Argive army was called on 'in the name of their ancient hegemony and their one-time equal share of the Peloponnese not to put up with being deprived forever' (5.69.1). Victory restored to the Spartans their reputation and authority (5.75.3), after which Argos relapsed into her secondary role. So in 433, the resurrection of Argive hegemony was conceivable. The Scholiast is likely to be correct.

8 Most notably Andrewes (1959), followed by Fornara and Samons (1991: 141).

9 One would like to know more of how the two sides regarded the oracle given to the Spartans (1.118.3). Thucydides could not take such things seriously, but the Spartans did. So in what sense did they have bad conscience about their conduct in 432/1? Likewise, how well informed about it were the Athenians? At 1.118.3 Thucydides treats it as a story (*hōs legetai*) of which he cannot be sure, but the Corinthians are made to speak of it as a well-known fact (1.123.1). Perhaps there were so many oracles being bandied about (2.8.2) that Athenians were not particularly impressed by this one until the Plague struck in 430 and Athens sued for peace (2.59.2). But it was much in Sparta's interest in 432/1 to give it maximum publicity. Of course, Thucydides 'cared for none of these things'.

10 That was not the line taken by Archidamus as Thucydides presents him (see p. 37), but some moral scruples would not be surprising. Cf. the situation in 371, when some demanded literal adhesion to the terms of the Peace despite it seeming to Sparta's manifest interest not to waste the military advantage (Xen. *Hell.* 6.4.2). The oft-quoted lines of Euripides' *Andromache* denouncing Spartan perfidy (445–9) reflect Athenian feelings 'in the beginning of the Peloponnesian War' when, according to the Scholiast at 445, the play was written – but it may not have been true at all times or of all Spartiates.

11 This is the inference, commonly made, from Pericles' proposed reply to the final Peloponnesian embassy which had demanded that Athens 'let the Hellenes be autonomous' (1.139.3). He says: 'and as to the cities, we will let them be autonomous if we actually had them autonomous when we made the treaty' (1.144.2). The Aeginetans had claimed that it was contrary to the treaty of Athens to infringe their autonomy (1.67.2), and Badian (1993: 137ff.) is right to argue for a general clause, not just a clause special to Aegina. De Ste Croix (1972: 293f.) leaves the question open.

12 Thucydides may have written 'fifty-seven'. Cf. Hornblower *ad* 2.86.4.

13 Cf. Cawkwell (1975a: 54n4).

14 Cf. Meiggs (1972: 244) ('In the list of 442 for the first time the cities are grouped in districts under district headings, Carian, Ionian, Hellespontine, Thracian, Island, and the order of the districts, though not of the names within the districts, is retained throughout the period.') The ordering may have been due to a tidy-minded *Hellenotamias*.

15 The rubrics are listed in *ATL* I 449–57 and discussed in III 80–8, Meiggs (1972: 249–53). Cf. Lepper (1962). The meaning of the *epiphora* entries remains unclear (Meiggs 247f. and 432).

16 It is argued by Schuller (1981) that '*the* individuals' are groups of dissident democrats from the cities concerned, acting contrary to the wishes of those in power. Perhaps this is less likely than the received view, but it must be admitted that all explanations are open to objections. [Xen.] *Ath. Pol.* 2.12 supports the 'protection racket' explanation. Cf. Isoc. 8.36, where the imperialists at Athens are said to 'dare to claim that we must imitate our forebears and not disregard ourselves being made fools of and those who are unwilling to pay their contributions (*syntaxeis*) sailing the seas.'

17 Cf. 8.64.4 for Thasian exiles in the Peloponnese, and Isoc. 8.79 for exiles in general.

18 See Hornblower ad loc.

19 According to Plut. *Cleom.* 9.1, there was a temple of Fear at Sparta. The Corinthians are represented as saying in their attack on Spartan character 'your way is to achieve less than you can and less than you have decided on and not to put your trust in what is secure but to think you will never get free of your fears' (1.70.3).

20 The latest (and most formidable) advocacy of this view is to be found in Badian (1993: 125–62).

21 For the five years, cf. Plut. *Per.* 13.12. The archon date Harpocration cites from Philochorus (*FGH* 328 F36). For Heliodorus see below p. 108f. For the Propylaea being the crowning glory, cf. Aeschin. 2.105 ('Epaminondas, not cowering before Athens' high repute, said expressly in the assembly of the Thebans that they must transfer the Propylaea of the Athenians' Acropolis to the forecourt of the Cadmea.').

22 Cf. Boersma (1970: 70 and 201).

23 See *ATL* III 64f. The theory is tentatively accepted by Badian (1993: 145).

24 Too little is known about tribute assessment for us to interpret with confidence changes in amount; e.g. Thasos suddenly increased from a payment of three talents to thirty in March 443 (*ATL* I 282), and one can only guess why, but it would not be sensible to presume that the change marked a serious intrusion on Thasian autonomy (which, formally speaking, had been lost in 462). If Potidaea's tribute was raised in 438 (or 435), it may not have been a flexing of imperial muscle. In 1.56.2 the abrupt orders to Potidaea are given out of fears of Corinthian revenge over Corcyra and there is no hint of Potidaea being previously suspected and chastened.

25 Cf. de Ste Croix (1972: 229f.).

26 Jacoby's habit of printing what he deems to be Philochorus' words may be deceptive. In fragment 121, the Megarian denunciation of the Athenians to the Spartans is given in inverted commas, the *ipsissima verba*. The explanation which follows in the Scholiast, namely the passing of the Megara Decree, may well have preceded in the text (indeed, one almost presumes that it must have), but could well have

been given fully under the archon Pythodorus (432/1). For a view similar to mine of the dating of the decree cf. Fornara (1975: 227n55).

27 Cf. Kagan (1969: 260).

28 Notably by Brunt (1993: 1–16), who consistently argued for an early date for whatever happened on Aegina, if indeed anything did happen. He declines (p. 12) to make any connection between Aegina's lowered tribute and the Aeginetan complaint. In this he stands alone.

29 It is to be noted that, at 1.118.1, Thucydides includes not only the Corcyra and Potidaea affairs, but also *hosa prophasis toude tou polemou kateste*, in which he presumably counts the complaints of Megara and Aegina. So whether or not these matters originally had anything do with the relations of Athens and Sparta, some further account was to be expected – which exposes the weakness of Brunt's method of argument.

For the temporal relation of the Megara Decree to the two other decrees concerning Megara recorded in Plut. *Per.* 30, see Appendix 2.

30 See the Register in *ATL* I 218.

31 Cf. *ATL* III 320.

32 Brunt (1993: 11ff.) argues that nothing in particular had happened with Aegina, that her complaint that she was not autonomous was no other than a protest, perhaps, at having to pay tribute. This is not likely in view of the cases recorded where tribute-payment and autonomy were clearly regarded as compatible (5.18.5; Xen. *Hell.* 3.4.25). His objection to the idea that a garrison was installed or 'any new action taken by Athens just before the meeting of the Peloponnesian congress' is that he is convinced 'that Thucydides would not have passed it over in silence.' Since, however, Aegina was so prominent in the diplomatic exchanges of 432/1 (1.139.1, 2.27; cf. Andoc. 3.6), there was some explaining to be done which Thucydides, for whatever reason, has omitted to do. Arguments from his silence are of little value.

33 Cf. Thompson (1973: 29).

34 Cf. Fornara (1970: 189).

35 By Pritchett (1971).

36 Kallet-Marx (1989).

37 Cf. Bradeen (1971: 469).

38 See pp. 107–10.

39 De Ste Croix (1972: 225–89, esp. 252–61).

40 Cf. Cawkwell (1975b).

41 *Esti gar dēpou en tais synthēkais tēn thalattan plein tous metechontas tēs eirēnēs, kai mēdena kōluein autous mēde katagein ploion mēdenos toutōn.*

42 Cf. Fornara and Samons (1991: 143).

43 P. 266. Even in Athens citizens were more engaged in foreign commerce than Hasebroek allowed; cf. Isager and Hansen (1975: 71).

44 *Malista ge pantōn kai endēlotata.*

45 Cf. Michell (1957: 258–83).

46 *Epigraphica* ed. H. W. Pleket, Leiden, Brill, (1964) vol. 1, no. 2, *SEG* 18 no. 337.

47 Badian (1993: 125–62).

48

> It has ... been the aim of this investigation, not to 'discredit' Thucydides, but to show that he must not be followed in slavish adoration and treated like a provider of revealed truth. He was an Athenian of his time, trying to convey the strong feelings that he himself naturally held about Periclean democracy and its disintegration owing to the war.
>
> (Badian 1993: 235)

Badian's viewpoint is not dissimilar from that of Rhodes (1987).

49 Cf. 1.139.2 *phoitōntes*, a word that normally has a frequentative meaning. It is used only six times (apart from the draft treaty of 8.18) in Thucydides. 1.146, 3.104.5, 6.104.7 have the normal sense, but 4.41.4 (*pollakis phoitōntōn*) raises doubt, as does 1.95.1, for frequent deputations seem a bit unlikely. (The use of imperfects in 1.139 is less persuasive; cf., for example, 1.138.1.) On the whole, however, it is probably right to accept Badian's picture of frequent embassies.

50 Churchill is alleged to have said 'History will bear me out, especially as I shall write that history myself.'

51 For the chronology of 432/1, see Thompson (1968).

52 De Ste Croix (1972: 170).

53 Cf. Bar-Hen (1977).

54 I take the demand of Gelon for a half-share of command of the whole alliance, as that of Argos (Hdt. 7.160.2, 148.4), to be mere embroidery on the real idea of separate command on land and sea.

55 I equate Thucydides' account in 1.95.7 of Sparta's withdrawal in 478 from seeking to command the Hellenic fleet with the account of Diodorus 11.50, the famous or infamous debate in which Hetoemaridas carried the day. No one acquainted with Diodorus' practice of putting chunks of epitomised narrative into vacant years in his chronographic framework will be deterred by the fact that Diodorus puts his account under 475/4. (Fornara and Samons (1991: 123) assert that 'the story of Hetoemaridas is one of the most transparent fictions of fifth-century history,' but if Ephorus wrote his account with characteristic fourth-century colouring, he got the fact of its having happened from somewhere and, in view of the exchanges about hegemony during the Persian invasion, it is wholly credible that it happened. Only if one insists on the Diodoran dating will one fail to see that Thucydides 1.95.7 describes the same occasion.)

56 For Gorgias (= Diels, *VS* II no. 82), fragments A1.4–5, B5b and 8a, which show that Aristophanes' Lysistrata was giving expression in her reconciliation speech to Panhellenist sentiments (*Lys.* 1128–34).

57 5.49 and 6.84.2 – proposals for an *Anabasis*. At 7.11, Xerxes is represented envisaging a Greek campaign to secure the subjection of the whole of the Persian Empire (*tade panta*)!

58 Badian (1993: 1–72) argues for two Peaces (one in the mid 460s). If he is right, this paragraph would need rethinking. I hope to deal with his theory elsewhere.

3 THUCYDIDES AND THE STRATEGY OF THE PELOPONNESIAN WAR

1 Accusations of accepting bribes or treasonable behaviour were common enough against Spartan kings, and despite the hardened historian's disinclination to take such talk in Greece at its face value, it is not inconceivable that Plistoanax was persuaded by Pericles to accept a handsome bribe and withdraw (cf. Schol. *ad* Ar. *Clouds* 859; Plut. *Per.* 22 and 23.1). However, Athens made the Thirty Years Peace because she was hard pressed (4.21.3 *kata xymphoras*, etc.) and it is likely enough that Plistoanax withdrew with a promise by Pericles that Athens would accede to Spartan demands, including a sweeping clause guaranteeing autonomy – cf. Badian (1993: 137–41). When Sparta realised that such a clause was hardly worth the stone it was inscribed on, they turned, perhaps, on Plistoanax and made him responsible and blameworthy. Cf. Hornblower *ad* 1.114.2.
2 In Ar. *Peace* 747, the whip applied to the slave *edendrotomēse to nōton*. The word for cutting trees down is *koptō* (cf. 4.69.2, 6.66.2). Cutting vines was an easy and effective way to cause damage (cf. Ar. *Acharnians* 512).
3 *Pace* Andrewes ad loc.
4 Cf. Hdt. 1.82.7f. for the victors in the Championship battle of 546 growing their hair long and the losers cutting theirs short.
5 Cf. Lazenby (1993: 59–61) who rejects this account. How long it took to embark horses is only to be conjectured, but horse-transports could not have been as convenient as tank landing craft!
6 Cf. Cawkwell (1975a: 54–60).
7 The tense of *epithumein* is to be noted. Cf. 4.41.4.
8 According to the Corcyran speaker (1.36.3), the three greatest naval powers in the Greek world in 431 were Athens, Corinth and Corcyra. By making all her old ships serviceable in 435, Corcyra sent out 120 ships (1.29.3 and 4). At the battle of Sybota in 433, the Corinthians had 90 ships (1.46.1), which was 20 ships more than they had sent out in 435 (1.29.1). In 431 Pericles said that Athens had 300 seaworthy ships (2.13.8; with which cf. Ar. *Acharnians* 545). The information of 3.17 is untrustworthy (see Hornblower ad loc.) and the statement in [Xen.] *Ath. Pol.* 3.4 about 400 trierarchs being appointed annually, even if accurate, argues nothing about the size of the navy, but clearly Athens had a large numerical superiority. Mere totals can be misleading. The real index of power, which we lack, would be the number of new ships constructed annually, and Thucydides could speak of the Samians coming close to depriving Athens in 440 of the command of the sea (8.76.4), though he may have meant that this was only temporarily so in the special circumstances of 1.116. However, in the early years of the war, Athens had the money to build as many ships as she needed.
9 As the Corinthian is made to remark of the Athenian navy at 1.121.3, 'the Athenians' power depends more on mercenaries than on their own citizens.'

10 The Spartans' desire to recover the prisoners was a major consideration in their seeking peace in 421 (5.15.1), just as they had abstained from invading Attica for fear that if they did, the Athenians would carry out their threat to execute the prisoners (4.41.1). For different views of Sparta's demographic problem, cf. Cartledge (1979: ch. 14) and Cawkwell (1983).

11 Pericles may have been over-optimistic about his financial provision. In 428, the Mytilenians judged the moment ripe for a revolt because the Athenians were ruined by plague and by expenditure of money (3.13.3), and Pericles could hardly have envisaged Sparta giving up by that year. He was well aware what a revolt could cost (cf. ML 55 for the cost of dealing with Samos) and the 2,000 talents expended on Potidaea (2.70.2) would have come as no surprise. Nor can he have failed to realise the heavy costs of the naval expeditions he advocated (1.142.4) and sent out (2.23.2, 100 ships in 431; 2.56.1, another 100 with large numbers of soldiers of various sorts on board in 430). If 3.17.4 may be believed in general, if not in detail (cf. Jordan (1972: 112–15)), 100 ships out for a month cost about 100 talents, and the *eisphora* imposed in winter 428/7 was a frank confession that Pericles' great reserve (2.13.3ff.) was draining away fast. Yet it is clear (cf. Kallet-Marx (1993: ch. 6)) that Athens was far from exhausted, for although 'forced levies' were not as good as 'reserves' (1.141.5), Athens had ample sources she could draw on. How far the less predictable evil of inflation had an effect is debatable (cf. Cawkwell, 1974: 54n4).

12 See below p. 48f.

13 Thucydides (2.65.12) gave an important part in the defeat of Athens to Cyrus' provision of money to the Peloponnesians. Andocides 3.29 said that the King gave Sparta 5,000 talents and Isocrates 8.97 speaks of 'more than 5,000'. Lewis (1977: 131n138) was sceptical about such a sum, but did not explain whence Andocides in 392 and Isocrates who lived in Athens during the Ionian War might have derived such a notion. The King originally sent a mere 500 talents (Xen. *Hell.* 1.5.3) despite ample promises (Diod. 13.70.3), an instance of the celebrated Royal niggardliness (*Hell. Oxy.* 22.2 in Chambers's edition; cf. Ar. *Acharnians* 103f.), but Cyrus did keep his word and provide money (Xen. *Hell.* 1.5.3, 1.6.10 and 18, 2.1.14). What Cyrus' support did for the Spartans was to encourage those in Sparta resolved to finish Athens off. (For the crisis at Sparta after the defeat at Arginusae see p. 58f.)

14 This is plain in 412/11; cf. 8.58.2 (both the preliminary drafts had been even more demanding; cf. 8.18.1 and 37.2). Following Wade-Gery (1958: 220), I believe that the Peace of Callias contained such a clause, as will be argued elsewhere. Demands for autonomy for the Greek cities of Asia made in the 390s (Xen. *Hell.* 3.2.20, 3.4.5, 3.4.25) could only be made against the King's claim that 'the cities in Asia were his' (cf. the Royal Rescript of 387/6, Xen. *Hell.* 5.1.31) – 'autonomy' was not 'freedom'.

15 Thucydides does not suggest that the first two documents were mere drafts. At 8.17.4, the first document is described as 'the first alliance with the King' and the document itself uses the term 'alliance' (18.1). The second declares itself (37.1) to be an 'agreement' (*synthēkai*) and is introduced at 36.2 as such, at which point the first document has the same term applied to it. At 43.3, both the first and second documents are referred to as 'treaties' (*spondai*). The third document terms itself an 'agreement' (58.1), but in describing it Thucydides speaks of Tissaphernes 'making this third treaty' (57.2 *spondas tritas tasde spendetai*). The third document, however, is properly dated and gives the names of the Persians involved in its making, and it is wholly unlikely that a treaty made by Chalcideus (17.4) should be so promptly superseded by another made by Therimenes simply because the Peloponnesians no longer liked it (36.2), and then both superseded by another because Lichas was dissatisfied (43.3). The reasonable presumption is therefore that the first two documents were drafts of treaties negotiated with Tissaphernes by Spartan officers, but repudiated by the authorities in Sparta to whom the draft was naturally submitted for approval (cf. Xen. *Hell.* 3.4.26 for comparable procedure). (For discussion of the three treaties, cf. Andrewes, *HCT* V 143–6.)

What is so curious about the first two drafts is that any Spartan official should have assented to a formula so blatantly damnable as the attempts to define the area of the King's authority (18.1 and 37.2), which appeared to recognise the right of the King to territories outside Asia. Brusque repudiation should have seemed certain, and one can only suppose that Chalcideus and Therimenes were shying away from the stark assertion of the final version: 'such territory of the King as is in Asia, is to belong to the King.' The word 'territory' rather than 'Territory and cities' (18.1 and 37.2) could gloss over the painful truth that Sparta was abandoning the Greeks of Asia.

Whatever one makes of these three 'treaties', one cannot accept Thucydides' account unreservedly, but since Book 8 is 'the workshop of Thucydides', he is not to be held at fault. (Cf. Westlake (1989: 176) who speaks of 'the unrevised condition of the eighth book which has led to other imperfections.')

16 Xen. *Oec.* 4.20, *Hell.* 1.5.1–7, 2.1.7, Diod. 13.104.4.
17 Cf. Westlake (1989: ch. 12).
18 Tissaphernes had certainly found the Spartans difficult to get on with (cf. 8.43.3f. where he goes off, angry that the clause so recently for whatever reason agreed to by Therimenes is objected to by Lichas). His bad relations with the Greeks of Asia, a sharp contrast with Cyrus, led to the Spartan intervention in 399 (Xen. *Hell.* 3.1.3). Pharnabazus was perhaps more agreeable. Certainly, Conon seems to have found him very satisfactory to deal with to judge by their joint voyage in 393 (Xen. *Hell.* 4.8.1ff.). When the Milesian *dēmos* fled from Lysander, who was at that time Persia's arch-friend, Pharnabazus both settled them and gave each of them a *stater* (Diod. 13.104.5f.); and when Pharnabazus had his meeting with Agesilaus in 395/4, he not

only cast away Persian formality, but also could assert that, unlike Tissaphernes, he had always kept faith (Xen. *Hell.* 4.1.29–38). He had Greek friends (8.6.1; Xen. *Hell.* 4.1.29). Apart from sheltering the useful Alcibiades, Tissaphernes did not, as far as we know, care for Greeks.

19 Cf. Lewis (1977: 56–8). Note, especially, Diod. 15.41.5.

20 Cf. Lewis (1977: 131):

> Despite Tissaphernes' failure to maintain good relations with the Spartans and his preference for a more even-handed policy, despite Pharnabazos' evidently growing conviction that the Athenians were a force which had to be reckoned with permanently, and that there might be a case for exploring their attitude further, the King himself has come down for a clear policy of supporting Sparta. Western Asia Minor will be put in the hands of one man with a larger satrapy than Tissaphernes had had and apparently with wider supervisory powers. That he is coming with the King's backing is made further clear by the fact that he is the King's son. His instructions are to collaborate with the Spartans and he is provided with money to make the policy work. There can be no doubt now that Darius himself is putting his full weight behind the Spartans.

Ancillary but not essential to this view is Lewis' hypothesis (pp. 123–9) that the embassy of Boiotios (Xen. *Hell.* 1.4.2) had made a new treaty superseding that made with Tissaphernes in winter 412/11 – the evidence he adduces for it is not compelling.

21 Lewis (1958) proposed that troubles in Egypt prevented Tissaphernes using the fleet that came to Aspendus (8.87), or that Tissaphernes pretended so, but no such explanation is to be found for the period of Cyrus' command.

22 The fact that Pharnabazus was prepared to escort, in person, the Athenian embassy (which was on its way up to the King, but was turned back on meeting the embassy of Boiotios on its way down in the train of Cyrus) does strongly suggest that Pharnabazus was wanting to reconcile the King and the Athenians (cf. Amit (1973)), but he cannot earlier have been seeking to undo the policy of Tissaphernes, his superior – for that policy must have been royal policy. In so far as he seemed more strenuously to support the Spartans (8.99 and 109; Xen. *Hell.* 1.2.16, 3.5), he was concerned to exclude the Athenians from his satrapy, but there is no reason to think that he was trying to secure victory for Sparta. Pharnabazus may well have resented Tissaphernes being senior to him, as he showed he was later (Xen. *Hell.* 3.2.13) and, quite apart from Cyrus' ambitious demand for a command (cf. Lewis (1977: 134f.)), Darius may have seen that the appointment of a royal prince would prevent rivalry between the two satraps. Tissaphernes was replaced but not discredited (cf. Xen. *Anab.* 1.1.2 and *Hell.* 1.5.8 where the Athenians choose to approach Cyrus through Tissaphernes).

23 Cf. Lewis (1977: 134n151).

24 Antiphon seems to have prosecuted him for making an illegal proposal (Plut. *Mor.* 833D). Several fragments of his speech survive (fragments 8–14 in Thalheim's edition), but are hardly illuminating. There is no reason to think that there was anything important at issue.

25 Cf. Develin (1989). (It is not clear from the ordering of the oath-takers' names in 5.19.2 that Demosthenes was not a general in 422/1.)

26 Cf. Cawkwell (1983: 391).

27 Cf. Hornblower (1985: 133).

28 See, for example, *CAH* V^2 387.

29 *Historia* 5 (1956: 447).

30 Cf. Henderson (1927: 396) ('. . . for Demosthenes, greatest of Athens' soldier generals in the war, Thucydides can spare no single word of regret or praise. It is hard to forgive the greatest of historians this silence.')

31 See p. 17f.

4 THUCYDIDES, PERICLES AND THE 'RADICAL DEMAGOGUES'

1 4.21.3, 8.65.2; cf. Finley (1974).

2 Cf. Lys. 13.12.

3 Cf. Rhodes on *Ath. Pol.* 28.3, ML p. 260.

4 Cf. Kagan (1987: 249–51).

5 Rhodes on *Ath. Pol.* 34.1 reviews scholarly opinion and inclines to the view that the author of the *Ath. Pol.* was confused and that there was no Spartan appeal after Arginusae. Kagan (1987: 377f.) takes the opposite view.

6 Most notably, Endios, son of Alcibiades (Thuc. 8.6.3), the Spartan who put the Spartan case for peace after Cyzicus (Diod. 13.52.2) and who was one of the three ambassadors who negotiated in mid-408 the exchange of prisoners of war (Androtion = *FGH* 34 F 44). He had been in favour of a compact with the Athenians as early as 420 (Thuc. 5.44.3).

7 Hyperbolus was named in the Acharnians (846) of 425, and, in the following year, he was treated as a figure of some importance (*Knights* 1300–4). By the date of the second version of the *Clouds*, both Eupolis and Hermippus had laid into him as had others (*Clouds* 551–9). Plato Comicus later wrote a play entitled *Hyperbolus* (schol. Ar. *Thesmo.* 808: fragments collected in R. Kassel and C. Austin (eds), *Poetae Comici Graeci*, vol. VII, 505–8). Cf. Connor (1971: 81f.) for Hyperbolus' career and importance.

8 One may suspect that behind *Knights* 1304 lies a widely recognised interest on the part of Hyperbolus in the extension of Athenian influence in the West.

9 If P. J. Rhodes in Osborne and Hornblower (1994: 85–98, esp. 91) is correct (as I believe he is) in supposing that, although Andocides IV is not authentic, it is evidence for dating the ostracism of Hyperbolus in 415, Thucydides' failure to notice it must be explained partly in terms of his lack of concern for what he regarded as the small change of

Athenian politics and partly by remarking that he prefers to concentrate on the dramatic moment of decisions; e.g. he treats of only the second Mytilene debate and likewise of the second debate in 415 when Nicias tried to get the decision to send aid to Sicilian allies reversed.

10 Both Thucydides and Aristophanes, according to Gomme and Cadoux in OCD^2 (250), 'were clearly prejudiced against him'; likewise in Woodhead (1960), an article to which all unblushingly appeal. Gomme (1962: 112) raises the real question – 'that Thucydides disliked Kleon and thought him a vulgar demagogue and a most mischievous politician is obvious; but was he also *biased* in his narrative when Kleon is prominent?' It does not suffice to show that Thucydides thought ill of him. Cleon may have deserved to be ill thought of and any rational man would think the same as Thucydides. If Thucydides is to be convicted of unfairness, he must be shown to have given an untruthful account.

11 Cf. Develin (1989: 491).

12 Fornara and Samons (1991: ch. 3) are concerned to deny that Pericles was 'the radical founder of a new imperialism', rather than 'the continuator of Cimonian rule' (110), all of which cannot be discussed here. The promotion of cleruchies is a crucial matter.

13 The view is based on Thuc. 2.37.1 ('no man is excluded on grounds of poverty') and [Xen.] *Ath. Pol.* 1.2 (*dikaion einai pāsi tōn archōn meteinai en tōi klērōi kai en tēi cheirotoniāi*). See Rhodes (1981) on [Arist.] *Ath. Pol.* 7.4, pp. 145f.

14 The commentary of Stadter (1989: 144–77) provides a convenient account of Pericles' building programme. Cf. Boersma (1970).

15 Isoc. 15.234 comments that the Periclean building programme in the 350s still made Athens seem a worthy capital of Greece. Presumably at the time when Epaminondas was urging the Thebans to acquire empire by sea (Diod. 15.78.4), he declared that 'they must transfer the Propylaea to the forecourt of the Cadmea' (Aeschin. 2.105), as if the Propylaea were the proudest symbol of the Athenian Empire.

16 By Andrewes (1978).

17 The opposition of Cleon (Plut. *Per.* 33.7f.) seems to have been over Pericles' refusal to have the army go out and confront the Spartans in 430.

18 Since Callias appears to have gone on an embassy to Persia at least twice, i.e. in 450/49 and in 461 (Hdt. 7.151), it may be correct to follow Mosley (1973) in dating the fining to the former occasion, but Demosthenes speaks as if Callias had actually concluded the peace.

19 The theme of the *Panegyric* of 380 is Panhellenist (cf. §3), but there is also *apologia* for the Athenian Empire (100ff.), and the bankruptcy of imperialism is not asserted until the oration *On the Peace* of 355.

20 5.49.3–50.3, 6.84.2, 7.11.2.

21 The date of Gorgias' *Olympic Oration* is unknown, but cannot be earlier than 424, for his Gorgianic prose was evidently a startling novelty in 427 (Diod. 12.53).

22 Accepting the argument of Andrewes (1978).

NOTES

23 Granted that the tract is during *the* war (3.2 *tou polemou*) and that the war must be the Peloponnesian (2.16 abandonment of Attica to ravaging), indications of date are for the most part *termini ante quem*, albeit not very precise; e.g. the allusion to 'pestilences of crops' (2.6) makes one think of the Plague which came from Zeus, which must have very powerfully affected most Athenians, and it would be more comfortable if the passage was written before 430. The mention of a 'prominent headland' (2.13) has been thought by some to refer to Pylos, but the whole passage (2.13–15) is more properly understood in the light of Pericles' discussion of the strategy of sea-borne raids (Thuc. 1.142, a passage which, like the Old Oligarch, perhaps draws on Pericles' own words). So there is no good reason to date the work after 425. The only precise indication of date may indeed be found in 2.16, where he seems to describe the transfer of farm animals from Attica to the islands which Thucydides (2.14.1) puts in the opening days of the War. The present indicative tenses suggest that the treatise belongs exactly to that time. Of course, they may be repetitive presents describing what happens annually, but it is very unlikely that the transfer to the islands was repeated year by year, and a simple aorist participle (*parathemenoi*) would have naturally respected that. If the tract does date from the very beginning of the War, it is testimony to the moderation of Pericles and to the soundness of Thucydides' judgement.

24 Consistently, those who preferred to accept the Spartan offer of peace were described as *sōphrones* (4.28.5), a 'good word' (cf. 1.79.2).

25 Indeed, only Woodhead (1960) has put up the sort of apologia that is offered by those responsible for atrocities. 'Total war, as we know, is a savage and bitter thing, but if it is to be fought at all it must be fought totally. ... Like the Melian Dialogue, Cleon's speech represents a direct and sensible, and in the circumstances properly drastic, implementation of accepted doctrine' (p. 299f.)!

26 For example, Kagan (1974: 232–7).

27 Marcellinus' *Life of Thucydides* 46 is cited as evidence, but it seems to be based solely on Thucydides' own words (for *diaballontos* cf. 4.27.4 and 5.16.1; for *memēnota* cf. *maniōdēs* 4.39.3; and for *kouphon* cf. *kouphologia* 4.28.5).

28 Cf. Plut. *Per.* 33.8, 35.5; Ar. *Ach.* 6, 300, 377–82, etc.

29 For example, Hornblower (1987: 167).

30 For jury pay, Hansen (1991: 188f.), and for the reduction of interest on loans, ML p. 215.

31 The name of the proposer of the Assessment Decree of 425, Thudippus (ML 69 1.4 and 1.55), is also found in Isaeus 9, which concerns a Cleon, son of Thudippus, and it is perhaps not improper to suppose that the proposer of 425 was son-in-law of the demagogue (cf. Davies (1971: 228f.)), even though the speech betrays no hint of its Cleon's ancestor (cf. Bourriot (1982 410–18)). It must be remembered that, regardless of whether Thudippus was so related, Cleon was the dominant politician in 425.

32 Kallet-Marx (1993: 164–70) belittles the importance of the Assessment of 425 and so finds Thucydides' silence palatable. My viewpoint is quite the opposite. The Assessment was indeed important, but was not the sort of thing Thucydides thought it important to record.

33 Woodhead (1960: 299f.).

34 Woodhead (1960: 298).

35 III 459. Cf. Hornblower (1987: 56), Kagan (1974: 232–8).

36 Cf. Gomme (1962: 112).

37 Woodhead (1960: 313f.).

38 Westlake (1968: 69–75) lays out the case against Thucydides' fairness in his account of the debate admirably, but concedes (73) 'he may well be perfectly right in his interpretation of each move by Cleon throughout the episode; the available evidence certainly does not provide adequate grounds for believing that any of his interpretations must be wrong.' Thucydides resorts to *gnous* and *gnontes* elsewhere (e.g. 3.52, 4.128.1, 6.19.2, 8.12.1, 8.50.1, 5.15.2). Is he to be abused whenever he uses the verbs *gignōskein* and *nomizein* and the like in his narrative?

39 Cf. 6.24.1 for comparable tactics of Nicias over the Sicilian Expedition.

40 Woodhead (1960: 314).

41 Kagan (1974: 318).

42 Cf. Pritchett (1973) and Mitchell (1991: 176–82).

43 Woodhead (1960: 306–10).

44 For the form of Thucydides' expression, cf. 2.36.4 and 7.75.6.

45 *Pace* Gomme (1962: 115).

46 For example, Gomme (1962: 119). Kagan (1974: 330) seems to think no defence is necessary ('since the plan was not to stand and fight, Cleon was right to flee and the hoplites of the right wing wrong to make a stand if there were any way to avoid it.')

47 Woodhead (1960: 309), Kagan (1974: 330) ('an ancient tradition clearly shows Cleon fighting bravely at Amphipolis'). Diodorus is prone to give generals who die in battle a good 'send off' (11.18.5, 31.2; 12.3.5; 13.51.6; 15.17.1, 33.6, 55.5, 64.4 and 5, 80.5, 89.1), but if Brasidas did die 'like a hero', to say that Cleon did the same because Diodorus uses the word *homoīōs* seems monstrous. It is one of Diodorus' favourite words (the Diodorus *Lexicon* records 128 uses) and, generally speaking, has about as much colour as the English word 'likewise'. Westlake (1968: 81n2) is right.

48 The phrase is Busolt's (*Griechische Geschichte*, Gotha (1904) III.2, 1181n2).

49 *Panourgos* echoes and re-echoes through *The Knights* 12 times, in one form or another, where Cleon is introduced as *panourgotatos kai diabolōtatos* (45).

50 Cf. Kagan (1974: 332).

51 Syme, R. (1958) *Tacitus*, Oxford: Clarendon Press, vol. 1, Preface p. v: '. . . conjecture cannot be avoided, otherwise the history is not worth writing for it does not become intelligible.'

52 Connor (1984: 116) ('... some coordination between Cleon and Demosthenes seems likely'). Cf. Roisman (1993: 38n71).

53 The question has been much discussed. Cf. Babut (1986: 72n39).

54 The Spartan attempt to prevent Athens allying with Argos (5.45) and the oligarchic revolution (8.66.1, 69.4, 70.1, 86.6).

55 Cf. Flower (1992) for the whole debate. Whether Cleon was a sort of supernumerary general is debated – cf. Develin (1989: 130).

56 The reports would have had to go first to the Council (cf. Rhodes (1972: 53), citing Dem. 19.185) and would have occasioned a *probouleuma* to accompany their presentation to the Assembly.

57 Hunter (1973: 71f.) supposed that Demosthenes purposely had the fire started. Even if he was so silly as to think that this would make things easier for the light-armed attackers, he needed the Spartiates on Sphacteria as hostages, not as charred corpses.

58 Cf. Hunter (1973: 66–9).

5 THUCYDIDES, ALCIBIADES AND THE WEST

1 Cf. Hornblower *ad* 3.115.4.

2 Cf. Hornblower ad loc. Gomme (1962: 95–7) finds the judgement 'hardly consistent', but 'this is not to say that Thucydides' judgement *contradicts* his narrative in VI–VII (it may only supplement it), still less that it is wrong' – an interesting example of Gomme's belief in the infallibility of Thucydides. Dover in *HCT* V 423–7 is clear: 'there is good evidence for a genuine change of mind on Thucydides' part' (427).

3 Westlake (1969: 168) pointed out that 'not so much an error of judgement' is a quite misleading translation, that Thucydides was not saying that it was not a mistake to go on the expedition, but simply that that mistake was not as great as later mistakes.

4 Cf. Dover *HCT* V 424.

5 Indeed, Thucydides has the Syracusans astonished at the size of the force brought by Demosthenes, 'equal to and about as large as the first' (7.42.2), which it was as far as the number of hoplites was concerned, but not in ships (7.42.1 and 6.31.2).

6 Cf. *CAH* V^2 464f.

7 1.36.2 envisages the possibility of two-way traffic.

8 Stadter (1989: 221) surveys Athens' relations with the West during the Pentekontaetea. Themistocles naming his daughters Italia and Sybaris (Plut. *Them*. 32.2), however, looks a bit *ben trovato*, as if one was now to name one's daughter Hiroshima!

9 See above p. 12f.

10 See above p. 127n1.

11 The hypothesis of a war between Segesta and Selinus in the 450s rests on an emendation of Diodorus 11.86.2 (cf. App. Crit. in Teubner edition) concerning the year 454/3 – hardly a satisfactory support for an alliance of Athens and Segesta in 458/7. If the archon's name in the Segesta decree (ML 37) which ends in *ON* is indeed that of the archon of 458/7, it might be best to forget about Diodorus and simply

presume that the reason why the alliance was made was Segestan fear of their neighbour and ancient enemy, Selinus (cf. Diod. 5.9.2).

12 Plut. *Per.* 20.4, *Alc.* 17.1. Whence Plutarch derived his story of men sitting round and discussing the geography of the West, drawing maps of Sicily in the sand (cf. *Nic.* 12.1) is beyond conjecture. One suspects some fourth-century embroidery.

13 To judge by the presence of embassies from Leontini and Rhegium, it would appear that the initiative came from those states.

14 For Syracusan help for Sparta in the fourth century, Xen. *Hell.* 5.1.26, 28 (20 ships in 387), 6.2.33 (10 ships in 372), 7.1.20 and 28 (20 ships with mercenaries in 369 and 368). Cf. Xen. *Hell.* 6.2.9.

15 It is uncertain whether Thucydides wrote the Sicilian parts of his account of the Archidamian War before or after 415. The operations he recorded seem fairly petty, but Hermocrates, the leading spirit of Syracusan resistance in that year 'second to none in intelligence' (6.72.2), is given an ample speech at the conference of Gela (4.59–64), which has been supposed to give two hints of the expedition of 415. At 4.60.1, Hermocrates is made to speak of the 60 Athenian triremes in Sicilian waters in 424 as 'few', and he goes on in §2 to envisage the Athenians 'coming with a larger expedition sometime and trying to subject the whole of Sicily to themselves.' This may be merely a prediction that happened to come true, but it is more likely a matter of hindsight. Likewise with Thucydides' claim (3.86.4) that in 427 the Athenians partly wished to make 'a preliminary attempt' (*propeira*, the sole use of the word in Thucydides, matching a single use by Herodotus at 9.48.2, and never in Xenophon). To what was the 'attempt' 'preliminary'? Gomme ad loc. was 'not sure that *propeira* does not point only to the greater expedition of Eurymedon and Sophocles in 425–4.' Of course, one cannot be 'sure', but 'a preliminary attempt to see whether the position in Sicily (*ta en tēi Sikeliai pragmata*) could be brought under their control (*hypocheiria*)' looks suspiciously like Thucydides' view of 415. If he did write the Sicilian parts of the Archidamian War after he learned of the departure of the expedition in 415, was he affected in his judgement of 427–4 by 415, or did he write up 415 under the influence of what he knew of 427–4? This chapter argues for the latter. He knew about 427–4, but he only thought he knew about 415 and, in his postscript, had to retract.

16 The optative of *apochōrēseian* denotes what the Athenians thought, i.e. the charge against the generals.

17 Brunt (1993: 22–34) argues that Thucydides, to a large extent, based his account of Alcibiades on information provided by Alcibiades himself. That is highly probable for Book 8 (see below p. 144n22). Alcibiades played so crucial a role in 412 and 411 that it would be amazing if the exile at the western end of Thrace did not consult the exile at the eastern end. In Book 6, however, there is absolutely nothing that could have come only from Alcibiades. He was, admittedly, the only survivor of the three generals who shared in the discussion of strategy in chapters 47–9, but it is wholly improbable

that some subordinate officers were not well aware of the different views. In Book 5 the account of the Spartan embassy at Athens (44.3–46.3) is problematic; it might derive from Alcibiades boasting how smart he had been, but it might equally well derive from people showing what a dishonourable trickster the fellow was. It certainly does seem to be the case that Alcibiades made much of himself as, for instance, in 8.45–6 he is pictured counselling the wily Tissaphernes, to pursue a policy which he probably was well able to excogitate for himself. (How much Greek did Tissaphernes understand? He used an interpreter to communicate with the Greek generals of the Ten Thousand (Xen. *Anab.* 2.3.17), but one suspects that Tissaphernes was well aware of what Alcibiades and the Athenian ambassadors said to each other in his presence in the scene described in 8.56.) But if Thucydides heard Alcibiades boasting, he did not have to believe him and the uncritical account of how Alcibiades tricked the Spartan embassy in 420 is more likely to proceed from dislike than from information derived from him.

18 Moderns have not all been as commendatory of Alcibiades' military performance. Brunt (1993: 20f.) is dismissive. Lewis (*CAH* V^2 497) says of Thucydides' judgement at 6.15.2 that

> Alcibiades' performance between his recall by the fleet in 411 and his return to Athens in 407 gives something of a base for this judgement, but it does not follow that he could have coped equally well with the combination of Cyrus and Lysander. . . .

Kagan (1987) argues that Alcibiades has received credit more properly to be given to others, at Cyzicus to Thrasybulus (245), at Byzantium to Theramenes and Thrasyllus (284) and in the summing-up (323f.) he finds Alcibiades over-praised and outshone by Thrasybulus. Since Athenian generals were equals, it is not possible to say who, in any battle involving more than one general, was chiefly responsible, but the series of successes in the Hellespont involved the destruction of Spartan naval power and the restoration of Athenian empire and moved the Spartans to seek peace. That was enough for the Athenians and should be for us. Perhaps the unhappy outcome of the operations off Notium, undertaken in Alcibiades' absence, has unduly affected judgement. Antiochus, the steersman, who as the real professional was left in command by Alcibiades, essayed a minor success with a small patrolling force, which turned into a minor disaster, and Alcibiades quite unfairly got the blame (cf. my note on Xen. *Hell.* 1.5.14 on p. 76 of the Penguin translation, *Xenophon, A history of my times*, 1978 edition).

19 Cf. Dover *HCT* IV 240–5.
20 *Pace* Brunt (1993: 18n2).
21 At least the alliance with Argos secured that Argos supported Athens not only in Sicily (7.57.9), but also in Ionia (8.25.1). Thucydides may have thought such military assistance negligible. But Alcibiades' Argos policy led to the Battle of Mantinea which, without endangering a large number of Athenian lives, brought Sparta very close to disaster.

In Thucydides' view, the policy can have done nothing to bring on a resumption of the war, for he thought the peace was unreal (5.25). In fact, the Argive alliance constituted an implicit check on Spartan action and Alcibiades' remark at 6.16.6 is not a mere empty rhetorical claim. Cf. Kagan (1981: 71–4).

22 Brunt (1993) is probably, if not certainly, right about Book 8, for there is a curious hiatus in Thucydides' account of Alcibiades, who disappears after the battle of Miletus (8.26.3) and does not reappear for 20 chapters until he is found at the court of Tissaphernes (8.45.1), no account being offered of how he had fallen out with the Spartans. If Alcibiades was the main source of 8.45ff., there is no reason why this hiatus should have opened up – save that Book 8 is so patently not complete that one is not entitled to say that what Thucydides omitted, he was not well informed about. Brunt, it should be added, never claimed that his case was more than probable.

23 For the role and importance of cavalry, see below p. 83.

24 Westlake (1968: 190–2) declares confidently that Thucydides' version of the letter from Nicias to the assembly 'is certainly not a copy of the original or even an abstract of its salient points.' It does not profess to be a verbatim report, nor would one ever expect such a thing of a Greek historian, but the contents may well be very much what Nicias actually wrote. There are no philosophical generalisations, and the points made are all practical and credibly Nician.

25 Cf. Westlake (1968: 187).

26 See Dover HCT IV ad 7.50.4.

27 Cf. Liebeschuetz (1968: 299–302).

28 The Athenian rebuff at Camarina (6.52) was due not to a failure of diplomacy, but to a misleading message from that city. The failure of diplomacy came after Alcibiades had departed (6.75.3–88.2).

29

> The combined resources of Gela and Syracuse, together with their allies, provided a strength in war that was nearly invincible. More than any other factor, it was their supplies of horses which brought about the downfall of the great Athenian expedition of 415 BC. . . .
>
> (Frederiksen, 1968: 10–12, see also p. 28n36)

In view of Thucydides' picture of the state of affairs on the eve of Gylippus' arrival (6.103.1–3), Frederiksen is wide of the mark. If the circumvallation had been completed as it would have been under the more energetic general, Athens had enough cavalry. There were ample horses in Sicily: Nicias had asked for and received horsemen (6.88.6, 93.4). Of course, Alcibiades would not have begun the circumvallation until he had all the necessary forces and manpower ready to complete it in double quick time.

30 The class of landholders, who were presumably the descendants of the original settlers, are alluded to as *gamoroi* only in this passage of Herodotus. (Diodorus (1.28.5) speaks of *geōmoroi* in Egypt, and

likewise Thucydides (8.21) of Samos.) The *dynatoi* at Leontini were no doubt the landowners, threatened by the *dēmos* with a redistribution of land (5.4.2).

31 For this Euboea, see Strabo 272c and 449c.

32 See Dover *ad* 7.55.2, and Lewis in *CAH* VI² 125.

33 Athenagoras was obviously important in 415, but Thucydides names him twice only and we have no idea who, apart from Hermocrates, was politically active in 424.

34 Westlake (1969: 174ff.) furnishes a useful survey of Hermocrates' career.

35 Sicels living on the coastal plain had been subjected by Syracuse; those in the hinterland were independent (6.88.4, 3.103.1; for Centoripa, 6.94.3). Morgantina had been handed over to Camarina in the peace of Gela (4.65.1), having earlier been taken by Ducetius (Diod. 11.78.5). (For the site of Morgantina, see Asheri in *CAH* V² 161f.)

36 This was the good question raised by Henderson (1927: 245–53), to which he gave the far from good answer that the Sicilians had heard of a proposal by Hyperbolus to send 100 ships against Carthage (witness Ar. *Knights* 1302–15), which Henderson regarded as no laughing matter.

37 The operations that Thucydides found 'most worthy of mention' seem petty (3.90). No large Syracusan naval force appears, an impression reinforced by the events described on the papyrus from Oxyrhynchus (*FGH* 577.2).

38 The Peace of Gela is a shadowy affair. The clause appealed to by Camarina in 415 (6.52.1) cannot belong to the Peace (see Dover *ad* loc.) and, in any case, it was part of a treaty of alliance (cf. 6.87.2); it must be part of an alliance made when Leontini and her allies appealed to Athens in 427 (3.86). There certainly does seem to have been a clause defining the limits of Sicilian waters (6.13.1), but the main clause declared that each 'signatory' should continue to hold what it held at the moment of operations ceasing (4.65.1). A clause guaranteeing joint assistance in case of attack is to be presumed.

39 Gone are the days when the silence of Thucydides was decisive. If Syracuse did seek to counter the Segestan appeal of 416/15, they would have done so months before the events recorded in 6.8. The most telling argument against Andocides is that, in the speech Thucydides put in the mouth of Athenagoras (6.36–41), he treats it as wholly unlikely that there is any truth in the report of an Athenian armada on its way. If Syracuse had tried to prevent Athens helping Segesta by offering alliance herself, there should have been nothing surprising about Athens coming west, as they had done before. The other point against Andocides' story is that he speaks of Catana as a central player, which certainly conflicts with Thucydides' account (6.51, cf. 20.3). At an interval of 23 years, Andocides could be confusing and confused (cf. §6 for another startling statement).

40 Dover *ad* 7.48.2 suggests that it was 'probably some of the wealthy citizens of Leontini who in 422 had become citizens of Syracuse and

had not broken away among the earlier malcontents' (5.4.3f.). The talks with Nicias (6.103.3) and the planned assembly (7.2.1) sound like the work of more than a few dissidents.

41 See Brunt (1993: 26f). One would dearly like to know when this speech was written. Alcibiades may indeed have advised the Spartans to establish a strong-point in Attica; to give the obvious advice, which was in no way needed, was the right way to establish credibility. The specifying of Decelea (6.91.6) may well be a piece of hindsight. Likewise, the assertion that such a fortification 'is the only thing amongst the hardships the war can bring which they think they have not experienced' followed in §7 by a listing of its ill consequences for Athens looks like wisdom after the event. Of course, the Athenians may have precisely envisaged the effects of the fortification of Decelea, but if they did it is surprising they did not fortify and hold it themselves. For a different view of the speech see Westlake (1968: 225–30).

42 Thucydides asserted that the Ephors and 'those in office' intended to send an embassy to Syracuse, but were not keen to send military aid (6.88.10). However, it is not clear what the proposal before the assembly was (cf. 6.93.1–2). If the Spartans already intended to campaign against Athens (6.93.1), what else could they have had in mind other than the *epiteichismos* they were preparing for in winter 422/1?

43 Plut. *Mor.* 237a, *Lycurgus* 16.10, Isoc. 12.209.

44 Brunt (1993: 42–4) accepted the story. Opposition was best expressed by Busolt, G. (1904) *Griechische Geschichte*, Gotha, III.2: 1327n3; the notice in Plutarch he supposed to derive from the Isocrates speech, which is not to be regarded seriously, and he found it unlikely that Alciabiades would even wish to go to Argos where the *dēmos* was opposed to his friends and on good terms with the Athenian *dēmos*, whose leaders had most vigorously agitated against him (6.61.3). But at least Alcibiades did have friends in Argos, so it would have been plain good sense to try his luck there. Nor is there any justification for the claim that Plutarch *Alcibiades* 23 derived from Isocrates 16; ch. 22 certainly did not.

45 Perhaps Thucydides was persuaded that Alcibiades from the outset intended to betake himself to Sparta and so felt no need to go into the matter of the sojourn at Argos.

6 THUCYDIDES AND THE EMPIRE

1 De Ste Croix (1954).
2 De Ste Croix (1981: 290).
3 De Ste Croix (1972: 40).
4 Perhaps it was this admission that moved Finley (1978: 310n57) to 'see no need to enter into the debate over "the popularity of the Athenian Empire"'.
5 Cf. the *apologia* of empire in Tacitus *Histories* 4.74; also Cicero *Ad Q.F.* 1.1.34.

6 The rise of piracy after the King's Peace is noted by Isocrates (4.115). In early times, piracy was widespread (1.5) and defence against it was attempted by not siting cities close to the shore (1.7) unless, of course, there was a strong naturally defensible position (as Xenophon in *Anabasis* 6.4.3–4 claimed to have found on the southern shore of the Pontus). The real defence was provided by strong naval power. The Minoan thalassocracy mentioned by Thucydides (1.4) has been questioned (see Hornblower ad loc.), but perhaps wrongly, to judge at any rate by the case of Thera. The ancient city at Akrotiri, brought to an abrupt volcanic burial, was situated on flat ground easily enough accessible to the sea-raider, whereas classical Thera, founded in the Dark Age, was on high ground, access to which could easily be controlled. Through the sixth century, piracy flourished, notably in the case of the pirate tyrant of Samos as the name of his son, Syloson, testifies, but with the Delian League things were different. Cimon cleared the pirates out of Scyrus (Plut. *Cim.* 8) and, no doubt, the constant movement of naval forces generally put the pirates out of business, for otherwise Athens would not have been able to require cities to pull down their walls and expose them to marauders (cf. especially 3.33.2 and Hornblower ad loc.). Indeed, Pericles' Congress Decree (Plut. *Per.* 17), which *pace* Seager (1969) I hold to be authentic, professedly aimed to secure the safety of the seas. Once the war began, however, pirates used by Sparta – just as in the 350s and the 340s they would be used by Philip of Macedon – re-emerged (2.69 and cf. 8.35 and Andocides 1.138). Such oscillation between strong naval power and, when it faltered, the return of piracy, continued throughout the centuries. Ormerod (1924) remains the best account in English. Amit (1965: 119–21) is useful.

7 See de Ste Croix (1961), who discusses in Part III (270–7) the 'political' cases.

8 Cf. Meiggs (1972: 265).

9 Hornblower ad loc. is excessively sceptical. Greek states would not have been equal, demographically speaking, to manning a large number of ships year in and year out.

10 See Appendix 3.

11 Seager (1967).

12 Cawkwell (1976).

13 Cawkwell (1973: 56–60).

14 'The cities' is the short phrase used in fifth-century inscriptions for the Empire, as is to be seen in decrees of general imperial scope, such as the Coinage Decree (ML 45), the Clinias decree (ML 46), the Collectors of tribute decree (ML 68), the Assessment decree of 425 (ML 69), and the First-fruits for Eleusis decree of 422 (ML 73). The full version, 'the cities which the Athenians control', is to be found in the decree honouring Leonidas of Halicarnassus (*IG* 1^3 156), but the short version sufficed for Aristophanes (*Acharnians* 642) and for Eupolis as a title. So when Isocrates and Xenophon used the phrase, it was loaded with imperial associations.

147

NOTES

15 Cargill (1981, especially 176–9) argues that it was only during the Social War of 357–5 that Athenian imperialism reasserted itself, that for the rest the record of Athens from 378 onwards was white as driven snow, and he appeals to Isocrates (8.141) as evidence of Athens' unblemished record. But that passage must be understood in the context of Isocrates' summary of the good consequences that will follow from the changes he has advocated (§§133–44). §142, which speaks of the ill-esteem in which Athens is currently held, shows plainly that in §141 Isocrates is speaking of the future. Isocrates has argued against the recrudescence of Athenian imperialism, which threatened the Second Athenian Confederacy, sidelined since Leuctra. Cf. Cawkwell (1981: 51–5).

16 Griffith (1978) omits all consideration of the external constraints on Athens' relations with her allies.

17 Cawkwell (1981).

18 Diod. 15.95.3. The status of Corcyra is made plain by ML 127, *pace* Cargill (1981: 72–4).

19 See above p. 5–7.

20 De Ste Croix (1954: 31).

21 De Ste Croix (1954: 4), Gillis (1971), Macleod (1983: 100 and n53). See Hornblower *ad* 3.27.3.

22 Cf. Andrewes (1962: 78 and n34).

23 In the event the Peloponnesians, among those captured at Torone, were released under the terms of the Peace of Nicias (5.3.4). Presumably, they had been intended all along to be used, along with the captives of Sphacteria, as bargaining counters. The rest were used to exchange for Athenians held in Olynthus (ibid.), thus escaping death, unlike the Scioneans who had chosen to revolt (4.120.1, 122.6).

24 De Ste Croix (1954: 11).

25 Hence the prominence of Samos in the narrative of Book 8; see especially 8.73.4 and cf. Andoc. 2.11. For the fourth century, see Polyaenus 6.2.1.

26 Harpocration s.v. *eklogeis* ('Those who collect and exact what is owed to the public chest. Antiphon in the speech about the Samothracians' tribute: "For we (*sc.* we Samothracians) have as collectors those who are thought to have the most wealth." Lysias in the speech against Aresandros "But now we register everything with the collectors of the tribute." ') is the only occurrence of the term, but its use in the supplementation of line 8 of ML 68 ('Appointment of Tribute Collectors: 426 BC') is justified by the phrase in line 55 (those 'who will collect the tribute'). Presumably, these rich men had to pay the tribute and reimburse themselves from their fellow citizens. Antiphon (frag. 51 Thalheim) seems to be arguing for a lesser tribute for Samothrace because the island, being to begin with small, has only small parts that can be worked and made to produce. Persian tribute was based on the size of a state's territory and this seems to have been followed in the Delian League (Hdt. 6.42.2). So perhaps it was the farming class that carried this burden of empire.

27 See above p. 93 and below n29.

28 *IG* 1³ 96, which concerns Samos, is a poor basis for generalisation, since with the formal grant of *autonomia* in 412 (8.21) that city may well have been far from typical. The amendment to the Chalcis Decree (ML 52 70–6) is similarly unreliable. First, it is the amendment from 'the floor of the House' of what the Council had given its blessing to, and while we do not know whether Archestratus was insisting on a mere rewording or was making a substantial change in procedure, it can hardly be relied upon as a statement of settled imperial policy. Second, it is concerned with *euthynai*, the term regularly used at Athens for judicial inquiries into the acts of magistrates, and it is wholly improbable, *pace* de Ste Croix (1961: 271), that this special word would have been used in an Athenian decree in the broad sense of 'proceedings involving criminal punishment'. Such a claim can only be made by those who do not understand that the decree to which Archestratus was making the amendment was itself a series of answers to queries from the Chalcidians, about 'hostages' (l. 47), about 'the foreigners' (l. 52). The clauses of 'the decree of the *dēmos*' (l. 76), to which Archestratus referred, i.e. *ta epsēphismena* of l. 49, we do not know. (They were perhaps published to the left of the inscription we have, that is, on one large broad *stēlē*, and that is why the left edge of ML 46 is rough-cut and why, uniquely, ML 46 does not carry the Secretary's name, the real indication of date, for that name would have been cut in large letters across the top of the complete *stēlē*, if (as is possible enough) both the original decree and the decrees of the inscription we have were passed within the same prytany – and this would explain why *horkos* is spread across the bottom of our *stēlē*. It was not the *syngraphai*, which were on the left.) So to generalise from the Chalcis Decree about the judicial arrangements of the Athenian Empire is somewhat unsatisfactory, but Archestratus' amendment may show the direction in which things were tending. How fairly the final state of affairs is represented by a statement of an Athenian orator (Antiphon 5.47), which may be highly tendentious, is very open to question; if every murder within the Athenian Empire was automatically tried in Athens, only the richest could contemplate seeking redress in a court of law.

Similarly, the evidence concerning privileges granted to favoured persons is provided by fragmentary inscriptions – cf. de Ste Croix (1961: 272–5). The best is *IG* 1³ 65, but one cannot be sure that the privileges of Apollonophanes were not peculiar to himself. There is much to be said for the view that, in the Athenian Empire, there was complexity and variety, not regularity, important matters being decided on the whim of an Archestratus.

29 We cannot know whether there was any truth at all in the charge against the generals who assented to the Peace of Gela, namely that they had been bribed (4.65.3), although in view of the frequency of such allegations one is sceptical (cf. the rubbish thrown at Timagoras in 367, which is described in Plutarch *Artax*. 22.9–12, when he was on trial for having accepted the Boeotian case – Xen. *Hell*. 7.1.35, Dem. 19.137). The trial of Pericles in 430 (2.65) was as unjust as it seems

absurd, for he was made responsible for the decision taken on his advice to go to war (2.59.2, 65.2) – a wonderful example of the irresponsibility of the *dēmos* (Xen. *Ath. Pol.* 2.17). Alcibiades was prudent in refusing to face Athenian justice (6.61.6). The Generals of Arginusae were executed in a fit of mob passion, for which repentance shortly followed (Xen. *Hell.* 1.7.34–5). There are ample cases of such 'political' trials in the fourth century. Aristophanes had written his *Wasps* in vain.

30 According to Androtion (*FGH* 324 F46), Dorieus was executed by the Spartans in the mid-390s, in the very period when the rest of the family, according to the Oxyrhynchus Historian (15.2 Bart = 1. 360 Chambers), was put to death with the connivance of Conon. Not a family of quislings, it would seem.

31 Whether reference to Athens was automatic or optional remains unclear.

32 The Old Oligarch (Xen. *Ath. Pol.* 1.14f.) might suggest that there were a large number of persons suffering major penalties, but the tone of the passage is intemperate. It seems much more likely that the main effect of Athens' judicial arrangements was to exclude independent-minded people from politics in the subject states.

33 See Appendix 3.

34 Cf. Rhodes (1981: 305). Balcer (1976) assembles the evidence for overseas magistrates. It is to be noted that the Old Oligarch (Xen. *Ath. Pol.* 1.19) could say that the Athenians have learnt to row in going out to serve as 'overseas magistrates', which perhaps suggests that there were a large number of persons concerned.

35 The '1,000 cities' of *Wasps* 707 is a joke, but there are nearly 250 cities listed on the tribute lists of the period before the War, and in 425 a great many more were assessed.

36 Collected in Meiggs-Andrewes Index III.4.10. The case of the *Hellespontophylakes* is arresting. They are once mentioned in the Methone Decree (ML 65 l. 37) and nowhere else, be it in literature or in lexicography; yet they are likely to have been in place all through the war and possibly earlier – cf. Cawkwell (1975: 55n4).

37 The word is supplemented in the Erythrae Decree (ML 40 l. 13) and in *IG* 1^3 13, which may be part of the same decree. The word is found on its own in a fragment, but in the Clinias Decree (ML 46 l. 7), although all but the last three letters are supplement, it seems sure that, unlike *archontes*, *episkopoi* are not 'in the cities'; which accords with the role of the *episkopos* in *Birds* 1050 as a roving commissioner.

38 The evidence for Athenian overseas settlements during the Empire is usefully collected in Jones (1957: 167–73). There is little to be gained by seeking to distinguish 'cleruchs' (3.50.2) from '*epoikoi*' (2.70.4, 8.69.3, etc.) or, indeed, '*apoikoi*' from '*epoikoi*' (4.102.2, 5.116.4). One suspects that Thucydides used the two latter terms indifferently. He used the word 'cleruchs' the once only. (Indeed, he spoke of the cleruchs sent to Mytilene almost as if such a thing was a novelty, which it certainly was not (Plut. *Per.* 11 etc.) – just as one would hardly suppose from 1.87.4 that there was settled procedure in the

Peloponnesian League. The novelty of Mytilene was perhaps that, although the cleruchs were sent out from Athens, the Lesbians took it on themselves to work the land and pay rent for it (3.50.2). See below n40.) Under one guise or another, a large number of Athenians were settled in the Empire and these were no doubt the majority of those sent home after Aegospotami (Xen. *Hell.* 2.2.9, Plut. *Lys.* 13.3f.), but not all. Athenians held property overseas (Finley, 1978: 115–17; Gauthier, 1973) and presumably this involved them visiting their estates and treating 'the citizens of petty states' (Xen. *Hell.* 2.3.10) in unendearing ways.

39 The commentary on ML 79 furnishes references to the full publication of the *stēlai*.

40 Gauthier (1966) proposed that since the two minas rent the Lesbians paid for each roughly amounted to a hoplite's pay, those sent out from Athens formed a garrison, but, *pace* Hornblower *ad* 3.50.2 who accepts the theory, the objection of Brunt (1993: 126f.) is compulsive; there is no trace of a garrison at the moments when it might have been expected to assert itself (cf., for example, 4.75). Nor would one expect a garrison to be chosen by lot, and 2,700 hoplites would be an astonishingly large number to be sent to the one island. The reasonable explanation is that those who were sent out (cf. *apepempsan* in 3.50.2) drifted home, just as in the fourth century the Samian cleruchy appears to have twice needed replacements (cf. Jacoby *ad FGH* 328 F154). The Lesbian cities did not need garrisons in 427; the Mytilenians had lost their fleet and their walls (3.50.1) and that sufficed. (*IG* 1^3 66, which concerns cleruchs and Mytilenians, is too fragmentary to be of use.)

41 We rely almost entirely on the Decree of Aristotle (ML 123) for the names. The total of 75 derives from Diodorus 15.28.3, 29.6 and 30.2, ultimately one presumes from Ephorus who was alive and aware in the 370s.

42 The history of the growth of the Confederacy is to be deduced almost entirely from the Decree of Aristotle, on which names were inscribed in groups by different hands (see commentary *ad* ML 123). Cf. Cawkwell (1981: 41–7).

43 ML 67 concerns 'contributions to the Spartan war-fund'. (For new fragment and improved text, see Loomis (1992).) If it is correctly dated to the Archidamian War – cf. Loomis (1992: 63–76) – the contributions of 'the Melians' may help to explain why Athens attacked Melos in 426 (3.91.1f.), but in no way condone the assault of 416.

44 Note the plural in *Birds* 1021.

45 Cf. *FGH* 392 F6 (= Athenaeus 13 603E-604D), where Ion of Chios describes a dinner-party given for Sophocles, as general, *en route* in 440 for Lesbos, by the Athenian *proxenos* in Chios. Ion himself had gone to Athens as a youth and recorded dining with Themistocles (Plut. *Cim.* 9.1) and was evidently of an atticising family (cf. 8.38.3 and Andrewes ad loc.). Similarly with Athenians, who were *proxenoi* of other states, such as Callias in the first four decades of the fourth century. Spartan envoys stayed with him (Xen. *Hell.* 5.4.22) and he

was constantly to the fore in business which concerned Sparta (id. 6.3.4), just as Alcibiades, another Spartan *proxenos*, as his ancestors had been (6.89.2), expected to be used by Sparta in making the Peace of Nicias (5.43.2).

46 Cf. the activities of Pithias at Corcyra (3.70.3).

47 De Ste Croix (1954: 11).

APPENDIX 1 A NOTE ON THE SO-CALLED 'FINANCIAL DECREES' OF CALLIAS, *IG* 1³ 52 (= ML 58)

1 ML (p. 157) follow Wade-Gery in declaring that the two decrees were cut by different hands. I follow Bradeen (1971: 469) who asserts the contrary. Cf. Kallet-Marx (1989: 95n6).

2 The absence of the definite article in line 13 was emphasised by Thompson (1973: 29). 'The normal Greek for reaffirming the office would be *tos de tamias apokuameuen*.' Cf. Kallet-Marx (1989: 105).

3 *Art. cit.* n1.

4 Pritchett (1971: 220–5).

5 As Kallet-Marx points out (p. 103), the total borrowings for the period 433–26 which are stated in the *logistai* accounts of the Archidamian War (ML 72 ll. 112–20) provide no proof that borrowings from the Other Gods began before the War.

6 The full entry of Harpocration is cited in Meiggs and Andrewes 121.

7 F. Jacoby in *FGH* IIIb (Kommentar) p. 145 says: 'Everything points to a work that was really informative and really learned, well based on documents. . . . '

8 Assuming that the Opisthodomos of l. 15 was 'the back room' of the Parthenon.

9 Cf. Fornara (1970: 189) – 'The explanation put forward in favour of 434/3 consequently stultifies Thucydides' entire exposition. . . . The speech of the Corinthians presupposes a set of possibilities already precluded by this alleged action of the Athenians; they have already evacuated their temple treasures in preparation for a Spartan invasion.'

10 In §7 the speaker would have it that the lateness of the *dokimasia* is due to some improper scheming by Evander.

11 Hansen (1991: 220).

12 Generals were elected much earlier than other magistrates (*Ath. Pol.* 44.1) to suit the campaigning season, but in general Athens was rather a 'last minute' society. Cf. the short time provided for preparation by those choosing to join the colony of Brea on their return from military service (ML 49 ll. 27–30), or the 10 days envisaged as sufficient for those who have been ostracised to settle up outstanding legal business (*FGH* 328 F30).

13 Meritt (1969: 217).

APPENDIX 2 THE MEGARA DECREES OF PLUTARCH, *PERICLES* 30

1 De Ste Croix (1972: 246–51).
2 Brunt (1993: 15). Fornara (1975: 218ff.) agreed with de Ste Croix. Cf. Stadter (1989: 174–6).
3 Mosley (1973a: 81–9, especially 84–7) for the differing roles of heralds and ambassadors.
4 Cf. Cic. *Ad Fam.* 8.8.9 (*At ille quam clementer: 'Quid, si filius meus fustem mihi impingere volet?'*). Most scholars have agreed that, behind Pompey's courtesy and reasonableness, there was a nasty threat.
5 Thucydides may have not deigned to dwell on these essentially religious excursions, or he may have thought the repetition of 'wide ravaging' would be boring.
6 Cf. Stadter (1989: 281).
7 The dates of the truces for the Greater and Lesser Mysteries are known from *IG* 1³ 6 B 17–47. The Greater fell in Boedromion (roughly September), and the Truce could be made for about two months in all, though no doubt for places as near as Megara it would have been much shorter.
8 Cawkwell (1969).
9 De Ste Croix (1972: 387f.).
10 Cf. Brunt (1993: 15).
11 Cf. Parke (1977: 135).
12 De Ste Croix (1972: 388) says that the view that the ban on Megarians entering Attica was related to the period of the Mysteries is 'flatly contradicted by the very words of the decree' which I proceed to quote. Not so, if the whole decree was about the Mysteries. Also, the decree was no doubt much fuller than Plutarch's account of it; very few decrees contain as few as 40 words. My hypothesis may be wrong, but it is not 'flatly contradicted' by the evidence.

APPENDIX 3 MILITARY SERVICE IN THE ATHENIAN EMPIRE

1 Blackman (1969) is concerned entirely with naval service before the Peloponnesian War. I am not aware of any discussion of allied contributions to armies.
2 At Delium in 424 there were 7,000 Athenian hoplites when the army went out 'in full force' (*pandēmei*) (4.90.1, 93.3, 94.1). The word is used freely by Thucydides in relation to a great variety of states in situations for which he is unlikely to have had precise knowledge of numbers, and one suspects that he used it to describe a comparatively large force and that it is no more precisely to be understood than *panstratiāi*, with which it seems interchangeable (cf. 2.31). Of course, if Athens had put every hoplite she had into the field in 431, there could have been 13,000 of them (2.13.6), but in practice armies were probably more modest in size.

3 Plut. *Cim.* 11.1 describes how Cimon dealt with allies who 'neither manned the ships nor despatched men' (i.e. soldiers). Those who came to the assistance of the Athenians on Lesbos in 428 were not rendering naval service (3.5.1).

4 Note particularly 1.99.2 (*oute xynestrateuon apo tou isou*). Eurymedon was a special effort with 200 Athenian ships and 100 allied (Diod. 11.60, Plut. *Cim.* 12).

5 It is curious that Thucydides did not mention them at 2.56, but did at 6.31.2.

6 In 361, when Leosthenes was engaged at Peparethos, he sent calls for help to Samos, Thasos and the Hellespont (Polyaenus 6.2.1), where presumably detachments of the navy were stationed. Thasos was certainly a base as Dem. 50 (esp. 48–52) shows. There is a helpful account of sailing conditions in the Aegean in *CAH* VI^2 519–22. Because Philip of Macedon so effectively exploited the Etesians (mod. *Meltem*) (cf. Dem. 4.31, 8.14), they are much discussed in connection with fourth-century history. We do not hear of them in the fifth century because Athens could afford to keep ships based in the north.

7 The Imbrians and the Lemnians engaged in the suppression of the Mytilene Revolt (3.5.1) were, of course, Athenian cleruchs (cf. 7.57.2).

8 Whatever military obligations Rhodes had were probably met by the provision of the two pentekonters (6.43).

9 I by no means accept the arguments of Seager (1969) against the authenticity of the Congress Decree.

10 Cf. *CAH* V^2 129f.

11 The Congress Decree (Plut. *Per.* 17.1) professes that part of Athens' purpose is to see 'that all may sail the seas free from fear'.

12 According to Gomme (*HCT* III 509), 'the numeral can hardly stand . . . in 8.25.2 the Milesians have only 800 when defending their own lands. Some figure such as 400 or 500 is doubtless right.' Diodorus 12.65.8 gives 2,000 as the total number of hoplites in Nicias' attack on Cythera.

13 In line 10 a 'trireme' and 'the troop carriers' appear; in line 11 there is allusion to 'hoplite status'; in line 15 there is mention of 'the soldiers'. D. M. Lewis (*British School at Athens* 49, 1954: 24n19) thought that these terms come too early in the decree to belong to a statement of Miletus' military obligations, but an alternative interpretation is not obvious.

14 See the bibliography cited at *IG* 13 21.

15 There is no trace of Miletus producing a trireme in the Archidamian War, and by 415 it is clear she did not (7.57).

LIST OF WORKS
REFERRED TO
IN NOTES

Abbreviations of titles of periodicals appear as in *L'Année Philologique*.

Adcock, F. E. (1963) *Thucydides and his History*, Cambridge University Press.

Amit, M. (1965) *Athens and the Sea, Collection Latomus* vol. 74, Brussels.

—— (1973) 'Le traité de Chalcédoine entre Pharnabaze et les stratèges athéniens', *Antiquité Classique* 42: 436–57.

Andrewes, A. (1959) 'Thucydides on the causes of the war', *CQ* 53 (N.S. 9): 223–39.

—— (1962) 'The Mytilene debate', *Phoenix* 16: 64–85.

—— (1978) 'The opposition to Pericles', *JHS* 98: 1–8.

Babut, D. (1986) 'L'épisode de Pylos-Sphactérie', *RPh* 60: 59–79.

Badian, E. (1993) *From Plataea to Potidaea*, Baltimore and London: Johns Hopkins University Press.

Balcer, J. M. (1976) 'Imperial magistrates in the Athenian Empire', *Historia* 25: 257–87.

Bar-Hen, E. (1977) 'Sparte et la guerre du Péloponnèse', *Ancient Society* 8: 21–31.

Blackman, D. (1969) 'The Athenian navy and allied naval contributions in the Pentecontaetia', *GRBS* 10: 179–216.

Boersma, J. S. (1970) *Athenian Building Policy from 561/0 to 405/4* BC, Groningen: Wolters-Noordhoff.

Bourriot, F. (1982) 'La famille et le milieu social de Cléon', *Historia* 31: 404–35.

Bradeen, D.W. (1971) 'The Kallias Decrees again', *GRBS* 19: 469–83.

Brunt, P. A. (1993) *Studies in Greek History and Thought*, Oxford: Oxford University Press.

Cargill, J. L. (1981) *The Second Athenian League: Empire or Free Alliance?*, Berkeley, LA: University of California Press.

Cartledge, P. A. (1979) *Sparta and Lakonia*, London: Routledge & Kegan Paul.

Cawkwell, G. L. (1969) 'Anthemocritus and the Megarians and the decree of Charinus', *REG* 82: 327–35.

—— (1970) 'The fall of Themistocles', in B. F. Harris (ed.) *Auckland Classical Essays presented to E.M. Blaiklock*, Auckland: Auckland University Press, 39–58.

—— (1973) 'The foundation of the Second Athenian Confederacy', *CQ* 23: 47–60.

—— (1975a) 'Thucydides' judgement of Periclean strategy', *Yale Classical Studies* 24: 53–70.

—— (1975b) Review of G. E. M. de Ste Croix, *The Origins of the Peloponnesian War*, *CR* 25: 258–61.

—— (1976) 'The imperialism of Thrasybulus', *CQ* 26: 270–7.

—— (1981) 'Notes on the failure of the Second Athenian Confederacy', *JHS* 101: 40–55.

—— (1983) 'The decline of Sparta', *CQ* 33: 385–400.

Chambers, M. H. (1992) 'Photographic enhancement of a Greek inscription', *CJ* 88: 25–31.

—— (1993) 'The archon's name in the Athenian-Egesta alliance (*IG* 13 11)', *Zeitschrift für Papyrologie und Epigraphik* 98: 171–4.

Chambers, M. H., Gallucci, R. and Spanos, P. (1990) 'Athens' alliance with Egesta in the year of Antiphon', *Zeitschrift für Papyrologie und Epigraphik* 83: 38–63.

Connor, W. R. (1971) *The New Politicians of Fifth-Century Athens*, Princeton, NJ: Princeton University Press.

—— (1984) *Thucydides*, Princeton, NJ: Princeton University Press.

Davies, J. K. (1971) *Athenian Propertied Families*, Oxford: Oxford University Press.

Derenne, E. (1930) *Les procès d'impiété intentés aux philosophes à Athènes au Vme et au IVme siècles av. J.C.*, Liège-Paris: H. Vaillant-Carmanne.

de Ste Croix, G. E. M. (1954) 'The character of the Athenian Empire', *Historia* 3: 1–41.

—— (1961) 'Jurisdiction in the Athenian Empire', *CQ* 11: 94–112 and 268–80.

—— (1972) *The Origins of the Peloponnesian War*, London: Duckworth.

—— (1981) *The Class Struggle in the Ancient Greek World*, London: Duckworth.

Develin, R. (1989) *Athenian Officials*, Cambridge: Cambridge University Press.

Dover, K. J. (1988) *The Greeks and their Legacy. Collected Papers II*, Oxford: Oxford University Press.

Finley, M. I. (1974) 'Athenian demagogues', in M. I. Finley (ed.) *Studies in Ancient Society*, London: Routledge & Kegan Paul, 1–25.

—— (1978) 'The fifth-century Athenian Empire: a balance sheet', in P. D. A. Garnsey and C. R. Whittaker (eds), *Imperialism in the Ancient World*, Cambridge: Cambridge University Press, 103–26 and 306–10.

Flower, H. I. (1992) 'Thucydides and the Pylos debate', *Historia* 41: 40–57.

Fornara, C. W. (1970) 'The date of the Callias Decrees', *GRBS* 11: 185–96.

—— (1975) 'Plutarch and the Megarian decree', *Yale Classical Studies* 24: 213–18.

Fornara, C. W. and Samons, L. J. (1991) *Athens from Cleisthénes to Pericles*, Berkeley, LA: University of California Press.

Frederiksen, M. W. (1968) 'Campanian cavalry: a question of origins', *Dialoghi di Archeologia* 2: 3–28.

Gardiner, E. N. (1910) *Greek Athletic Sports and Festivals*, London: Macmillan.

Gauthier, P. (1966) 'Les clérouques de Lesbos et la colonisation athénienne au Vme siècle', *REG* 79: 64–88.

—— (1973) 'A propos des clérouquies athéniennes du Vme siècle', in M. I. Finley (ed.) *Problèmes de la terre en Grèce ancienne*, Paris: Mouton, 163–78.

Gillis, D. (1971) 'The revolt at Mytilene', *AJPh* 92: 38–47.

Gomme, A. W. (1962) *More Essays in Greek History and Literature*, Oxford: Blackwell.

Griffith, G. T. (1978) 'Athens in the fourth century', in P. D. A. Garnsey and C. R. Whittaker (eds) *Imperialism in the Ancient World*, Cambridge: Cambridge University Press, 127–44 and 310–14.

Guthrie, W. K. C. (1969) *A History of Greek Philosophy* III, Cambridge: Cambridge University Press.

Hansen, M. H. (1991) *Athenian Democracy in the Age of Demosthenes*, Oxford: Blackwell.

Heichelheim, F. M. (1964) *An Ancient Economic History* II, Leyden: Sijthoff.

Henderson, B. W. (1927) *The Great War between Athens and Sparta*, London: Macmillan.

Henry, A. (1992) 'Through a laser beam darkly,' *Zeitschrift für Papyrologie und Epigraphik* 91: 137–45.

—— (1995) 'Pour encourager les autres: Athens and Egesta encore', *CQ* 45: 237–40.

Hornblower, S. (1985) *The Greek World 479–323* BC, London: Methuen.

—— (1987) *Thucydides*, London: Duckworth.

—— (1991) *A Commentary on Thucydides* I, Oxford University Press.

Hunter, V. J. (1973) *Thucydides the Artful Reporter*, Toronto: Hakkert.

Isager, S. and Hansen, M. H. (1975) *Aspects of Athenian Society in the Fourth Century* BC, Odense: Odense University Press.

Jones, A. H. M. (1957) *Athenian Democracy*, Oxford: Blackwell.

Jordan, B. (1972) *The Athenian Navy in the Classical Period*, Berkeley, LA: University of California Press.

Kagan, D. (1969) *The Outbreak of the Peloponnesian War*, Ithaca: Cornell University Press.

—— (1974) *The Archidamian War*, Ithaca: Cornell University Press.

—— (1981) *The Peace of Nicias and the Sicilian Expedtion*, Ithaca: Cornell University Press.

—— (1987) *The Fall of the Athenian Empire*, Ithaca: Cornell University Press.

Kallet-Marx, L. (1989) 'The Kallias Decree, Thucydides, and the outbreak of the Peloponnesian War', *CQ* 39: 94–113.

—— (1993) *Money, Expense and Naval Power in Thucydides' History 1–5.24*, Berkeley, LA: University of California Press.

Lazenby, J. F. (1993) *The Defence of Greece*, Warminster: Aris & Phillips.

Lepper, F. A. (1962) 'Some rubrics on the Athenian quota lists', *JHS* 82: 25–55.

Lewis, D. M. (1958) 'The Phoenician fleet in 411', *Historia* 7: 392–7.

—— (1977) *Sparta and Persia*, Leiden: Brill.

Liebeschuetz, W. (1968) 'Thucydides and the Sicilian Expedition', *Historia* 17: 289–306.

Loomis, T. W. (1992) *The Spartan War Fund* (*Historia* Einzelschriften 74) Stuttgart: Steiner.

Macleod, C. W. (1983) *Collected Essays*, Oxford: Clarendon Press.

Marinatos, N. (1981) 'Thucydides and oracles', *JHS* 101: 138–40.

Meiggs, R. (1972) *The Athenian Empire*, Oxford: Oxford University Press.

Meritt, B. D. (1969) *The Athenian Year*, Berkeley, LA: University of California Press.

Michell, H. (1957) *Economics of Ancient Greece*, Cambridge: Heffer.

Mitchell, B. (1991) 'Kleon's Amphipolitan campaign', *Historia* 40: 170–92.

Mosley, D. J. (1973a) *Envoys and Diplomacy in Ancient Greece* (*Historia* Einzelschriften 22), Wiesbaden: Steiner.

—— (1973b) 'Callias' fine', *Mnemosyne* 26: 57–8.

Ormerod, H. A. (1924) *Piracy in the Ancient World*, Liverpool: Liverpool University Press.

Osborne, R. and Hornblower, S. (eds) (1994) *Ritual, Finance, Politics*, Oxford: Oxford University Press.

Parke, H. W. (1977) *Festivals of the Athenians*, London: Thames & Hudson.

Parker, R. C. T. (1983) *Miasma*, Oxford: Oxford University Press.

Pritchett, W. K. (1971) 'Kallias: fact or fancy?', *California Studies in Classical Antiquity* 4: 220–5.

—— (1973) 'The Woodheadean interpretation of Kleon's Amphipolitan campaign', *Mnemosyne* 26: 376–86.

Rhodes, P. J. (1972) *The Athenian Boule*, Oxford: Oxford University Press.

—— (1981) *A Commentary on the Aristotelian Athenaion Politeia*, Oxford: Oxford University Press.

—— (1987) 'Thucydides on the causes of the Peloponnesian War', *Hermes* 115: 154–65.

Roisman, J. (1993) *The General Demosthenes and his Use of Military Surprise* (*Historia* Einzelschriften 78), Stuttgart: Steiner.

Schuller, W. (1981) 'Über die *IDI^{m}TAI* Rubrick in den attischen Tributlisten', *Zeitschrift für Papyrologie und Epigraphik* 42: 141–51.

Seager, R. (1967) 'Thrasybulus, Conon and Athenian imperialism 396–386 BC', *JHS* 87: 95–115.

—— (1969) 'The Congress Decree: some doubts and a hypothesis', *Historia* 18: 129–41.

Stadter, P. (1989) *A Commentary on Plutarch's Pericles*, Chapel Hill, NC: University of North Carolina Press.

Syme, R. (1962) *Thucydides. Proceedings of the British Academy* 48: 39–56.

Thompson, W. E. (1968) 'The chronology of 432/1', *Hermes* 96: 216–32.

—— (1973) 'Internal evidence for the date of the Kallias Decrees', *Symbolae Osloenses* 48: 24–46.

Wade-Gery, H. T. (1958) *Essays in Greek History*, Oxford: Blackwell.

Wallace, W. P. (1964) 'Thucydides', *Phoenix* 18: 251–61.

Westlake, H. D. (1968) *Individuals in Thucydides*, Cambridge: Cambridge University Press.

—— (1969) *Essays on the Greek Historians and Greek History*, Manchester: Manchester University Press.

—— (1989) *Studies in Thucydides and Greek History*, Bristol: Bristol Classical Press.

Woodhead, A. G. (1960) 'Thucydides' portrait of Cleon', *Mnemosyne* 13: 289–317.

Woodman, A. J. (1988) *Rhetoric in Classical Historiography*, London: Croom Helm, 1–69.

Woolley, C. L. (1938) 'Excavations at Al Mina, Sueidia', *JHS* 58: 1–30.

INDEX

160